Islamic Fundamentalism   3rd Edition

Also available from Continuum:

*Fundamentalisms and the Media*, Stewart M. Hoover and Nadia Kaneva
*Interpreting the Qur'an*, Clinton Bennett
*A Mirror For Our Times*, Paul Weller
*Religious Cohesion in Times of Conflict*, Andrew Holden
*Religious Diversity in the UK*, Paul Weller
*Understanding Christian-Muslim Relations*, Clinton Bennett
*Young, British and Muslim*, Philip Lewis

# Islamic Fundamentalism   3rd Edition

## The Story of Islamist Movements

Youssef M. Choueiri

continuum

**Continuum International Publishing Group**

| | |
|---|---|
| The Tower Building | 80 Maiden Lane |
| 11 York Road | Suite 704 |
| London SE1 7NX | New York NY 10038 |

www.continuumbooks.com

**British Library Cataloguing-in-Publication Data**
A catalogue record for this book is available from the British Library.

ISBN:   HB: 978-0-8264-9800-7
        PB: 978-0-8264-9801-4

**Library of Congress Cataloguing-in-Publication Data**
Choueiri, Youssef M., 1948–
   Islamic fundamentalism/Youssef M. Choueiri. – 3rd ed.
      p. cm.
   Includes bibliographical references and index.
   ISBN 978-0-8264-9800-7 – ISBN 978-0-8264-9801-4
   1. Islam–20th century. 2. Islamic fundamentalism. I. Title.

   BP60.C45 2010
   297.09–dc22

         2009050380

Typeset by BookEns, Royston, Herts
Printed and bound in Great Britain by the MPG Books Group

# Contents

# Preface to the Third Edition

Since the last edition of this work, the world of Islamic fundamentalism has become, more or less, a daily preoccupation, not only of journalists and scholars, but, more importantly, of almost all governments and security services across the globe. This new phase was inaugurated by the 9/11, 2001 attacks on the Twin Towers of the World Trade Center in New York, and on the Pentagon. These attacks, launched by al-Qa'ida under the leadership of Usama Bin Laden from his base in Taliban-dominated Afghanistan, shifted the entire debate and our perceptions of what was to be dubbed later as 'Jihadism' to an entirely different level. Islamist radicalism had become a worldwide phenomenon, with the United States marked out as its main enemy. From being a movement straddling different factions and engaged in skirmishes with its own national governments, it was now transformed into an internationalist campaign against all enemies of its version of Islam.

However, another no less significant movement was making its own inroads into the territories of an ideology based exclusively on the idea and practice of *jihad*. Thus, Islam was once again dissected and reinterpreted by Muslim intellectuals and leaders as well as western scholars and research institutions.

In revising the second edition I have added a new chapter dealing with these issues and developments. I have also corrected some minor errors in other chapters and updated some of their contents.

I would like to thank all colleagues who have over the years debated with me the relevance of my general approach to fundamentalism in its Islamist version. I would also like to thank all my students over the last ten years who have never hesitated to discuss its contents or ask me probing questions on almost all its aspects.

Exeter, 29 September 2009

# Preface to the Second Edition

In this revised edition the definition of fundamentalism is refined and restated. I have also added a new section in Chapter 7 dealing with the activities and discourse of Islamist movements which came to the fore in the 1990s. These include, in particular, Hamas, the Islamic Salvation Front of Algeria, the Taliban and the Egyptian Islamist Association.

A number of minor corrections were made, pertaining to dates and names of individuals.

Youssef M. Choueiri
Exeter
March 1997

# Acknowledgements

I owe a great debt of gratitude to the Department of Arabic and Islamic Studies, University of Exeter, for placing at my disposal its collection of documents, pamphlets and books on modern Islamic movements.

My thanks are due to Dr Roger Eatwell who, from his academic base in the city of Bath, never lost hope of receiving the final draft. I must also pay my tribute to Dr Iain Stevenson, Editorial Director of Pinter Publishers, for his subtle encouragement, despite hitches and delays. I would like to thank Paul Auchterlonie for his invaluable help in locating sources and compiling the index.

My thanks go to Mrs Sheila Westcott for her diligence in word-processing the manuscript of the book.

Finally, this work would not have been possible to write without the moral support of my wife, Amal, and my son, Tarek.

All quotations from the Qur'an are from A.J. Arberry's translation, *The Koran Interpreted*, George Allen & Unwin, London, 1955.

# Introduction to the Second Edition

Most Islamist writers and intellectuals, along with a number of western scholars, object to the use of 'fundamentalism' as a generic term, considering it to be either irrelevant to Islam or, at best, a dubious concept alien to the cultural heritage of Muslims. Consequently, earnest efforts have been exerted to find a more neutral designation deemed less tainted by European or American categories. The list of alternative terms has so far included 'Islamism', 'political Islam', 'Islamic resurgence' and a host of other, but no less controversial ones, such as 'Salafism' and the 'Islamic Renaissance'.

However, being fundamentalist or *usuli* is an eminently indigenous Arabic designation, originally reserved, at least since the ninth century of our era, for two categories of Muslim scholars: legists and dialecticians. While legists were specialists in the principles of jurisprudence (*usul al-fiqh*), dialecticians expounded the principles of religion (*usul al-din*), using Greek logic and Aristotelian categories.

Thus, *fundamentalism* in historical Islam was in its early development associated with a scholarly and religious activity, undertaken for the purpose of elucidating the principles and sources of a particular discipline. In addition to law and religion, the study of Arabic grammar, poetry and philosophy gave rise to theoreticians who expounded respective first principles and underlying assumptions. Subsidiary or secondary issues were, moreover, presumed to flow from these theoretical foundations. Needless to say, students of primary principles dominated the intellectual scene, determining the development of high culture in Islam.

Modern and contemporary Islamic fundamentalism combines political action with an ardent desire to discover the original blueprint of a pious community and its ideological principles. Hence, the rediscovery of the fundamentals of religion, and irrespective of its multiple theoretical configurations and social contexts, enjoys a long historical presence in Islam. It is also the hallmark of revivalism, reformism and radicalism as studied in this book.

It is then quite legitimate to use fundamentalism, in spite of its Anglo-Saxon and evangelist connotations, in order to designate intellectual, theological and political movements in the Muslim world. Nevertheless, this insistence on the use of a deep-rooted term is not meant to postulate continuity of cultural forms or revolutionary movements. It is rather a linguistic device that could be harnessed to the advantage of a generic appellation. Nor does it require a corresponding commitment to upholding its incidental appearance in western discourse as being the yardstick of correct classification.

Moreover, while words such as *dimuqratiyya* (democracy) and *ishtirakiyya* (socialism) were coined by Arab grammarians in the nineteenth century in order to express novel concepts and institutions, the words *usul*, *usuli* and *usuliyya* (fundamentals, fundamentalist and fundamentalism) have continued to figure in Islamic theological and theoretical discourses since the rise of the religious movement of Mu'tazilism at Basra, Iraq, in the first half of the eighth century. This movement, despite its eclipse after the eleventh century, became one of the most influential philosophical schools of Islam. Its creed was adopted in the first decades of the ninth century by the 'Abbasid state, and its tenets determined the course of subsequent theological debates throughout the world of Islam.

The Mu'tazilites developed a doctrine that consisted of five principles (*al-usul al-khamsa*): (1) the unity of Allah; (2) Allah's absolute justice; (3) the promise and threat of punishment and reward in the afterlife; (4) the intermediate position of a transgressor, deeming sinners to be neither Muslims nor unbelievers; and (5) the obligation to command the good and prohibit the evil.

It is perhaps more than a sheer coincidence that the pillars of Islam are also divided into five categories, with the first being shared by the Mu'tazilites.

The principles of jurisprudence, on the other hand, received their most elaborate exposition and refinement under the guidance of the legist Muhammad b. Idris al-Shafi'i (d. 820). These were: the

Qur'an, the *sunna,* or the deeds and words of the Prophet, *qiyas* or analogy, and *ijma'* or consensus of the community of believers.

In the wake of these theological and jurisprudential elaborations, the stage was set for a new synthesis that would take account of the contributions of the science of dialectics (*'ilm al-kalam*) and that of jurisprudence (*'ilm al-fiqh*). This was accomplished by the former Mu'tazilite Abu al-Has an al-Ash'ari (d. 935). Using the methods of his former Mu'tazilite masters, al-Ash'ari proceeded to establish a new theological system that has had an enduring and overwhelming influence in Sunni circles. One of his works was entitled *al-Ibanah 'an usul al-diyana* (*The Elucidation of Islam's Foundations*). In it he elaborated his theory of the essence and attributes of God, refuting in the process beliefs and opinions held by heretical or non-orthodox sects.

This amalgamation of theological, judicial and philosophical arguments became by the eleventh century an established tradition, so much so that someone like the celebrated 'Abd al-Qahir al-Baghdadi (d. 1037) included in his work *Kitab usul al-din* (*Fundamentals of Islam*) a systematic treatment beginning with the cosmos, God's attributes and the five pillars of Islam, and ending with the significance of *jihad,* laws of property and the necessity of appointing an Imam to lead the community (al-Baghdadi, 1980). In the twelfth century, another celebrated theologian and exegist of Islam, Fakhr al-Din al-Razi (d. 1209) wrote a compendium under the title *The Characteristics of the Foundations of Islam – Ma'alim usul al-din.* His modern editor calls him:

> The most learned religious scholar, the fundamentalist (*al-usuli*), the dialedician, the rhetorician, the exegist [...] A Shafi'ite jurist in law and an Ash'arite by doctrine [...] he surpassed all his contemporaries in the rational and traditional sciences, particularly in the fields of the principles of jurisprudence (*usul al-fiqh*) and the principles of religion (*usul al-din*) [...] He is indeed peerless and unique in his kind.
>
> (al-Razi, n.d.)

Thus, al-Razi's compendium treats the fields of dogmatics, the principles and methodology of law and the rules governing differences of opinion.

It is, moreover, no accident that the names of the spiritual or intellectual founders of the three modern movements studied in this book are associated with texts dealing with the foundations of Islam or its ultimate principles and questions.

The spiritual founder of revivalism, Muhammad b. 'Abd al-Wahhab, composed a number of tracts under the titles: *Kitab al-Tawhid* (*Allah's Unity*), *Thalathah al-usul* (*The Three Fundamental Principles*) and *Usul al-iman* (*The Principles of Faith*) (Ibn 'Abd al-Wahhab, 1976).

Muhammad 'Abduh, the most prominent leader of the reformist movement, published in 1897 *Risalat al-Tawhid* (*Treatise on God's Unity*). One of the most popular and cogent works of 'Abduh, it served to re-establish the study of dogmatics and religious first principles as a prerequisite for launching the mission of Islam in the modern world. Throughout the treatise, the importance of recapturing the spirit of Islam's first principles (*usul*) is argued with all the authority of textual and historical evidence ('Abduh, 1981: 17, 21, 23, 24, 25, 124). He, moreover, called the theology of unity 'the cornerstone' of Islam and religions in general.

Sayyid Qutb, the intellectual founder of radicalism, devoted most of his literary and religious output to the exposition of the first principles of Islam. Indeed, his main contribution to contemporary Islamist discourse is this recurrent theme. A work of his, published posthumously, reiterates this line of thought in a systematic and panoramic manner. Written shortly before his death, under the title *Fundamentals of the Islamic Conception* (*Muqawwimat al-tasawwur al-islami*), it declares these fundamentals to be immutable and not amenable to change. They moreover, form 'The permanent principles (*al-usul al-thabita*) which are capable of keeping humanity within the orbit of God's straight path' (Qutb, 1986: 33).

Hence, Qutb's last testament, in addition to 'Abd al-Wahhab's and Abduh's published works, justifies the use of the term 'fundamentalism' as an authentic Islamic signifier, having as its premise, in the apt argument of Qutb, 'the determination of the fundamentals of the Islamic worldview (*usul al-tasawwur al-islami*) or its first principles (*mabadi'ihi al-asasiyya*) (Qutb, 1986: 370).

Modem fundamentalism is understood in this context to be based on a clear differentiation between the fundamental assumptions of Islam and those which are related to practices and are thus of a derivative nature. This distinction encompassed, in varying degrees of clarity and emphasis, revivalists, reformists and radicalists.

It goes without saying that the delineation of the distinction between first principles and their subsidiary branches led to divergent interpretations which often assumed the character of novel discoveries. Moreover, one should in this respect differentiate between fundamentalism as a global phenomenon and the particular manifestations of its Jewish, Christian and Muslim movements. It is in this sense that one could encounter fundamentalism in both the United States of America and the Arab world.

## Utopia or Dystopia?

Islamist movements have sometimes been dubbed Utopian, with no precise definition of such a designation. It is, however, assumed that the Utopia of the Islamists is an imaginary ideal that has become untenable, or at best, an unrealistic harking back to a lost world.

This untenability is particularly seen to derive from the irreconcilable differences between modernity and an obsolete system that was basically medieval in its outlook and institutions. Being pre-modern, Islamic civilization cannot thus be recreated in a world that has irrevocably left behind all the cultural and political baggage of the ancient and medieval communities, be they occidental or oriental.

While such an argument has much to recommend it, its premise of Utopian ideals falls far short of an accurate depiction of the subject in question. This depiction is questionable because an Islamist scheme of things, despite its modern and contemporary affiliations, is diametrically opposed to the tradition of Utopian thought as it has developed in the West.

Although there is no general agreement among scholars as to the desirability of Utopias such as those propounded in Plato's *Republic*, Thomas More's *Utopia* (1516) and Francis Bacon's *New Atlantis* (1627), most students of the subject consider Utopian thought to be oriented towards the future. Or as Benedict Anderson points out in discussing Europe's discoveries of the sixteenth century:

> All these tongue-in-cheek Utopias 'modelled' on real discoveries, are depicted, not as lost Edens, but as *contemporary* societies. One could argue that they had to be, since they were composed as criticisms of contemporary societies, and the discoveries had ended the necessity for seeking models in a vanished antiquity.
> (Anderson, 1993: 69)

In other words, the futuristic orientation of Utopian thought precludes its reliance on past models, thereby constituting a clear rupture with both the present and antiquity.

In this sense, Utopia is an ideal or imaginary society endowed with hitherto unknown institutions, and organized on the basis of equal citizenship. Moreover, the citizens themselves are empowered to devise their own laws and reach a stage of social harmony and terrestrial perfection. Both of these characteristics – equal citizenship and legislative authority – are either totally excluded or severely restricted by the ideological presuppositions of islamist notions.

Furthermore, Utopias are first and foremost secular schemes deemed to be the most perfect creation of a rational human community. Being secular and rationalist, Utopian thought delegates to the members of its society the authority to invent laws and devise institutions commensurate with the highest ideals of humanity. These laws and institutions are projected as the best guarantee for creating order and stability out of chaotic conditions, degenerate values and wicked impulses.

By postulating the creativity and rationality of human beings, Utopian thought rejects instinct and primitive desires, seeking to transcend nature in order to infuse society with civic consciousness (Davis, 1981: 379).

Having sketched the elementary notions of Utopian ideals, one could not fail to see the chasm between this system of ideas and that propounded in the contemporary literature of Islamic radicalism. It is for this reason that Islamist concepts of state organization and social regeneration are more akin to dystopia with all its attendant negative aspects.

# Introduction to the First Edition

Islamic fundamentalism is a vague term, currently in vogue as a catchphrase used to describe the militant ideology of contemporary Islamic movements. It is, however, adopted in this book to refer to Islamic systems of thought and political movements that emerged from the eighteenth century onwards in countries as far apart as Saudi Arabia, Indonesia, Nigeria and India.

Whereas the term 'fundamentalism' has an obvious Protestant origin, denoting the literal yet creative interpretation of the Bible, it is here redefined, for lack of a better word, in order to convey a less rigorous connotation. Its direct meaning is assumed to indicate a certain intellectual stance that claims to derive political principles from a timeless, divine text. Thus, three separate movements are identified and studied within this convenient framework: revivalism, reformism and radicalism. Each movement is treated as a distinct entity with its own historical genesis, socio-economic environment and conceptual frame of reference. Moreover, although all their followers appealed to the Qur'an in formulating responses to certain questions, their respective appeals issued in different results and interpretations.

Revivalism denotes Islamic movements that emerged in the eighteenth and nineteenth centuries. It was mainly confined to peripheral areas lying beyond the reach of central authorities, while its social basis had a predominant tribal formation. Moreover, it articulated its political outlook in the form of an internal Islamic dialogue. The movement's first and perhaps most celebrated manifestation occurred in Central Arabia under the guidance of a religious leader and a local chief. Hence, 1749, the date of the final consolidation of a political alliance, struck between Muhammad b., Abd al-Wahhab and Muhammad b. Al-Sa'ud, marks the starting-point of a revivalist current covered in Chapter 1.

Islamic reformism was, by contrast, an urban movement that came into being in the nineteenth century and lasted well into the twentieth. Its leaders were state officials, intellectuals or *'ulama* fiercely opposed to traditional interpretations of religion. It conducted an open dialogue with European culture and philosophies in an attempt to grapple with what it perceived to be an intolerable state of Islamic decline. By studying the pre-industrial phase of European civilization, its exponents hoped to discover the pre-requisites of building viable political structures and a sound economic basis. This is the subject of Chapter 2.

By the middle of the twentieth century, both revivalism and reformism were superseded by the emergence of sovereign nation-states throughout the Islamic world. These states carried out varied programmes of development and relegated Islam to a personal sphere or subordinated its fundamental tenets to the requirements of politico-economic interests. Chapters 3 and 4 chart the course of this new phenomenon.

Chapters 5 and 6 deal with Islamic radicalism, with a view to delineating its system of thought and theoretical frame of reference. It is primarily seen as a direct reaction to the growth of the nation-state and the peculiar problems of the twentieth century. Its constituency embraces recent rural migrants to cities and towns, or a declining social stratum of artisans and shopkeepers. Moreover, it finds a fertile source of recruitment in the ranks of young Muslim men and women who grew up under largely secular and nationalist systems of government. Hence, radicalism does not revive or reform. Rather, it creates a new world and invents its own dystopia.

The inclusion of a book on Islamic fundamentalism in a series on right-wing politics and ideology calls for an explanation. By and large, Islamic activists define the characteristics of their movements according to a modern system of classification that originated with the advent of the French Revolution in 1789. They thus judge their ideological formulations to be of a centrist nature, asserting that this notion is derived from a Qur'anic verse (11:143). Although this particular verse does not imply a political stance, referring as it did to the direction of prayer, it is certainly a convenient source, conducive as other verses are to a creative act of semantic manipulation.

It was in the second half of the nineteenth century that Muslim intellectuals began to discuss political issues in terms of right and left tendencies. There is, moreover, no doubt that the adoption of this new vocabulary signified the way European cultural norms and politics had become internal features of Islamic and other societies. It seems that the itinerant reformist Jamal al-Din al-Afghani (1839–97) was one of the first Muslims to popularize such political notions throughout the Islamic world. By the middle of the twentieth century, political parties in most Muslim countries came to be classified in the light of European, American or Soviet concepts. Movements which called for the restoration of Islam as a system of government were consequently considered by their nationalist, socialist and communist opponents as being either reactionary or right-wing. This political scheme of classification highlighted the conservative policies of these Islamic movements, particularly in matters related to land reform, class struggle, secularism and the rights of women.

However, not all movements designated 'Islamic' are necessarily right-wing or fascist. In Egypt, for example, Hasan Hanafi, Professor of Philosophy at Cairo University, leads a school of thought that calls itself 'the Islamic Left'. This particular instance only goes to show that political classifications have become a worldwide phenomenon, bypassing local cultures or purely religious beliefs. It also serves to draw attention to the multifaceted attributes and specifications of Islamic ideologies.

In this book, three Islamic movements, mentioned above, are deemed to fall within the purview of right-wing politics. The criteria which Muslims themselves have adopted in discussing various socio-economic and cultural issues are used in reaching such a conclusion. Each movement is shown to have been a belated reaction to internal and external forces, a fact that tended to place its respective political articulation in conflict with more progressive currents. Hence, these reactions became decidedly conservative and sometimes openly outmoded.

Nevertheless, it is important to bear in mind that fundamentalism is not simply the hallmark of a fanatic or a traditionalist. Contrary to common belief, it is an ardent endeavour that is imbued with an activist stance and an earnest determination to grapple with overwhelming odds. It is thus not to be belittled, taken lightly or derided. The ideological pronouncements of fundamentalism reveal a hostile attitude towards both traditionalism and official religious institutions. In other words, it is neither tradition-bound, nor a literalist transcription of the statements of a divinely inspired book. This is true of Jewish, Christian and Islamic fundamentalism.

Intellectually and politically, it espouses a creative interpretation of its revealed text, be it the Bible or the Qur'an. However, such an interpretation is thoroughly non-critical, apologetic and didactic. There is as a result a marked hostility towards historical criticism and all attempts to question the accuracy of certain events or the validity of circumstantial prescriptions. This paradoxical approach, straddling simultaneously creativity and adherence to fundamentals, leads to a constant updating of the text in order to keep abreast of new developments and discoveries.

As far as Islam is concerned, each movement studied in this book rediscovered a vital and central principle of the Qur'an. Revivalism saw renewal of Islam by a Mahdi or his forerunner as an overriding task in the face of prevalent superstitions and religious innovations. Reformism reasserted the quest of knowledge and the function of consultation in the life of the community. Radicalism highlighted God's sovereignty and the role of *jihad* as the most important aspects of Islam. The act of assigning particular aspects a dominant position entailed the subordination of other Qur'anic injunctions, or their outright abrogation for the sake of more urgent tasks. Furthermore, these new priorities were often in direct contrast to the prevailing customs of traditionalist or official Islam. It is at this juncture that one must be aware of a superficial resemblance between two similar statements – one Qur'anic and another fundamentalist. The same statement, joined to a different configuration of concepts, conveys a totally separate significance and performs a new function quite distinct from the original one. It consequently loses its former association with other objects and becomes an integral part of a novel frame of reference. Islamic reformists, such as Rashid Rida (1865–1935) for example, were often refreshingly frank in admitting the innovative nature of their ideas, albeit in an implicit line of analysis discussed in Chapter 3. Similarly, the sheer absence of Sufi orders as well as the concept of Mahdiship during the formative period of historical Islam points up the peculiar response of revivalism.

While scholars have generally succeeded in isolating the distinctive characteristics of revivalism and reformism, their analysis of radicalism has so far been less amenable to a straightforward treatment. Perhaps this is only to be expected when one studies a contemporary event that has not yet disclosed its multifarious ramifications. The scholar's task in this particular instance is rendered more difficult by the voluminous quantity of Qur'anic verses which pervades almost all radicalist texts and treatises. It is this overgrowth of quotations, often supplemented by a selected array of the sayings *(hadiths)* of the Prophet Muhammad, which often obscures the substratum of a political current deeply affiliated with modern right-wing ideologies. These extensive quotations, however, can be easily shown as a convenient device of building up a new edifice by using the scattered bricks of a demolished castle. The ideology of the founders of Islamic radicalism, al-Mawdudi and Qutb, are thus studied in this light, whereby a direct influence of European fascist notions is clearly uncovered and delineated.

Chapter 8 explores the world of Islamic radicalism and Jihadism in the wake of the 9/11, attacks and their repercussions both in the West and the Muslim world. Radicalism represents the latest and perhaps last attempt to establish a totalitarian Islamic state. It is both an urban response and an ideological articulation of contemporary dimensions, highlighting and condensing the social divisions and problems of Islamic cities and towns. The rise of radicalism is consequently linked with the developments which these urban centres underwent after 1945. Its ideology is closely related to the anxieties and ambitions of certain strata of society: small merchants, middle traders, artisans, students, teachers and state employees. Hence, it is an ideology shot through with the precarious position of these social groups. However, whereas the ideologues of Islamic radicalism were largely the product of the 1960s, their popular appeal did not become apparent until the late 1970s. In this sense, theoretical discussions of the second phase, in which disciples and followers attempted to apply the ideological analysis of the leaders of the first phase, assume a redundant character unless socio-economic factors are fully considered.

Finally, whatever definition is adopted in a study that aspires to understand the characteristics of fundamentalism, one particular chain of reasoning links revivalism, reformism and radicalism. It is their rejection of secularism in all its schools and manifestations that marks these movements and serves to highlight their fundamentalist constructions. So long as a revealed text is constantly judged to be the final arbiter of human affairs, or of truth and falsehood, fundamentalism is bound to appear under various labels and systems of thought.

# Chapter 1

## Islam and Islamic Revivalism

It is the contention of this study that the term 'Islam' indicates different systems of organization and thought under different historical circumstances.

By and large, one may speak of two broad periods, encompassing 'historical Islam', on the one hand, and 'modern Islam', on the other. The first period opens with the career of the Prophet Muhammad (*c.* 610–32 CE), and reaches its zenith with the fall of Constantinople under the assault of Ottoman artillery in 1453. The second period finds its threshold at the moment Europe left behind the Renaissance, and embarked on a new venture of commercial expansion and military conquests. This modern stage coincided with the rise of three territorial states in the Islamic world: the Ottoman Empire, the Safavid monarchy of Persia and the Mughal Empire in India (Ghorbal, 1958: 75–6).

These two broad periods are, in turn, subdivided into distinct phases. First, the age of conquests, which roughly extends from 634 to 838 CE, witnessed the consolidation of an Islamic polity based on a partnership of tribal confederacies, urban merchant families and Arab statesmanship. Its economic system was centred on major cities acting as nodal points of long-distance trade and commerce. Islam itself as a system of rules and values was imperceptibly integrated into the official structures of the state. Second, between 945 and 1492, Persian administrative norms and Turkic military standards set the pace of a new phase. The army, built as a Mamluk institution in possession of military fiefs, monopolized the state and dominated the economy. The Crusades, launched between 1099 and 1250, only served to accentuate the trend towards the militarization of Islam. In conjunction with these developments, Sufi orders sprang up both as a reaction to official Islam and an expression of popular discontent.

Philosophy was another vehicle which conveyed an intellectual endeavour seeking to mitigate the harsh nature of military oppression. Historical Islam reached its full fruition towards the end of this highly original and rich phase. It was under these conditions that the world of Islam became a truly universal domain, ruled by varied and numerous dynasties.

Historical Islam gave way to a new period of political, economic and cultural organization. In its initial stages, modern Islam derived its specific features from the three gunpowder empires of the Ottomans, the Safavids of Persia and the Mughals of India (Hodgson, 1974). The first phase of this period, extending from 1500 to 1770, was the era of territorial and absolutist Islam: almost every facet of public life tended to take on a systematic form of institutional arrangements, bureaucratic precision and politico-economic rationality. Both Sufi orders and artisan guilds were intertwined as entrenched means of spiritual and material endeavours. Whereas historical Islam unfolded in its last phase within the fluctuating fortunes of city-states and urban centres, the modern period bore the marks of developments taking place towards the end of the fifteenth century throughout the Mediterranean. These developments were aptly summed up by Fernand Braudel as follows:

> Everywhere the city-state, precarious and narrow-based, stood revealed inadequate to perform the political and financial tasks now facing it. It represented a fragile form of government, doomed to extinction, as was strikingly demonstrated by the capture of Constantinople in 1453, the fall of Barcelona in 1472 and the collapse of Granada in 1492.
>
> (Braudel, 1973: 657)

Thus the city-state became an obsolete form of political organization doomed to be absorbed by larger entities. Moreover, this phenomenon was characteristically Mediterranean, having no peculiar Islamic origins. The territorial state was superseded in the sixteenth century by the rise of empires which 'in the Mediterranean means essentially that of the Ottoman Empire in the East and that of the Hapsburg Empire in the West' (Braudel, 1973: 660). This periodization was to a large extent mirrored in the development of Arabic historiography from the early days of Islam down to the nineteenth century.

Viewed in its metaphysical dimensions, Islam represented an endeavour to rectify the false Scriptures of Judaism and Christianity. By doing so, it envisaged the restoration of Abrahamic monotheism to its pure origins. Its message was deemed to consist of a timeless reality, rooted in the eternal reaffirmation of God's permanent laws. Nevertheless, Islam as a system of thought and social organization came into being stamped with historical temporality. It unfolded in time and space, denoting the continuation and culmination of other unitarian religions. Its Arabian nucleus expanded within a short period to encompass a far-flung empire, extending from China to Spain. By becoming cosmopolitan, the survival of Islam was contingent on the specific fortunes and institutions of its multitudinous adherents. History and Islam were thus intertwined in a journey of expansion, conquest or gradual regression.

The Prophet Muhammad (*c.* 570–632) had a career that unfolded over time. His message and life were acted out as a drama, with a beginning, a plot and a glorious end. The revelations that he received and were later embodied in the Qur'an, spelt out a divinely-inspired response to the immediate problems of both Mecca and Medina. His other utterances and activities complemented and often shed light on obscure verses. Both the Qur'an and his sayings (*hadiths*) entered history as textual inspirations in renewed contexts and novel circumstances, whereby worldly and scholarly historicity never ceased to throw up innovative interpretations.

Not unlike other branches of knowledge, Islamic historiography emerged to meet the needs of a flowering religion and a new political community. It was first regarded as an auxiliary branch of literature designed for practical purposes. By the tenth century, it had, however, carved out for itself an autonomous space, delimited by its own object of study – the dynastic state – as well as its primary materials, or reports of events.

Early historical writings were concerned with the life of the Prophet Muhammad as the ultimate arbiter of truth. His death, the conquests of the first three rightly-guided Caliphs (Abu Bakr, 'Umar b. al-Khattab and 'Uthman b. 'Affan), and the civil wars which split the community into various factions, set the themes of this genre of history-writing. Soon, each faction produced its own version of the Sayings of the Prophet. The career and deeds of the Messenger of God opened up a new field of investigation and narration. Thus, the realms of factual happenings and legends were merged, or dressed up in the guise of an unswerving loyalty to the ideals of Islam.

In addition to Muhammad's biographies, there developed a new legal activity concerned with the collection of his sayings and doings. The authenticity of these traditions (the *hadiths*) depended on establishing a chain of transmitters (*isnad*) consisting of a succession of pious and prominent companions of the Prophet. This art of *isnad* was both fictional and practical. Its fictionality was invented in the process of confronting unexpected problems and unforeseen situations. Hence its practicality, which consisted of solving the daily issues of the Muslim community. The Qur'an, local customs and the science of *hadith* formed the basis of Islamic *fiqh* or jurisprudence. The literature of conquests complemented and completed the first aim. Its graphic depiction of various battles and military expeditions helped to trace the genealogy of Muhammad's companions, ascertain the priority of one tribe over the other, and define the role a particular tribal group played in the early conquests. It also fixed the date of conversion, and the services rendered to the community by a leading individual or his followers. Utilitarian interests were thus an integral part of the divine message: financial remuneration and the triumphant destiny of the new religion were juxtaposed in a chronological or annalistic narration glorifying the graded social strata of the community.

The literary chronicles of military conquests demonstrated with irrefutable evidence the power of Islam. As a result, historical anecdotes became the handmaid of expansion and settlement in liberated territories. History echoed in its detailed reports of events the aims of a political community represented and led by the Caliphate. While al-Waqidi (747–823), in his chronicle of *al-Maghazi* (*Expeditions*), endows this whole phase with its distinct character, al-Tabari (d. 923), in his multi-volume chronicle, *History of the Messengers and Kings* (*Tarikh al-Rusul wa al-Muluk*) embodied its ultimate consummation.

The second phase in Islamic historiography (*c.* 900–1370) was characterized by the advent of chronicles bearing a humanist outlook and a multicultural approach. The purely military and chivalric accounts were relegated to the background in a society teeming with a wide spectrum of races, cultures, social classes and customs. War reports became almost obsolescent, except for official chroniclers and court historiographers. The geographer and historian al-Mas'udi (d. 957) in his work *Meadows of Gold and Mines of Gems* (*Muruj al dhahab wa ma 'adin al-jawhar*) expresses this era in its infinite varieties. Even the title of his book, bearing no religious connotations, was highly significant, and captured the spirit of the age.

It was the North African historian Ibn Khaldun (1332–1406) who first highlighted al-Mas'udi's status as an embodiment of his age. The reader is informed that *Meadows of Gold* represented an exhaustive work, dealing with the general history, conditions, geography, political life and cultural aspects of all nations and regions in the West and in the East. So much so that his chronicle 'became the standard authority for historians and their reliable source for verifying numerous reports of events'. According to his own testament, Ibn Khaldun aspired to follow in the footsteps of al-Mas'udi, and depict for his age the new conditions which obtained between the eleventh and fourteenth centuries. He thus ushered in a novel phase, and heralded the transition to a higher level of historical comprehension in Islamic culture.

Ibn Khaldun thought he was witnessing 'a total alteration' in the urban and rural structures of his civilization: first, the emigration of nomadic tribes from Egypt into North Africa led to the decline of the indigenous Berbers; second, the plague in the fourteenth century destroyed entire communities; finally, these developments coincided with a general disintegration in the political authority of dynasties throughout the Islamic world. Thus:

> It was as if the voice of the universe in the world had called for the advent of lethargy and depression, and the world had responded to its call. When there is an entire alteration of conditions, it is as if the whole creation had changed and all the world been transformed, as if it were a new creation, a rebirth, a world brought into existence anew. Thus this new age stands in need of someone to register the situation of its inhabitants, regions and generations, as well as their changed customs and creeds, doing for this period what al-Mas'udi did for his, so as to become a model for future historians to follow.
>
> (Ibn Khaldun, 1967: 64–5, 1900: 32–3)

Ibn Khaldun's celebrated *Muqaddima* (*Prolegomenon*) adumbrates the theory of the territorial state, ruled by its particular dynasty, as the pivot of Islamic civilization. His delineation of the mechanisms which lead to the rise and fall of political entities transformed the intellectual debate in the world of Islam, marking the advent of new forms of theoretical conceptualization. Furthermore, the main currents of Islamic thought – the jurisprudential, the historical and the philosophical – converged in his theory to constitute a fresh synthesis (Laroui, 1981: 100).

By positing '*asabiyya (esprit de corps*, group solidarity) as the agency of bringing about the foundation of states, our great historian paved the way for the integration of Islam into the networks of an absolutist polity permeated by a secular ethos. Although he did not effect a complete rupture of Islamic cosmology, adhering as he did to 'a hierarchical gradation of beings', noted by a number of modern scholars (Mahdi, 1964: 190–3), he nevertheless breached the classical paradigm by focusing attention on the gradual and logical stages of socio-economic transformations. His cyclical view of the prescribed course of each dynastic state – the periods of foundation, prosperity, complacency and rapid disintegration – has repeatedly been taken up by various Muslim thinkers and historians down to the present time. In the Ottoman Empire, for example, Ibn Khaldun was intermittently rediscovered, appropriated and reinter-preted. Far from leading to despair or resignation, his empirical diagnosis of inevitable decline seemed to have acted as a stimulus for recovering the original conditions of energy and power. The French invasion and occupation of Egypt in 1798–1801 evoked in the Egyptian chronicler, 'Abd al-Rahman al-Jabarti (d. 1825), an array of apocalyptic images similar to Ibn Khaldun's description of his age. He, too, saw the emergence of a new order, the disruption of the natural sequence of events and the utter destruction of ordinary life. To him, the year 1798 heralded the beginning of:

major battles; formidable happenings; calamitous occurrences; terrible catastrophes; the multiplication of evils; the succession of great events; the incessancy of ordeals; the disruption of time; the inversion of the natural order; the *bouleversement* of man-made conventions; the concatenation of horrors; the alterations of conditions; the corruption of political management; the advent of destruction; and the prevalence of devastation, as well as the recurrence of ordained causes. 'That is because thy Lord would never destroy the cities unjustly, while their inhabitants were heedless.'

(Qur'an 6:131; al-Jabarti, Vol. 2, n.d.: 179)

However, unlike al-Mas'udi or Ibn Khaldun, al-Jabarti came into contact with a modern European scheme of things. Accordingly, the conceptual elements of his outlook began to undergo subtle shifts of emphasis. The defeat of his admired Mamluks by Napoleon's superior military power, his inspection of new scientific instruments and observation of experiments conducted by the *savants* of the French expedition made a lasting impact on his personality. His participation in the General Council, set up by Napoleon Bonaparte to run the affairs of Egypt, whittled down his religious objections, and led him to realize the hopelessness of restoring the former order in its golden days (al-Jabarti, Vol. 1: 9).

In spite of his apocalyptic imagery, al-Jabarti conveys in his chronicle the tense anxieties of a disappearing world. His fulminations against the innovative policies of Egypt's governor, Muhammad 'Ali (1805–48), only served to widen the gap between his 'withdrawal into solitude' and the inevitable march of historical change. Hence, words had ceased to be signs implanted in things as their marks and true resemblance, and 'the original text' was flung into the whirlpool of a totally negative environment. In this sense, the Islamic world had acquired in al-Jabarti its own Foucauldian *Don Quixote*, embarking on its journey towards an alluring landscape. In the words of the French philosopher, Michel Foucault, Cervantes's *Don Quixote* was:

> the first modern work of literature, because in it we see the cruel reason of identities and differences make endless sport of signs and similitudes [...] because it marks the point where resemblance enters an age which is, from the point of view of resemblance, one of madness and imagination.
>
> (Foucault, 1977: 48–9)

In the Egyptian *Don Quixote* both Islamic revivalism and reformism cohabited as two facets of an evolving society. Wahhabism and Ottomanism were on the verge of claiming the loyalty of a community destined to resolve its problems in a constant confrontation with an alien power: European capitalism. The fortunes of the Ottoman, the Indian and the Persian empires thus became entangled in worldwide developments.

## Revivalist Islam

The three Muslim empires, mentioned above, entered after 1700 a phase of relative decline. This was the result of financial crises, demographic dislocations and agricultural stagnation. Thus, the eighteenth century was generally characterized by extortionate abuses of the taxation system and the rise of autonomous principalities, often competing with the political centre for the same resources. Furthermore, luxury consumption of the upper classes was coupled with decreasing revenues. As trade was either diverted to new routes, especially after the emergence of the European naval powers, or taken over by foreign merchants, local chieftains and governors were increasingly inclined to concentrate their efforts on their own administrative units. The central authorities were thus faced with the intractable tasks of fending off foreign competition and mounting local opposition. Finally, these transformations of imperial authority and functions led to a breakdown of military discipline and efficiency. Consequently, tribes, Bedouin and nomads, sought to lessen the effects of agricultural and commercial stagnation in repeated encroachments upon cultivated areas, thereby forcing agriculturalists to withdraw into urban centres. Hence, Sufi orders congealed into formal ritualistic organizations, a fact which throttled the inventive outlets of various artisanal guilds.

It was against this background that religious revivalist movements began to sprout in order to reinstate Islam in its pure and original state. Islamic revivalism made its appearance and exerted an enduring impact in the outlying areas stretching from Sumatra and the Indian subcontinent to central Arabia and northern Nigeria. These revivalist currents were to be encountered even in the second half of the nineteenth century, such as the Mahdist uprising in the Sudan. This delayed action of revivalism suggests the peculiar history of a particular region, the lateness of European commercial repercussions or the slow maturation of social and economic crises. There are, however, clear indications that Islamic revivalism was a reaction against the gradual contraction of internal and external trade, brought about by the mercantile activities of European nations, particularly the Portuguese, the Spanish, the Dutch, the British and the French. Slaves, gold, spices, coffee, tea and textiles were the major bone of contention between various central Islamic governments and the seaborne empires of Europe. Tribal confederations, pastoralists and nomads often depended for their livelihood on their role as guides and guards of trade caravans, protégés of merchants or governors, suppliers of livestock and receivers of illegal taxes by the mere fact of occupying strategic positions lying astride major trade routes. Before the Industrial Revolution, European mercantile penetration confined itself at the outset to coastal stations and garrison enclaves, thus rarely venturing into the interior, or, having succeeded in establishing a foothold in the hinterland, such as the Dutch in Indonesia and the British in India, European mercantile companies and governments were content to conduct their transactions under the umbrella of royal courts and princely families. Revivalism echoed to a large extent this 'peripheral' penetration.

One of the first revivalist movements was launched in central Arabia, inspired by the teachings of Muhammad b. 'Abd al-Wahhab (1703–92), who had travelled and studied in both Ottoman Iraq and Syria. Dubbed Wahhabism, this particular brand of revivalism was consolidated into an alliance between tribes led by a local chieftain, Ibn Sa'ud (d. 1765) and its religious founder. Although Arabia was the cradle of Islam, its tribes, in particular those of Najd, the birthplace of Wahhabism, had lapsed into a state of semi-paganism. More importantly, the dominant position of the British in Indian textiles, spices and indigo diverted the Gujurat–Red Sea trade route away from Arabia. The British ascendancy precipitated the commercial collapse of the foremost Arabian ruler, the Sharif of Mecca. He consequently lost his ability to act as patron of various tribes or continue to employ those of central Arabia in his trading activities. Wahhabism managed to rally under its banner tribes which were most adversely affected by this turn of fortunes (Abir, 1971: 185–200).

In northern India, as the Mughal Empire began to crumble under British economic and military penetration, in addition to the rise of locally-based dynasties, Sayyid Ahmad Shahid (1786–1831), and Isma'il Shahid (1779–1831), called for the purification of Islam and proclaimed *jihad* (holy struggle) against Hindu and Sikh influences. This movement derived its inspiration from the puritanical teachings of Shah Wali Allah (1703–62) and his son Shah 'Abd al'Aziz (d. 1824). Both had argued in various tracts and commentaries the urgent need of reviving authentic Islam and the elimination of Hindu customs among Muslim Indians. Sayyid Ahmad led a militant movement with the sole aim of stamping out the harmful effects of Hinduism and the corrupt aspects of polytheism. He succeeded in establishing a short-lived state in the tribal regions of the North-West Frontier and parts of Afghanistan. However, his hastily built Imamate, being based on a loose tribal confederation, began to crumble soon after its foundation. Finally, the Sikhs dealt the final blow to his forces at the battle of Balakot in 1831.

In northern Nigeria, Shaykh 'Uthman Dan Fodio (1754–1817) launched in 1804 his holy struggle, and set up between the River Niger and Lake Chad the Caliphate of Sokoto (1809–1903). His revivalist movement was based on a coalition of Fulani pastoralists (herdsmen) and Muslim traders against the corrupt and oppressive practices of Hausa agriculturalists. As English and Dutch traders initiated at the turn of the seventeenth century the introduction of firearms into West Africa, in exchange for slaves and gold, the balance of power tilted in favour of settled communities organized into political entities. The Hausa rulers of the State of Gobir and their policies of enslavement were the main target of Dan Fodio's *jihad*. Another West African revivalist movement was that of al-Hajj 'Umar Tal (1794–1865). It spread throughout the lands of contemporary Guinea, Senegal and Mali. He was greatly influenced by the exemplary rise of the Caliphate of Sokoto, and formed with its ruler, Muhammad Bello, a close matrimonial alliance and an association based on mutual conviction of waging *jihad* against unbelievers and idolators. Hajj 'Umar Tal's call for holy struggle was proclaimed in 1852. His was mainly a war against local traders and rulers engaged in capturing slaves for western markets and plantations.

Between 1803 and 1837 the puritanical Padri movement witnessed its most powerful expansion in Sumatra (Ricklefs, 1981: 133). It concentrated its fiercest attacks against local customs and corrupt chiefs. It emerged in the interior of a region undergoing 'a commercial revolution', associated with pepper, gold and tin, and fought over between indigenous kings and the British or Dutch trading companies. The Padri directed their attacks against the lax practices of their community exemplified by the royal family of Minang-Kabau in West Sumatra. As trade in gold and pepper declined or collapsed, a new cash crop, coffee, was introduced by new groups based in the interior, and linked to the British and Americans, rather than the Dutch. It was in these areas of new commercial activities that a revivalist movement was launched upon the return of three Sumatran pilgrims from Mecca in 1804. It had as its main objective the protection of traders and farmers against robbery or slavery. Defeated by the Dutch, after a long and bloody struggle, the revivalist trend petered out, and was replaced, towards the end of the nineteenth century, as in other Muslim regions, by Islamic reformism (Dobbin, 1974: 330–2; 1983).

Another revivalist movement which arose as a response to

European commercial penetration was that of the Fara'idis in Bengal. Founded by Hajji Shari'at Allah (1781–1840), it called for the strict observance of Islamic law and Qur'anic injunctions. Under the terms of the Permanent Settlement, initiated by the Director of the British East India Company in 1793, a new landowning class was brought into being. *Zamindars* (revenue-collectors) and tax-farmers, who were Hindus in their overwhelming majority, were turned into a class of large landlords receiving rent from their Muslim tenants. Moreover, the commercialization of agrarian life saw the appearance of Hindu moneylenders. Caught between the increasing demands of his *zamindar,* and his equally spiralling debts, the Muslim peasant joined forces with landless indigo plantation labourers in reasserting the strict application of the *shari'a.* Shari'at Allah's son, Dudu Miyan (1819–62), while adhering to his father's rejection of non-Islamic regulations and institutions, transformed the movement into organized militant groups bent on reinforcing a comprehensive revivalist programme (Khan, 1965).

In the tribal region between the Mediterranean coast and Chadian territories, a new Sufi order, the Sanusiyya, was established in 1842. Adhering to orthodox Islam and fiercely opposed to saint worship, its founder, Muhammad 'Ali al-Sanusi (1787–1859), chose the Bedouins of Cyrenaica to build an extensive network of lodges and agricultural colonies. However, this was an order which avoided coming into open conflict with the Ottoman authorities, who had reoccupied the autonomous Libyan province in 1835 in order to prevent it from falling into the hands of the French or another foreign power. It was thus a highly pragmatic organization. Apart from effecting reconciliation between Sufism and orthodox Islam, it did not forsake its peaceful penetration of the interior of Africa along well-established trade routes until the Italian invasion of Libya in 1911 (Cordell, 1977: 21–36).

Two late revivalist movements were launched in both the Sudan and Somalia. Sayyid Muhammad 'Abdallah Hasan (1864–1920) organized Somali clans and nomads of the interior against the British, Italian and French presence in the main coastal centres of Somalia. Preaching the doctrine of *jihad* against 'foreign infidels', and vehemently opposed to 'pagan innovations', such as seeking the intercession of dead saints with God, he sustained his resistance from 1899 to 1920, scoring major victories against his internal and external enemies. He was finally defeated by the superiority of British bombers and machine guns. Sudanese Mahdism (1881–98) suffered the same fate, and opened the Sudan to large-scale British penetration. Muhammad Ahmad b. 'Abdallah (1844–85) was the only prominent Muslim revivalist who openly declared himself the Expected Mahdi (the divinely guided one). Re-enacting the career and message of the Prophet Muhammad, he announced his Mahdiship in 1881, administered an oath of allegiance to his disciples and urged upon his followers the obligation of *hijra* from the territories of unbelievers as well as the concomitant duty of launching *jihad* in order to purify the world of idolatry and innovations.

The Sudan was initially conquered in 1821 by Muhammad 'Ali, the governor of Egypt, in order to acquire military recruits and exploit its gold reserves. Both objectives were total failures. However, his conquest ushered in a new era of political unification and administrative reforms, modelled on those he had introduced into his Egyptian province. His grandson, Khedive Isma'il (1863–79), completed this process by opening up the Sudan to European commercial and trading activities. Having introduced a regular system of taxation and charged a number of western officials with the task of suppressing the slave trade, Isma'il's policies disturbed the vested interests of various tribal groups, religious orders and powerful slave merchants.

The eruption of the 'Urabi revolt against European financial control of Egypt, following the deposition of Isma'il in 1879, paved the way for the spectacular rise of the Mahdi. However, whereas 'Urabi and his supporters advocated modern notions of patriotism and government, revivalist Mahdism reasserted purely Islamic principles and messianic claims (Holt and Daly, 1983: 47–95).

## Common Characteristics

All these revivalist movements shared a common denominator of conceptual and practical characteristics, clustered around the sequential phases of *hijra* (migration) and *jihad* (holy struggle). The preceding discussion of various revivalist groups may serve to identify the following theoretical assumptions:

1. The return to original Islam as the religion of oneness of God (*tawhid*). This belief led to the insistence on purifying Islam of pagan customs and foreign accretions. A pronounced hostility

was thus displayed towards innovations and traditions, particularly the excessive veneration of saints, the practice of magic and association with unbelievers.

2. The advocacy of independent reasoning in matters of legal judgements (*ijtihad*), coupled with an abhorrence of blind imitation (*taqlid*).

3. The necessity of fleeing (*hijra*) the territories dominated by unbelievers, polytheists and heathens. The practice of migration was the initial step towards the concomitant adoption of *jihad* (struggle in the path of God), whereby an open war would be declared against the enemies of Islam. Hence, the world was divided into two mutually exclusive geographical units: the abode of unbelief (*dar al-kufr*) and the House of Islam (*dar al-Islam*).

4. The fervent belief in one single leader as either the embodiment of the 'renewer' and just imam or as the Expected Mahdi.

The last theme constituted the linchpin of all the other vital characteristics. Upon the emergence of a renewer (*mujaddid*), or the manifestation of the Mahdi, depended the ability to initiate the return to unadulterated Islam, the lawful declaration of migration and *jihad*, as well as the building of a new Muslim community adhering to, and ruled by, the prescribed indigenous laws. It may be safely assumed that this belief in renewal and Mahdism became the hallmark of Islamic revivalism; so much so that the title of Mahdiship was bestowed even on those revivalist leaders who categorically refused to be designated as such. Thus, 'Uthman Dan Fodio, the founder of the Sokoto Caliphate, wrote a treatise refuting the claims of his followers, yet he went on to say: 'I am not the Expected Mahdi, though it is his garment that I wear. I am the clouds that precede the awaited Mahdi, and it is for this that I am associated with him' (Sulaiman, 1986: 177–8).

Dan Fodio believed himself to be the forerunner of the divinely-inspired one, and whose imminent appearance was widely believed by Central and West African Muslims. Such a popular expectation reveals the millenarianist background against which Islamic revivalism operated. This was premised on the idea in Islamic tradition of the coming of the Mahdi or his forerunner (the renewer) at the turn of every century according to the Islamic calendar. Thus the Sudanese Mahdi timed his manifestation at the beginning of the fourteenth Islamic century: 1300/1881–2. However, there was no watertight date for the advent of a religious saviour. The Indian revivalist Ahmad Shahid, for example, was held by his followers to be 'the promised Messiah' (Malik, 1980: 8) in the wake of his relentless battles against the Sikhs in 1829–31. Muhammad al-Sanusi was more prudent, being satisfied with naming his son and successor al-Mahdi (b. 1843) as he looked forward to the approach of a new century. When the Sudanese Muhammad Ahmad called upon al-Mahdi al-Sanusi to acknowledge him as the Expected One, the latter was quite explicit in his negative response (al-Dajjani, 1967: 182–91).

Although the idea of Mahdiship does not appear in the Qur'an, nor is it mentioned in the two 'most authoritative and authentic' collections of the sayings of the Prophet, Islamic revivalists were all unanimous in upholding its validity and eventuality. Muhammad b. 'Abd al-Wahhab, the most uncompromising revivalist who stead-fastly opposed Sufism and superstitious innovations in words and deeds, cites an extensive series of 'sound sayings' dealing with 'the Signs of the Hour', the appearance of the Antichrist, followed by the Second Coming of Jesus ('Isa) and the advent of the Mahdi. This doctrine is in fact an imaginative innovation fusing two separate traditions. The first was derived from Christian apocalyptic beliefs. The other embellished an Islamic political legend which flourished after the assassination in 661 CE of the Prophet's son-in-law and the fourth Caliph, 'Ali b. Abi Talib, and the foundation by Mu'awiya (661–80) of the Umayyad dynasty (661–750).

However, the belief in the Mahdi did not develop into an elaborate apocalyptic scheme until the emergence of the 'Abbasids (750–1258) and the transformation of the Caliphate into a cosmopolitan state. It is thus not possible to credit Islamic revivalism, even in its most puritanical expression, with the simple ambition to reinstate the true and pristine authority of Qur'anic Islam. Furthermore, the original concept of the advent of the Mahdi was envisaged as a sequence of three momentous events. Before the onset of these successive phases, portents and omens were required as clear indications of the end of the age. Hence, the Signs of the Hour would be preceded by civil wars, numerous false prophets, earthquakes and the obliteration of Islamic rules and laws resulting in the prevalence of unbelief. These omens would also be mingled with purely apocalyptic visions such as the rise of the sun in the West, the emergence of the beast of burden (al-dabba) at the crack of dawn and the appearance of the Antichrist (al-dajjal). The advent of the Antichrist, as well as the Second Coming of Jesus are expressly stated in the 'two sound collections' of al-Bukhari and Muslim. Subsequent compilers of the Prophet's sayings, such as Ibn Majah (d. 896) embroidered these traditions whereby Jesus would slay the Antichrist, break the cross, kill the swine, establish the exclusive worship of God (*Allah*) and bring about a reign of abundance, prosperity and harmony. Christ, in other words, would adopt the religion of Islam, bringing about its final triumph and dominance. This particular drama underwent further embellishment and rearrangement, forming a mere episode in the eventual manifestation of the Mahdi. The traditionalists Ibn Dawud (817–89) and al-Tirmidhi (824–92) were perhaps the first collectors of *hadiths* who expounded a comprehensive theme of Mahdiship, conflating the purely eschatological omens and the Signs of the Hour with the belief in the inevitable coming of a divinely-guided descendant of the Prophet. In this scenario the Mahdi would inaugurate the sequence of events, confirming the faith and making justice manifest in the reconquered Islamic realms. Then the Antichrist would appear on the scene. He would be followed by the descent of Jesus who would kill the Antichrist and perform his prayer behind the Mahdi (Ibn 'Abd al-Wahhab, 1978, Vol. III).

In so far as these revivalist movements were confined to the Sunnite adherents of Islam, the doctrine of Mahdiship was bound to suffer gradual erosion in the wake of the tragic defeat or failure of its successive claimants. On the other hand, The Shi'ite concept of Mahdiship, being openly millenarian, dogmatically binding and genealogically precise, stood the test of time, down to the twentieth century.

## The Hidden Imam

The main bulk of the Shi'ites, known as the Twelvers (*al-Ithna 'Ashariyya*), believe in the infallible imams (divinely chosen leaders of Islam) who are direct descendants of the fourth Caliph 'Ali b. Abi Talib (656–61) by his wife Fatima, the Prophet's daughter. The first Imam was 'Ali himself, followed by his two sons, al-Hasan (d. 669) and al-Husayn (d. 680). An uninterrupted succession of nine other infallible imams ensued, ending with the disappearance of the last twelfth, while still a boy, in 873–4 CE. He is believed by the Twelvers to be in a state of Occultation (*ghayba*), awaiting the opportune moment to return, sword in hand, and fill 'the earth with justice, as it is filled with oppression'. Moreover, the Imamate is conferred by explicit designation (*nass*), whereby the father singles out one of his chosen sons (except in the case of the first Imam who was supposed to have been appointed by the Prophet towards the end of his career). The Shi'ite Imam is, therefore, the legatee (*wasi*) of Muhammad, delegated to carry out his commands, irrespective of the opinion of the rest of the community. Thus, unlike the Sunni Caliph, whose selection was theoretically supposed to be based on the consensus (*ijma'*) of the Muslims or their prominent leaders, the Shi'ite Imam is appointed by God's will and as a sign of His grace (*lutf*) (Mughniyya, 1979a: 87–126).

Apart from Caliph 'Ali and his son al-Husayn, the other imams led a fairly pacifist and subdued style of life, shunning political disputes and avoiding open opposition to the powerful 'Abbasid Caliphs of Baghdad. Clustered around groups of merchant families, often claiming descent from the family of 'Ali (*Sayyids*), the Twelvers remained a quiescent sect throughout the 'Abbasid period. Their geographical distribution consisted of compact communities surrounded by an overwhelming Sunnite majority. Such was the case of the Shi'ite Karkh quarter of Baghdad, or the Arab garrison town of Qumm in western Persia. Other Twelver groups were located on the island of Bahrain, the eastern coast of Arabia and in the interior of Syria. The rise to power of the Shi'ite Buwayhid dynasty (945–1055), which exercised effective control over the appointment and deposition of 'Abbasid Caliphs, offered the Twelvers a golden opportunity to consolidate their separate sectarian identity within the wider Orthodox Islam. It was under the Buwayhids that Twelver jurists such as Ibn Babawayh (d. 991/2), al-Nu'mani (d. 970/1), al-Mufid (d. 1022/3) and al-Tusi (d. 1067) elaborated the themes of Shi'ite jurisprudence. Building on the work of al-Kulayni (d. 940), the Bukhari of the Shi'ites, these jurists reconciled the Twelvers with the new political authorities, while, at the same time, endowing the concept of the Hidden Imam with its final configurations.

The occultation of the Expected Imam, Muhammad al-Mahdi, was neatly divided into two separate phases. In the first phase, extending from 874 to 941, he was deemed to have maintained secret communications with his followers by means of using four designated agents or couriers (*safirs*). This was specified as the Lesser or Short Occultation (*al-ghayba al-sughra*). In the second one, he severed all contacts with the temporal world and began his complete occultation (*al-ghayba al-kubra*) (Mughniyya, 1979a: 252–3).

By divorcing the Imamate from the temporal world and its political sphere, the Shi'ite jurists opened the door to the paradoxical justification of supporting a wide variety of dynasties, as long as they proved able to enforce order and justice. This utilitarian precaution was in large accordance with similar jurisprudential arguments advanced by Sunnite scholars. Hence, the inevitable rejection of political violence, mitigated by the profession of dissimulation (taqiyya) in dealing with established states, paved the way for prominent Shi'ite families to enter into the services of various Sunnite dynasties, such as the Saljuks (1055–1194), or the Ilkhanids (1256–1336), and the Timurids (1370–1506) of Persia.

Deprived of divinely vouchsafed leadership, assuming the exercise of direct political power as blatant usurpation of the authority of the Expected Mahdi, the Twelvers theoretically denied the legitimacy of all governments pending the return of the Hidden Imam – Master of the Sword and of the Age. Even the founder of the Safavid state, Isma'il (1501–24), had to abandon his claims to be the incarnation of the Mahdi and the Messiah as soon as he decided to proclaim Twelver Shi'ism the official religion of his new empire. Originally based on a Sufi order of Turkomans, the Qizilbash, the Safavid dynasty was established as a millenarian movement endowed with the spirit of holy conquest, and led by the representative of God's light and his long-awaited redeemer. However, with the formalization of Twelver Shi'ism as the state religion, Sufism, including Isma'il's own order, Shi'ite extremism, and Sunnism, were combated, or forcibly banned. Learned men of Twelver Shi'ism were brought from Syria, Bahrain and Iraq to propagate and institutionalize the new state religion. These jurists of Arab origin, being specialists in jurisprudence (fiqh), tended to act as prayer-leaders, teachers and mujtahids, while their Persian counterparts, more inclined towards philosophy and rational theology, and drawn from notable families, dominated religious endowments, the judiciary and educational institutions of the state. The relationship between the two clerical camps was often marked with bitter conflict and rivalry (Arjomand, 1984: 123–9).

Towards the end of Safavid rule, Iranian society, which comprised Persia and western Afghanistan, began to break up into autonomous enclaves dominated by tribal chiefs, local notables and rival dynasties. As in other Islamic territories, religious jurists and teachers entered a period of readjustment and reappraisal. In Iran this internal debate in the face of socio-economic disintegration took the form of a jurisprudential conflict between two strands within the religious institution: the *Akhbari* and the *Usuli*. The first reasserted the traditions of the Shi'ite community in its strict adherence to the literal ordinances of acknowledged texts. The second school proclaimed the necessity of a *mujtahid* (practitioner of independent legal judgement), a claim which tallied with the teachings of Sunni revivalist leaders. Whereas the *Akhbari* stance echoed the quietist and conservative attitude of previous Shi'ite jurists, that of the *Usuli* aspired to carve out for its followers a separate space, thereby detaching the practice of religious law from the authority of a crumbling or weak state. However, the *Usuli* position did not reach beyond the non-political domain of the jurists. Its parameters were confined to rituals or the essential legal matters of marriage, inheritance and alms-giving. The belief in the rulership of the Hidden Imam as the only legitimate authority remained the supreme tenet of both schools. It was in this context that Shi'ite Mahdiship revealed itself as a tenacious and persistent millenarianism, forcing its supporters to limit the scope of their political engagement. In Sunnite Islam, a particular leader could simultaneously claim to be a renewer (*mujaddid-cum-mujtahid*) as well as the Expected Mahdi or his forerunner, whereas Shi'ite Islam created a dichotomy that was humanly impossible to bridge.

The doctrine of the Hidden Imam subsumes in its ramifications the separate roles assigned in Sunnism to Jesus as the killer of the Antichrist, on the one hand, and that of the Mahdi as the restorer of the Golden Age, on the other. Moreover, the Sunni Mahdi is at liberty to manifest his mission without having to attend the appearance of his companion, or wrestle with the indomitable task of physical resurrection – his mere emergence is sufficient to precipitate the consummation of the divine event. In Twelver Shi'ism, the rule of justice and equity is not fully initiated without the participation of Caliph 'Ali and his martyred son al-Husayn.

The tragic death of al-Husayn at the battle of Karbala in Central Iraq on 10 Muharram (10 October 680), was gradually transformed into the epitome of the struggle between absolute justice and ungodly evil. His defeat by the forces of Yazid I (680–3), Mu'awiya's son and successor, has been annually commemorated, while his shrine at Karbala has become a holy site of pilgrimage, often superseding Mecca for some extremist Shi'ites. The first ten days of Muharram have ever since become occasions of re-enacting al-Husayn's martyrdom as a focus of venting varied grievances and demands. Under the Safavids the commemoration of the tenth day, known as 'Ashura', was made an integral part of adhering to Twelve Shi'ism as the state religion. The Safavid concentration on al-Husayn's suffering was developed in its popular reiteration to serve as a constant reminder of the perfidy of Sunnite leaders, and an ideal pretext to vilify the Ottoman sultans who were the most formidable opponents of Persian Shi'ism. The reign of the Qajars (1785–1924) witnessed the introduction of passion plays as a religious vehicle of legitimating the reduced authority of the new Iranian rulers. Fath 'Ali Shah (1797–1834) fostered and promoted these theatrical re-enactments of the martyrdom of al-Husayn at a time when the state had effectively surrendered the control of the religious sphere to the *mujtahids* and other clerics. These jurists reasserted their right to receive *zakat* (alms) and levy the *khums* (one-fifth) tax on all gainful activities, and made it incumbent upon all Shi'ite believers to follow the rulings (*taqlid*) of a living *mujtahid*. Thus, the *mujtahid* became the sole competent authority (*marja' al-taqlid*) whose legal judgements were to be accepted as the only valid interpretation of Islamic law. The common people, being ignorant and evil, and contrary to the pious arguments of the *Akhbaris*, were under constant obligation to seek the services and guidance of their religious leaders in matters pertaining to spiritual and mundane transactions. The wider issues, such as declaring war or concluding peace, as well as the collection of the land tax (*kharaj*), were reserved for the state and its ruler (Arjomand, 1984: 239–49).

The demarcation of the functions of the state as temporal authority and those of the jurists as representatives of religious legitimacy, resulted in neutralizing the direct relevance of the Hidden Imam by the mere fact of sharing out the spoils of his legacy between the king and the *mujtahid*. Furthermore, both Shi'ite jurisprudence and rational theology served to detach the community from direct action or participation by means of assigning the management of its affairs to absolute agents. Far from leading to the liberation of jurisprudence from stagnation, the *Usuli* triumph over *Akhbari* traditionalism reinforced its arbitrariness by arrogating its domain of interpretation to one qualified individual. The ultimate authority was withdrawn from the community and vested in a new deputy of the Imam (*marja' al-taqlid*), whose knowledge and exemplary character would facilitate the return of the Twelfth Expected Mahdi. This dichotomy was the challenge which faced Iranian radicals as they sought to reverse the secular policies of the Shah.

# Conclusion

These movements conducted a purely internal dialogue, centred on the tenets and prescriptions of early Islam. Thus, there was no reference to other systems of thought, either for comparative purposes or in order to introduce new elements, and no recognition of the superiority of other cultures was contemplated. This deficiency was, however, acutely felt by both Islamic reformists and radicalists. One of the pioneers of Islamic radicalism, Abu al-Ala al-Mawdudi, while fully appreciative of the intellectual and practical contributions attributed to the revivalist movement of Shah Wali Allah, his son Shah 'Abd al Aziz and Sayyid Ahmad, was keenly aware of its shortcomings:

> The more surprising fact is that the English had seized the Bengal in the time of Shah Waliullah and their influence had reached as far as Allahabad, but he did not seem to take due notice of this fast-emerging power. In the days of Shah 'Abdul 'Aziz, the King of Delhi had become a pensioner under the British suzerainty and the latter had brought almost [the] whole of India under their sway. But even he did not seem to bother himself about the supremacy of this nation and the reasons for this supremacy. Even Sayyid Ahmad and Shah Isma'il, who had risen with the sole objective of bringing about an Islamic revolution and practically made all possible preparations and arrangements for its success, did not think of sending out a deputation of worthy 'ulema to Europe with a view to investigating and inquiring into the causes of the material superiority of her people.
>
> (Mawdudi, 1979a: 118–19)

The revivalist centres of action were often the geographical peripheries of areas lying outside the direct control of central authorities; their social composition consisted in the main of tribal confederacies or alliances organized into new orders. All these puritanical brotherhoods were invariably defeated by either urban political forces possessing superior firearms and methods of organization (such as the defeat of the Wahhabis by the Ottoman reformist governor of Egypt in the second decade of the nineteenth century), or by European military might (such was the fate of the *Padri* movement and all western and Central African revivalist states). Moreover, some of these movements underwent profound structural changes and were consequently transformed into reformist or fairly modernistic entities. This was the case of the Sanusiyya order which emerged in the twentieth century as a national liberation movement struggling for the independence of Libya. Even Wahhabism became after the foundation of the Kingdom of Saudi Arabia in the 1920s and 1930s a subordinate ingredient in the evolving institutions of the new state.

The defeat, slow disintegration and transformation of revivalist currents and political structures constituted opportune moments for the rise and articulation of Islamic reformism. Revivalism was thus eclipsed as an outdated reaction against European commercial expansion, agricultural stagnation and corrupt practices.

# Chapter 2

## *Islamic Reformism*

Islamic reformism was a modern movement which came into being in the wake of European supremacy and expansion. It first emerged in the nineteenth century in the face of external pressure. This particular movement differed from the response of Islamic revivalism to foreign challenges in a number of ways. It has, moreover, adopted a variety of political programmes.

## Europe and Islamic Decline

It was in the nineteenth century that Muslim religious leaders and politicians began to perceive their religion, or more correctly their societies, as being in a state of decline in comparison with various European nations. This painful concession made them aware of defects and weaknesses that had to be remedied or overcome. The European penetration of Islamic societies, financially, militarily and industrially, changed both the historical context and the intellectual perspectives of Muslims. It is true that Islam had previously suffered defeat, and its lands were occupied by foreign armies, yet no perception of decline, or the need to borrow from the enemy, was ever poignantly felt as an exigency. When the Muslims were defeated in the eleventh century and lost Jerusalem to the leaders of the First Crusade, no Muslim scholar questioned the self-sufficiency of Islam or its capability to renew itself. Nor did the Mongol invasions of Islamic territories two centuries later provoke the Hanbalite Ibn Taymiyya to venture beyond condemning the *yasa* of Genghis Khan as being man-made and contrary to the divine laws of Islam. The European encroachments in the eighteenth century were still absent in the normative system advocated by Muhammad b. 'Abd al-

Wahhab. Having discarded the existence of a foreign rival worthy of imitation, he based his teachings on the school of Ibn Taymiyya, calling for the exclusive Lordship (*rububiyya*) and Divinity (*uluhiyya*) of God and obliteration of polytheism (*shirk*) which resulted in the worship of 'humans, trees and stones' (Ibn 'Abd al-Wahhab, 1978: 150–6, 172).

The European civilization which the Muslims faced in the modern age was no longer that of Richard the Lionheart or of Louis IX. It was rather a new Europe refashioned and regenerated by the Enlightenment, the French and the Industrial Revolutions. Awareness of decline became at this crucial juncture of international events an integral theme in the discourse of Islamic reformists. The normative Islam of Ibn Taymiyya or Ibn 'Abd al-Wahhab suddenly ceased to be a searchlight illuminating the blemishes of a disrupted social order. Islam was for the first time dissected and re-evaluated under the watchful eyes of an advancing expansionist West. European norms and concepts were inevitably adopted or borrowed in this comparative endeavour, and the self-sufficiency of Islam was irredeemably shattered.

This new phase in the history of modern Islam was to a large extent succinctly expressed by the Ottoman reform movement, known as the *Tanzimat*. Launched at the turn of the nineteenth century, this movement was initially confined to military and technical measures conceived as an adequate response to the deficient operation of an originally sound political system. However, the perception of decline was accentuated by the relentless advances of European powers throughout Islamic territories. Military and administrative reforms were thus extended to encompass political, financial and educational institutions. By 1839 the Ottoman state was prepared to contemplate the application of a new notion of citizenship which entailed the equality of all its subjects before the law, irrespective of religious or national affiliation.

As a result of the direct occupation of other Islamic territories by European forces, or the collapse of state authority as in Iran, the Ottoman Empire gradually emerged as the last hope and refuge of Muslim power. Its Sultan, who increasingly stressed his dual function of being both emperor and caliph of all Muslims, tended to exert moral and political influence well beyond his ever-decreasing demarcated boundaries. A vigorous Muslim public opinion was consequently brought into being, bent on modern reform in order to encounter European penetration. However,

Europe had in the meantime fully grasped the possibility and beneficial results of seizing the unprecedented opportunity to exercise direct control over the vital economic resources and strategic position of the Islamic world. The triumphant power of successive European states reinstated the erstwhile relationship of almost two equal adversaries on a new footing. As the momentum of the Industrial Revolution gathered pace and turned the world into a vast network of market-oriented economies, various Islamic countries became a source of raw materials and cash crops as well as recipients of manufactured goods and articles.

Thus, Islamic reformism embarked on a search of viable cultural paradigms capable of checking the advance of industrial Europe. Its appropriation of concepts propounded during the Reformation and the Enlightenment adumbrated its specific objectives: it studied the pre-industrial phase of European civilization in order to discover the preconditions of building a strong state and a sustained economic growth. As its adherents deemed European progress the direct outcome of intellectual developments rather than socio-economic factors, their analytical tools were forged to probe the significance of standard laws, the use of reason, consultation as a sign of enlightened governments and the cultivation of science. Hence, Martin Luther was often considered a latter-day Muslim anxious to combat superstitions and restore religion to its original progressive nature. The Enlightenment, with its paradigm of the world as a machine obeying constant mechanistic laws, its deist *philosophes* who sought to bypass the Church and its intolerant bigotry, and the emphasis it placed on civilization as the product of science, reason and education, appealed to the intellectual predispositions of Islamic reformists. Furthermore, the stress which the Reformation and the Enlightenment laid on gaining the confidence and support of monarchs, princes and courtiers struck a responsive chord with urban Muslim scholars who were themselves either bureaucrats or state officials.

While Islamic revivalism was satisfied with its own homespun mode of analysis, Islamic reformism operated within a global system which informed its underlying terms of reference. Islamic revivalism invoked Islam as a coherent system of principles and laws. Islamic reformism directed its attention to the plight of Muslims who had lagged behind in the fields of military power, political organization and technological progress. Thus, retardation entered the vocabulary of Muslim reformers and became a historical dilemma rooted in the recent past and intolerable present of the community. The most influential and highly renowned current of Islamic reformism emerged in its political and cultural ramifications within the wider movement of Ottomanism. The general tenor and connotations of Ottomanism spanned a diverse body of intellectuals and reformers encompassing the exiled young Ottomans, the tempestuous Persian orator and agitator Jamal al-Din al-Afghani, the Indian aristocrat and ingenious pioneer of political accommodation with British sovereignty, Sayyid Ahmad Khan, the Tunisian statesman and scholar Khayr al-Din and the Egyptian rationalist cleric and meticulous educationist Muhammad 'Abduh. The same analytical approach authorized their theoretical level which targeted the state for implementing practical measures. The institutions of the state were perceived as a clock that had become rusty through lack of proper use. It therefore took the hand of a skilful ruler, aided by prudent advisers, to wind it up and reunite in its newly coordinated motions true Islam and modern civilization. This felicitous result was considered highly feasible since universal laws operated at parallel planes of linear progression.

It was inevitable that the diagnosis of western power as an efficient machine, based on just laws and scientific rules, would lead to a fundamental reinterpretation of historical Islamic concepts as well as the appropriation of European intellectual categories. Liberty, constitutionalism and the public interest were henceforth judged to be the key that unlocked the door to progress and material achievement. The practice of *shura*, enjoined by the Qur'an on believers as a worthy activity, and which meant mutual consultation with no clear institutional or procedural machinery, was redis-covered and turned into parliamentary democracy. *Ijma'*, a concept used by jurists to denote the consensus of their colleagues or that of the Companions of the Prophet, was held to be synonymous with public opinion. *Maslaha*, another legal term, indicating the necessity of arriving at new interpretations of the *shari'a* in the absence of a conclusive text or precedent, as long as the well-being of believers was kept in sight, developed into the liberal notion of utility. *Bay'a*, the act of allegiance performed by the members of the community to a new caliph, became equivalent in meaning to the right and process of universal suffrage, while *ahl al-hall wa al-'aqd*, a loose appellation alluding to prominent individuals in society, were transformed into a full-fledged body of elected representatives. Finally, *ijtihad*, a jurisprudential device used to elucidate obscure injunctions or solve new problems within the strict requirements of the *shariʿa*, was recast to stand for freedom of thought (Berkes, 1964: 202–18).

This voyage of rediscovery was a cumulative process, performed by specific groups of scholars and reformers based in the main cities and urban centres of the Islamic world. Distributed over wide geographical areas, and responding to almost identical challenges, these groups formulated similar intellectual concepts and categories. Initiated by the central Ottoman establishment in Istanbul, this movement gradually spread, in its first phase, to Egypt, Tunisia, Syria and India. At the turn of the twentieth century it had encompassed Indonesia, Algeria, Iran, Iraq, Morocco, the Sudan and almost all the urban centres of Islamdom. Hence, as an urban movement, Islamic reformism aimed at penetrating the rural interiors, breaking up the autonomy of regional potentates and bringing tribal confederations under the control of the new institutions of the state. These objectives were designed to introduce a regular and universal system of taxation, and stimulate agricultural expansion in order to finance the envisaged military, fiscal and educational reforms. In this sense, Ottomanism, Islamic reformism and colonial policies, such as those pursued by Britain in India, Holland in Indonesia and France in Algeria, displayed fundamental similarities in carrying out their programmes of action. Their points of divergence were concerned with the identity of the social agency charged with the political tasks rather than the contents of the policies and their desirable implementation.

Under the impact of internal reforms and European expansionism, the territorial empires experienced far-reaching changes. Their imperial style and organization shifted in the direction of national political entities advocating notions and norms of citizenship and patriotic allegiances. The reassertion of state authority, whether at the initiative of Ottoman or European officials, entailed the integration of large sections of social and economic structures into a hierarchy of international production and exchange. However, the cultural and intellectual responses were not issued in identical formulations, since the prominence or recession of Islamic pronouncements was often determined by the intensity and scope of the western-inspired reforms.

Territories which came under direct European control, or were in the grip of massive economic and political penetration, witnessed the emergence of a new social stratum – the class of landlords. These proprietors acquired large tracts of land in almost absolute ownership. Having previously served as tax farmers directly responsible to central authorities for collecting the imperial tribute from petty producers and independent peasants, the new landowners became employers of tenants and share croppers. Their novel function and legally-endorsed status emerged hand in hand with the adoption of western norms of private ownership. This fairly universal phenomenon appeared under different names in regions as far apart as Egypt, India and Indonesia. Its beneficiaries dedicated their energies to the cultivation of cash crops such as cotton, grain, sugar, rubber and raw silk, destined for European markets and industrial plants.

The introduction of monetary transactions into the economy of cash crop cultivation made the local producers totally dependent on the fluctuation of world prices and demand. The financial network, which tied the new landowner and his tenants to the world market, spread by means of a graded system, with a financial company or merchant bank at the top, and intermediaries or moneylenders at the local level. The last were in most cases non-Muslims enjoying extraterritorial rights under the capitulations agreements. The creation of various state institutions, such as local councils, municipalities, governmental departments and assemblies of delegates, gave the landowners the opportunity to voice demands for a more direct role in running the affairs of their communities. This type of political agitation obtained in India, Egypt and Tunisia. The intellectual debate on reform, or resistance to foreign occupation, was generally articulated in the terminology of Islamic categories. Although monetization and agricultural commercialization did gain a foothold in Ottoman Anatolia, the phenomenon of large landownership, or feudalization, was not as prevalent in that region as in other parts of the Islamic world. In Anatolia, Ottoman state officials generally managed to maintain a centralized system of tax collection whereby revenues were directly extracted from petty producers and small farmers. The entrenchment of state authority in lands which were later transformed into what became known as the Republic of Turkey, allowed Ottoman reformers to adopt by the early twentieth century a secular approach to politics. Islam, as a political or philosophical source of inspiration, was largely bypassed or submerged long before the emergence of Ataturk, who abolished the Caliphate in 1924. Furthermore, in territories where the simultaneous impact of Ottoman reform and intensive European penetration took place, as in the Fertile Crescent, there developed an ambivalent conceptualization of the functions of the state, straddling secular and Islamic strands. In regions which escaped both European penetration and Ottoman reform or did not become the target of early western exploitation, such as Afghanistan, central and western Arabia, Morocco and even Iran, Islamic reform and European notions of state and national affiliations were slow to develop and take root in local institutions.

Towards the end of the nineteenth century, three strands converged in most Islamic territories: European expansionism, Ottomanism and Islamic reformism. The first served to expose the internal weakness of Muslim societies. The gradual awareness of decline accelerated the pace of reforms which, in its turn, gave rise to new perceptions of Islam. The original text to be commented upon as the arbiter of truth and knowledge suddenly ceased to be enclosed in the revealed word of God. Another text, with no specific author or format, had made a permanent intrusion. It was the West in its political systems, military presence and economic domination, which appeared in the background as an authoritative code of practice.

## Science and Education

The gripping awareness of decline manifested itself in the unfavourable appraisal by Islamic reformists of their contemporary conditions. Not only did all defects become apparent and infamous, but new deficiencies were unreservedly uncovered as well. Whereas revivalists, such as Ibn 'Abd al-Wahhab of Arabia, would inveigh against visiting saints' tombs and the violations of true Islamic rituals, Sayyid Ahmad Khan and Muhammad 'Abduh highlighted the accomplishments of European culture as a yardstick of measuring the state of Muslims. During his first sojourn in France and England in 1869–70, Sayyid Ahmad Khan (d. 1898) wrote a series of letters to his friends in India, expressing his impressions and sentiments. Having visited and inspected clubs, mansions, private houses, museums, engineering works, shipbuilding establishments, gun foundries, ocean-telegraph companies and vessels of war, his native land was precipitately perceived from a new perspective:

Without flattering the English, I can truly say that the natives of India, high and low, merchants and petty shopkeepers, educated and illiterate, when contrasted with the English in education, manners, and uprightness, are as like them as a dirty animal is to an able and handsome man. The English have reason for believing us in India to be imbecile brutes. What I have seen and seen daily is utterly beyond the imagination of a native of India.

(Graham, 1909: 125–6)

This utter revulsion at the miserable conditions of Muslims became the hallmark of Islamic reformism. Islam, compared with European civilization, began to undergo a trial of questioning and cross-examining. It was bound to lose its absolute inviolability and become amenable to change and adaptability. Consequently, Europe loomed in the horizon of Islamic reformists as a gigantic power that had discarded its theological face, and embarked on a new adventure of science, industry and prosperity. Europe, moreover, ceased to be the distant ambiguous continent of the unbelievers, and was steadily penetrating with its goods, soldiers and administrators the urban and rural conglomerations of the Islamic world. It was a new power that ought to be imitated, emulated or challenged. It offered the Ottoman, the Persian and the Indian a glaring contrast between stagnation and dynamism, backwardness and progress. The Egyptian educationist, Muhammad 'Abduh (1849–1905), thought he was witnessing a new age in which:

the torrent of science has rushed forth and engulfed the entire globe, drowning the unsuspecting ['ulama] in the process. It is an age which has formed a bond between ourselves and the civilized nations, making us aware of their excellent conditions [...] and our mediocre situation: thus revealing their wealth and our poverty, their pride and our degradation, their strength and our weakness, their triumphs and our defeats etc.

('Abduh 1980a, Vol. II: 18)

Addressing the new landowning class in his county, Muhammad 'Abduh urged its members to draw the appropriate lessons which their contact with European nations for many years might have taught them. He particularly asked the wealthy landowners and civil servants to learn from the European associations whose members were farmers, industrialists and merchants, and whose entire income, amounting to more or slightly less than £30 million, was spent on the dissemination of knowledge and the sciences, as well as the expansion of crafts and the arts ('Abduh, 1980a, Vol. III: 47–8).

Jamal al-Din al-Afghani was quite categorical in pinpointing the causes of the Muslims' decline. Exhorting an audience in Calcutta in 1882, he exclaimed:

> The Europeans have now put their hands on every part of the world. The English have reached Afghanistan; the French have seized Tunisia. In reality, these acts of usurpation, aggression, and conquest have not come from the French or the English. Rather it is science that everywhere manifests greatness and power. Ignorance had no alternative to prostrating itself humbly before science and acknowledging its submission.
>
>                    (Pakdaman, 1969: 240–1; Keddie, 1983: 102–3)

Science is thus the source of all prosperity and industrial progress. It is the product of reason, proof and the spirit of philosophy. Rationality has always been the paramount attribute of human beings. Islam, being a rational religion, sanctions science and provides it with its ultimate substance and goals. Human nature, in its pristine essence, and true Islam, cleansed of traditions accumulating over centuries, are both eminently qualified to study the world as God's book. Hence, rational interpretation (*ijtihad*), rather than blind imitation (*taqlid*), was made an article of faith and the best instrument capable of countering the onslaught of the West. The diminution of the Muslims' position was, moreover, considered a temporary setback brought about by reversible causes. Overcoming such a fleeting and anomalous condition could be accomplished by reviving 'the spirit of the Qur'an' (al-Afghani and and 'Abduh 1958: 133). Reviving the spirit of the Qur'an meant a return to origins and rejection of subsequent distortions. Traditions were mere accretions obscuring the true essence of Islam. In this sense, the use of the Qur'an as an heuristic device enabled Islamic reformists to rescue the abstract principles of the faith and mould them in accordance with their own modern ideas. To someone like al-Afghani, whose main intellectual preoccupations were 'the rational sciences', or philosophical speculation, the Qur'an became the stimulus that made the early Muslims aspire to acquaint themselves with Hellenistic philosophy and Persian cosmology. He then proceeded to demolish all the edifice of Islamic philosophy by pointing out its anachronism and futility in the era of modern science and technological innovations. He scornfully ridiculed the way his contemporary Muslim scholars and 'ulama had divided science into two diametrically opposed branches: European and Islamic (Pakdaman, 1969: 243).

To al-Afghani, philosophy and science should no longer be concerned with celestial souls and bodies, the Platonic Idea, the four elements of water, earth, air and fire, the incorruptibility of the soul, or passive and active categories. Rather their subject matter would thenceforth have to include questions such as the causes of the inferiority and backwardness of the community; the proper remedy for such a distressing condition; and the best available means to be used in bringing about reform. The 'ulama of India, for example, had to ask questions and investigate problems, even if these were not raised by former outstanding Muslim philosophers. Telegraph lines, photography, electricity, steam power, railways, the camera, the telescope, the phonograph and the microscope – these are some of the new devices and inventions which ought to claim the attention of a new breed of believers (Pakdaman, 1969: 275–89; Keddie, 1983: 121–2).

Ahmad Khan, whom al-Afghani vilified as a British lackey, adopted Adam Smith's laws of supply and demand and applied them to the cultural field. Whenever, he contended, a branch of culture was no longer in demand, it would stagnate, paving the way for a better and more refined commodity. Thus, traditional Islamic disciplines centred on reports of traditions (*hadith*), jurisprudence (*fiqh*) and speculative theology (*'ilm al-kalam*), had lost their validity and were destined to be replaced by science and modern education (Malik, 1980: 182–6).

## The Politics of Consultation

Apart from science, rational thought and dissemination of modern knowledge, Islamic reformists were anxious to introduce European notions of political authority, administration and bureaucracy. These notions were supposed to be translated into technical devices that would complement the diffusion of knowledge and act as safety valves against regression or violation of proper governance. It was therefore thought that once the institutions of the state were reformed and refurbished, society would be set on a course of renewal and revival. These reforms were, moreover, to be accomplished between a ruler and his subjects, whereby the former would willingly heed the advice of enlightened religious leaders and state officials. Islamic decline became in this context the ineluctable result of 'oriental despotism'. The dichotomy of an advancing West confronting a declining East entered the field of ideological argumentation, revealing despotism as the main culprit responsible for the neglect of science or the requisites of true education. The leading Egyptian Islamic reformist, Muhammad 'Abduh, expressed this trend in the following way:

> I took upon myself to plead the cause of two great issues. The first was the liberation of thought from the shackles of blind imitation, and the comprehension of religion according to the rules laid down, before the emergence of conflict, by the ancestors of the community, and the return, in acquiring religious knowledge, to the original sources, considering them in the light of human reason. The second issue was the reform of the Arabic language [...] The other issue that I espoused [...] and is the pillar of social life was the differentiation between the entitlement of government to obedience from the people, and the people's right to justice from their government. Yes, I was one of those who called upon the Egyptian nation to recognize its right over its ruler – a suggestion that had not occurred to it for over twenty centuries. We urged it to believe that the ruler, although his obedience is obligatory, is only a human being, liable to err and be overwhelmed by his whims, and that nothing can dissuade him from his error and check the preponderance of his whims except the advice that the nation proffers him by word and deed.
>
> ('Abduh, 1980a, Vol. II: 318–19)

The duty of a ruler to seek the advice and expert opinion of his ministers or trusted companions was widely disseminated by Ottoman reformers after 1839. These reformers, having entrenched themselves in the highest echelons of the state, were staunch believers in sharing power with the sultan. Represented by able and thoroughly modern statesmen, such as the Grand Vizier Mustafa Rashid Pasha (1800–58), and his two disciples, Fu'ad Pasha (1815–69) and 'Ali Pasha (1815–71), they were the most visible symbols of Islamic modernity and progressive politics. The reforms initiated by such high officials and bureaucrats made it possible for new groups to emerge and voice more radical changes in the cultural and institutional domains. These groups gradually coalesced into a loose movement led by the New Ottomans, who were graduates of a new system of education: government employees, military officers, journalists, writers and poets. One of their prominent sympathizers, Midhat Pasha (1822–84), succeeded in 1876 in promulgating a new constitution that circumscribed the absolute authority of the Sultan, forcing him to accept the election of an Assembly as a junior partner in conducting the affairs of the empire. The New Ottomans, who elaborated their ideas in the 1860s and 1870s, were the pioneers of the main themes of Islamic reformism. It was upon his arrival in Istanbul in 1869 that al-Afghani first began to expound modern political views (Berkes, 1964: 181–7), having previously confined himself to the vague concepts of Sufism and traditional Islamic philosophy (Pakdaman, 1969: 37).

However, the New Ottomans, by opposing the 'secular' reforms of their senior statesmen, such as 'Ali and Fu'ad, unwittingly played into the hands of the Sultan 'Abd al-Hamid (reigned 1876–1909) who suspended the constitution in 1878, embraced pan-Islamism, and proceeded by autocratic dictates to implement the most extensive programme of modernization in the history of the Islamic world. Islamic reformism echoed the two facets of Ottomanism, often combining elements of the Tanzimat, the thought of New Ottomans, and the policies of 'Abd al-Hamid.

The first generation of Islamic reformists (Khayr al-Din al-Tunisi, Jamal al-Din al-Afghani, Ahmad Khan and Muhammad 'Abduh) counselled against the introduction of a representative form of government directly elected by a popular vote. Public security, a regular tax system, sound administrative structures, consultation in government, modern schools and education based on science and rationalism – these were the main items of their political agenda. From a practical point of view, Ahmad Khan opposed representative government as this would have allowed the Hindus, being the majority, to gain the upper hand over the Indian Muslims. However, opposition to popular elections and parliamentary liberalism sprang from the theoretical assumptions underlying the political analysis of Islamic reformists. Hence, their initial endeavours were concerned with the demarcation of a field of politics extending beyond the court of the monarch, and occupied by persons of the same persuasion. In order to do so, they offered a new definition of political rights and duties, centred on the idea of close co-operation or consultation between the ruler and his new body of western-educated officials. The reformists' appeals to the 'ulama at large to support the new movement were meant to widen their circle of recruitment and win over an influential pressure group. Khayr al-Din, who served both as Prime Minister of Tunisia (1873–7) and Grand Vizier (1878–9), sought to demonstrate the basis of European civilization by stating: 'know that the European nations have decided after much experience that the granting of a free hand to Kings and statesmen in the governance of the Kingdom leads to oppression resulting in the ruins of the realms'. In order to avoid such a disastrous outcome, he highlighted the prerequisites of security, justice and liberty and 'the duty of consultation' as a tradition incumbent upon all rulers (Tunisi, 1978: 118–20, 218–19; see also Brown, 1967: 81–2, 170).

Writing in 1881, Muhammad 'Abduh thought that, in so far as political life was concerned, the Egyptians were still in their infancy. This was premised on his division of human development into three stages: natural, social and political. The first was essentially instinctive, having as its main purpose the basic needs of human beings such as food and shelter. The second involved the struggle for self-preservation and the survival of the species, two activities necessitating co-operation and congregation. While the first two tendencies were strictly inborn abilities, the third became viable only as a result of hard learning and long experience. It was for this reason that Muslims longing for freedom needed 'a wise guide and educator', and whom 'Abduh identified as none other than the Khedive of Egypt, Tawfiq. Political science was thus an artificial skill, and a talent acquired after diligent practice applied by a selected number of people. Egypt could not adopt a fully-fledged constitutional government for generations to come. It was imperative that a political elite should first be formed. This elite, before entertaining the ambition of leading the nation, ought to formulate a clear objective and achieve an indissoluble national unity. The determination of a specific end had to precede all the required means for its achievement. Such a condition obtained in the developed European nations. In other words, loyalty to the fatherland took precedence over all differences of opinion and competing ideologies ('Abduh, 1979: 336–45).

'Abduh's line of reasoning was based on the premises of speculative and dialectic theology ('*ilm al-kalam*), particularly the rationalist school of Mu'tazilism that flourished in Baghdad under the 'Abbasids. According to the Mu'tazilites, there were two types of knowledge: necessary (*'ilm daruri*) and acquired (*'ilm muktasab*). However, 'Abduh departed from classical Islamic philosophy and political theorization by stressing the characteristics of the body politic as a process of humanly-devised institutions and concepts.

Having posited national affiliation as the focus of political activities, and the fatherland as the location of individual rights and duties, 'Abduh differentiated between tyranny, on the one hand, and autocracy, on the other. To him, the first was forbidden by the *shari'a*, while the second was not, since the execution of the law by one person was permitted by both religion and human reason. However, Islam had made it incumbent upon the ruler to consult those who were experts in religion and the application of its injunctions ('Abduh, 1979: 350–6).

Even at the height of the 'Urabi revolt in February 1882 (see above, p. 24), and the emergence of the Egyptian army and the Consultative Assembly of Deputies as the effective authorities, 'Abduh never ventured to vest legislative power in a freely-elected parliament. For him, the source of legislation remained a vague partnership between the Council of Ministers, the Khedive and an assorted elite of landowners and civil servants. What he aspired for was the installation of a government based on standard laws enshrined in a deontic charter or a code of moral obligations. In the terminology of Islamic reformism, constitutional rule denoted the mere restraining of absolute power by means of a code of laws ('Abduh, 1979: 380–1).

After the failure of the 'Urabi revolt and the British occupation of Egypt in September 1882, both al-Afghani and 'Abduh settled in Paris in order to continue their endeavours for Islamic solidarity, reform and political independence. They consequently founded a newspaper, *al 'Urwa al-Wuthqa* (*The Indissoluble Bond*) to propagate their political views, and of which only 18 issues appeared between 13 March and 17 October 1884. In one of its articles entitled 'State officials and the Monarch's entourage' (al-Afghani and 'Abduh 1958: 88–97), al-Afghani took up the familiar theme of 'consultation' and elaborated the concepts of nationality and patriotism. Conceding the importance of building fortresses, raising armies and acquiring good weapons, he went on to highlight the crucial role of experts and skilful technicians 'who knew how to operate and maintain' military machinery. There were, moreover, 'constant laws' which governed the rise of nations to power and ensured the realization of prosperity. One of these laws was love of the fatherland, the *sine qua non* of high moral motivation. All experts and technicians employed by the monarch ought to be related to the country in question, either by the bond of nationality or religion. Foreigners in the service of Muslim rulers only thought of furthering their own interests, and followed practices that invariably led to corruption and ruin. Moreover, a just ruler would give each citizen his due, and delegate responsibility of governance to the able and qualified. The suspension of consultation between the ruler and his trusted officials would always result in despotism and destruction. The 'Ulama, as the spokesmen of the community, should take upon themselves the duty of communicating these self-evident truths to their compatriots (al-Afghani and 'Abduh 1958: 115–20).

In 1889 'Abduh returned to Egypt, and reconciled himself to the British occupation of his country. Al-Afghani went to India, Persia and Russia, and then settled in Istanbul in 1892 at the invitation of Sultan 'Abd al-Hamid. Both ended their careers as frustrated reformists: 'Abduh conducted fruitless campaigns against the traditional scholars of al-Azhar, and al-Afghani became a virtual prisoner of his pan-Islamist Sultan. Nevertheless, al-Afghani and 'Abduh, together with Ahmad Khan, Khayr al-Din al-Tunisi and the New Ottomans, left behind a substantial legacy of concrete reforms and intellectual contributions which transformed the political outlook of a whole generation of Muslims. It was their school, growing as it did against the background of institutional changes and European expansionism, that pronounced slavery an aberrant system, discounted Mahdism as a superstitious belief, and advanced the concept of patriotism to be the embodiment of the spirit of the age.

The striking innovation of Islamic reformism is better appreciated when the arrangement of its priorities are demarcated. One cannot fail to notice how both al-Afghani and 'Abduh addressed themselves to the problems faced by Muslims as a political community. In other words, Muslims as people and citizens were given priority, whereas Islam, as a normative system, assumed the function of a defensive weapon that had to be restored in order to stop deterioration and check decline. If the economy, independence and culture of Muslims were being eroded, such erosion could be redressed by refurbishing Islam, turning it into a progressive religion whose essence was in harmony with modern science and education. Islam, in this sense, played the role of an available instrument that would yield the best desired results and enhance the well-being of the community.

Furthermore, the attack that Islamic reformism directed against Sufi orders, associating their beliefs and practices with superstitions and backwardness, accompanied the more devastating assault of European capitalism. Sufi orders were traditionally linked to artisans' guilds, traders or other socio-economic groups (Baer, 1970: 28–50). The penetration of Islamic territories by European commerce and manufactured goods undermined the economic basis of these orders. Sufism began to be transformed, and often became an empty shell, or a mere spiritual association bereft of its material ambience. It was at this juncture that Sultan 'Abd al-Hamid intervened in the name of pan-Islamism, and extended his patronage to various crumbling Sufi orders and their impoverished leaders. From being autonomous associations of producers and active agents, Sufi orders were turned into state-sponsored organizations toeing the official line of Islam ('Abd al-Hamid, 1978: 68, 74). Islam was thus restricted to specific fields and applications. Popular and spontaneous Islam became less and less viable.

## Salafism and Patriotism

It was towards the end of the nineteenth century that Islamic reformism widened its political scope. This occurred at a time when various secular movements were struggling for sweeping constitutional changes or outright independence from foreign occupation. The New Ottomans were gradually replaced by the Young Turks, radical military officers and intellectuals who upheld the doctrines of liberalism, secularism or popular sovereignty. In Egypt, two political strands emerged. One, led by Mustafa Kamil (1874–1908), argued the case of a constitutional government inspired by European models, as well as the necessity of putting an end to British occupation. The other, represented by Lutfi al-Sayyid (1872–1963), stressed the positive connotations of John Stuart Mill's liberalism, while eschewing the question of full independence. Both strands, however, emphasized the characteristics of Egypt as a distinct nation whose identity had been forged by factors that overrode or disregarded religion. After 1919, landowners, lawyers and civil servants managed under the leadership of Sa'd Zaghlul (d. 1927) to set up a parliamentary system and achieve partial independence.

In 1909 the Indian Councils Act was promulgated by the British authorities to demarcate separate electorates for Hindus and

Muslims. This act was welcomed by the All-India Muslim League that was established in 1905 to counter the growing assertiveness of Hindu patriotism, particularly after the foundation of the Indian National Congress in 1885. Being the spokesman of a minority which harboured fears of Hindu domination, the Muslim League advocated loyalty to the British government, and called for the promotion of the interests and rights of its Muslim constituency. It represented, in the main, landowners and prosperous members of India's urban centres. The league first put forward the idea of an Indian federal structure, and co-operated with Mahatma Gandhi (1869–1948) in his policy of civil disobedience. After 1918, Hindus and Muslims joined forces under the banner of the Khilafat Movement. Having as its main slogans the integrity of the Ottoman Empire and the legitimacy of its sultan as the Caliph of all Muslims, this movement marked the transformation of Indian struggle. However, the divergent interests and perceptions of the two main communities were bound to reassert themselves, particularly with the abolition of the Caliphate by the Turkish republican government in 1924. By 1930, and with the onset of a worldwide economic crisis, the two parties began to drift apart. Thenceforth, Indian Muslims resorted to articulating purely communalist demands based on their 'Two-Nation Theory' (Hussain, 1985: 205). The Muslim League detached itself from its former pro-British stance and demanded the autonomy of Muslim majority provinces within an independent Indian federation. It also worked for separate educational, commercial and industrial institutions. The Indian Congress responded by asserting Hindu symbols and practices, including the prevention of killing cows, and adopted Hindi as the official language of the state. Hence, Islam in India became a new national identity that entrenched itself in a highly vague manner. It led in 1947 to the foundation of Pakistan as a homeland of Muslims who wished to lead an independent life and avoid the hegemony of Indian Hindus.

In Iran the 'ulama, acting as local notables, merchants and administrators of religious endowments, opposed the drive towards modernization. While Sultan Mahmud finally succeeded in 1826 in disbanding the Janissaries as the main Ottoman military force, and proceeded to build a new model army, the Iranian 'ulama managed in the same year to thwart their Shah's efforts to follow in the footsteps of the Ottomans.

It was not until the last decade of the nineteenth century that a genuine pan-Iranian movement crystallized in reaction to commercial and financial concessions granted to foreigners. The Shah, by granting to a British firm the virtual control of Persian tobacco production, galvanized into action local merchants and artisans, as well as religious leaders opposed to foreign loans and European influence. The Tobacco Revolt (1890–2) led to the cancellation of the concessions and emboldened the urban classes in their agitation against British loans contracted by the Shah. In 1896 a follower of al-Afghani assassinated Shah Nasir al-Din (1848–96). His successor, Muzaffar al-Din (1896–1907), notwithstanding his weak personality, continued the policies of his predecessor by relying on foreign loans and advisers. His increasing reliance on Russian protection and commerce proved disastrous: in 1905 the Russian army suffered a crushing defeat at the hands of Japan, a defeat that opened the way for constitutional revolutions in both Russia and Persia.

A constituent national assembly was convened in 1906, dominated by merchants, artisans, 'ulama and liberal intellectuals. A new constitution was promulgated, limiting the authority of the Shah. However, the latter, with the aid of Russian military intervention, put an end to the new experiment. Most of the Iranian religious leaders were, moreover, opposed to an outright representative government, insisting on forming a permanent committee of *mujtahids* to approve all legislation and ensure its compatibility with Shi'ite tenets (Wilber, 1963: 66–77). Furthermore, the leading religious authority opposed economic reforms, such as an equitable system of land ownership, and exhibited a fierce hostility towards vesting the national assembly with the ultimate legislative power.

Iran emerged from the First World War a divided country, weakened by Anglo-Russian competition, tribal conflicts and a backward economy. The Russian Revolution of 1917 put an end to Russian intervention, an event that enabled the Iranians to prevent their country from becoming a British dominion. In 1925 an officer in the modern Cossack Brigade emerged as the effective ruler of the country. This was Reza Khan (1925–41), who upon assuming power declared himself the Shah of Persia. The policies of the first monarch of the Pahlavi dynasty launched Iran on the road of a full-scale programme of modernization. The state gradually asserted its authority over tribal and provincial areas, turning in the process into a precarious partnership of two socio-political sectors: the armed forces and a new class of absentee landlords (Lambton, 1953: Ch. VIII; Upton, 1970: 55–6). The emergence of a landowning class as a vigorous political force was a common feature of most Islamic countries after 1900.

The Shah, by setting up a secular system of education and judicial institutions under state control, partially deprived the 'ulama of their crucial socio-economic base and function. He further undermined the authority of the clergy in the way he sought to transform the cultural heritage of his subjects. The ancient past of Persia was thus resuscitated, and its historical landmarks and symbols were deployed as corroborative evidence of an Aryan identity. The Shah built new industries, introduced for the first time railway and telegraph lines throughout Iran, abolished the veil for all women, ordered men to don European hats and made the wearing of western clothes compulsory for both sexes. However, the oil industry remained under the control of Britain, while Germany acted as the main trading partner. German experts, technocrats, norms of propaganda and cultural influences were much in evidence until 1941. It is true that Reza Shah was an admirer of Ataturk, and often borrowed his slogans and strove to implement similar policies, yet he never declared secularism an official aim of his ideology, nor did he manage to eliminate the traditional preserves of clerical influence. His campaign in 1924 which extolled the beneficial attributes of a republic came to a halt as soon as the religious leaders voiced their opposition (Wilber, 1963: 70–1). His was a programme that echoed to large extent Ottoman reforms implemented between 1839 and 1919.

Suspected of his pro-Axis sympathies, Reza Shah was forced to abdicate by the Allies in 1941. His abdication inaugurated the reign of his son, Muhammad Reza, who was in his turn overthrown by the 1979 Revolution. From 1941 to 1945 Iran came under the effective joint control of the Anglo-Soviet forces. The first modern political organization to emerge as a result of the new situation was the *Tudeh* or Communist Party. It was also in this period that the religious leaders regained part of their lost influence. Some embarked on a course of political activities and intellectual argumentation which did not differ in substance from those of the Egyptian Muslim Brotherhood. In 1943 the future leader and guide of the Islamic Republic of Iran, Ayatollah Khumayni, published a polemic book, *Kashf al-Asrar*, aimed at refuting secular and socialist opponents of the religious establishment and its Shi'ite *mujtahids*. His proposal for an assembly of learned *mujtahids* to choose 'a just monarch' was in line with demands put forward by other reformist

Muslim leaders, such as Rashid Rida and Hasan al-Banna. Thus 'the principle of the monarchy' was kept intact provided Islamic laws did not suffer repeated violations (Rajaee, 1983: 57–8).

This relatively free political environment, occasioned by the intervention of the Soviet Union and Britain, came to an end in 1953. The liberal Prime Minister Mosaddeq was initially supported in his drive to nationalize the oil industry in 1951 by one of the leading religious leaders, Kashani. However, when the US administration refused to back the Iranian government, Kashani turned against Mosaddeq and welcomed the CIA-sponsored *coup d'état* of 1953 that restored the Shah's authority.

Between 1920 and 1945, various Islamic organizations sprang up, echoing the general political and economic motivations of urban social groups. The most important were those of the Muslim Brethren in Egypt, the Association of Algerian 'ulama led by 'Abd al-Hamid Ibn Badis, and the Masyumi movement in Indonesia. They all suffered the same fate as their ideologies or programmes lagged behind more radical parties.

Islamic reform in Indonesia began at the turn of the twentieth century as a modernist and Salafist movement. It propagated its teachings by publishing newspapers, and established a network of schools to inculcate its brand of Islam and combat Christian missionary activities. It derived its theoretical and religious interpretations from the same trend set in motion by Muhammad 'Abduh and Rashid Rida. The Muhammadiyya, founded in 1912, was the first organized effort by Indonesian 'ulama and merchants to propagate such ideas. It controlled mosques, schools, orphanages, libraries and clinics. These institutions clearly suggested its foremost priorities: welfare activities and educational pursuits. Sarekat Islam, another reformist organization, came into being during the same period. It was mainly an association of Indonesian traders opposed to Chinese and Dutch commercial interests. However, the political and intellectual secular school of Ki Hadjar Dewantara (d. 1959) gradually asserted itself as the prevalent ideology of Indonesian urban circles. The future leader of independent Indonesia, Sukarno (d. 1970), became in his early political career one of its prominent adherents. In 1928 he founded the Nationalist Party, and succeeded in bringing about a provisional broad coalition of most Indonesian associations, including the Islamic reformists. Indonesian national-ists, struggling against Dutch colonialism, tended to draw their inspiration from Turkish secularism and the tactics followed by

Gandhi in India (Ricklefs, 1981: 160–75), a fact that reduced Islam to a mere set of rituals and metaphysical beliefs.

The Japanese occupation of Indonesia (1942–5) saw the emergence of Masyumi as a mass rural movement, combining a number of reformist associations and directly assisted by the new masters of Indonesia. By that time, the Indonesian Islamic leadership had rescinded its positive attitude towards nationalism and radical social reforms. This negative stance rebounded to the advantage of secularist, socialist and communist tendencies. Indonesian independence was achieved in 1949, after the surrender of Japan and the brief return of direct Dutch rule. Sukarno's Nationalist Party, the Indonesian Communist Party (PKI) and disparate guerrilla bands thus played the decisive and central role in the national liberation struggle. Masyumi, the main Islamic party, re-emerged after 1945 as an urban movement that was more involved in hostilities against the nascent Republic rather than foreign occupation. After independence, it moderated its strident religious programme and avoided raising the issue of Islam as a political system. The bulk of its supporters became increasingly restricted to the upper and middle classes (Peacock, 1978: 73–9).

During the first years of the Indonesian Republic, Masyumi co-operated with Sukarno, and its leader joined various cabinets. However, as Sukarno moved closer into a formal alliance with the PKI, which claimed in 1953 party membership in rural and urban areas of over 1 million (Ricklefs, 1981: 236), Masyumi veered towards right-wing policies associated with the direction of official American perceptions of the Cold War and the containment of communism. The Asian-African Conference held at Bandung in April 1955 constituted a turning point in modern Indonesian history and heralded the radicalization of Sukarno's ideology, particularly his idea of 'guided democracy'. By 1959 Sukarno had abolished all political parties, and inaugurated his presidential regime based on his five principles of nationalism, humanity, people's sovereignty, social justice and belief in God. Masyumi, being an umbrella organization of various Islamic associations and parties, began to break up into its constituent parts as early as 1948. In that year Partai Sarekat Islam re-established itself as an Islamic party in its own right, while in 1950 Nahdatul Ulama (founded in 1926 as an anti-reformist association) entered the political arena as an independent force. The increasing co-operation between Sukarno and the Communist Party, as well as his strident secular nationalism, led to direct confrontation between Masyumi and the Nationalist government. It was not until 1965, with the elimination of the PKI after an attempted *coup d'état,* and the downfall of Sukarno in 1967, that Masyumi resumed its electoral activities in close association with the Muhammadiyya. However, the new government under President Suharto, supported by the armed forces, forced all Indonesian Muslim parties in 1973 to adopt a new non-Islamic appellation and operate under one single organization: the United Development Party.

The Algerian reformist movement known as Salafism (the return to the original Islam of the early forefathers) emerged in the 1930s in response to intensive French colonial policies. Algeria was one of the few Third World countries whose indigenous society, economy, culture and religion were targeted for total destruction by French colonialism. Between 1830 and 1871 the Algerians staged various revolts against foreign occupation. The initial resistance came to an end with the surrender in 1847 of the Algerian leader 'Abd al-Qadir al-Jaza'iri. Another revolt in 1871, launched after the occupation of Paris by Prussian troops, was ruthlessly suppressed. Thus, the option of military defiance was finally closed. After 1880, western-educated Algerians satisfied themselves with less ambitious aims, confining their demands to equality within a colonial state or even complete assimilation as citizens of a French commonwealth. Both aims met the fierce exclusiveness of French colonials. Demands for equality and autonomy were frequently raised throughout North Africa in the first three decades of the twentieth century. Algeria, Tunisia and Morocco, placed under French rule, experienced similar phases of national reassertion. Whereas in the first phase revivalist or tribal reactions prevailed, the second phase was closely linked to Islamic reformist articulations of cultural specificity and religious regeneration, tinged with an attachment to a common Arab legacy. The third phase, leading to political independence, subordinated Islam to the requirements of nationalist or socialist directions.

Between 1920 and 1940 'Abd al'Aziz al-Tha'alibi in Tunisia, 'Abd al-Hamid Ibn Badis in Algeria and 'Allal al-Fasi in Morocco adopted a programme of political reforms and patriotic slogans based on Salafism. This particular brand of Islamic reformism laid the foundations of educational and welfare institutions increasingly independent of state control, be it foreign or indigenous. In 1920, the Tunisian al-Tha'alibi founded the Destour or Constitution Party in order to promote political and cultural reforms. Its leadership, derived from prominent urban families, was replaced in the 1930s by provincial functionaries, landowners and traders. In 1934, Habib Bourguiba founded the Neo-Destour Party which succeeded in wresting independence from France by 1956. The new party was openly nationalist, secular and thoroughly modernistic (Anderson, 1986: 162–77).

In Morocco, independence was achieved in 1956 as the result of close co-operation between the Sultan Muhammad V and the Istiqlal (Independence) Party of 'Allal al-Fasi. The latter, however, despite his undeniable contributions, was overshadowed by the restoration of the prestige and authority of a nationalist Moroccan Sultan known to his countrymen as the Commander of the Faithful.

The Algerian Salafist 'alim, Ibn Badis, formed in 1931, along with other religious leaders, the Association of Algerian 'ulama. The Association published newspapers, pamphlets and books, founded a network of schools and sought to revive native crafts. By stressing the need of a modern education, both religious and secular, Ibn Badis aspired to achieve a number of interrelated objectives. His principal aim, and that of his associates, was to counter French persistent endeavours to deny the mere existence of Algeria as a political or national entity prior to its occupation. His was a patriotic struggle, undertaken to propagate the idea of an Algerian nation endowed with all the characteristics that qualified it for joining other nations in serving the common purposes of humanity (Ibn Badis, 1968: 277–81). In addition to its patriotic aims, the Association campaigned for regaining control of Muslim institutions and their properties so as to provide its members with a solid material base. Moreover, it waged a relentless war against traditionalist practices of Islam, particularly those associated with rural organizations and Sufi orders. Hence, Salafism in North Africa attacked Sufism or Murabitism not simply as an anti-Islamic innovation, but, more importantly, as a collaborationist political force (Vatin, 1983: 189). In this sense, the main function of Maghrebi reformism resided in its drive for crystallizing a separate national identity in the face of an aggressive colonial system. Nevertheless, the aggressiveness of French settlement, land confiscation, commercialization of agriculture and cultural deprivation sapped the educational, social and legalistic energies of Salafist leaders. It was a new generation, drawn from a different social background, which after 1945 gained the upper hand and forced France to accept the idea of an independent Algeria.

# The Muslim Brethren

In Egypt, the Muslim Brethren Association (MBA), founded in 1928, did not attract the attention of British authorities until 1936. This was the year that witnessed the beginning of a large-scale revolt in Palestine against British occupation, Zionist policies and Jewish immigration. The Palestinian revolt marked a new phase in Arab politics and served to draw Egypt back into the wider Arab world after an absence that had lasted for almost half a century. Thus, various Egyptian political parties and groups responded by holding meetings to discuss the Palestinian question. They organized demonstrations, collected funds and sent petitions of protest to the British government and its representatives in the Middle East. At that time, Hasan al-Banna, the founder and Supreme Guide of the MBA, was still considered a religious preacher, more concerned with moral and metaphysical issues rather than political affairs. The Palestinian revolt represented for him a golden opportunity to break out of his narrow mould and launch his movement onto the national and Arab stage.

Hasan al-Banna represented the culminating phase of Islamic reform and Salafism. His theoretical assumptions did not constitute a new departure from those advanced by Muhammad 'Abduh, Rashid Rida and Ibn Badis. His speeches, pamphlets and political attitude reveal a constant endeavour to reconcile Islam with the modern world. Consequently, concepts such as nationalism, patriotism, the nation-state, constitutionalism and socialism are reworked so as to become an integral part of his Islamic terminology. However, he was perhaps the first Islamic reformist to lay stress on the importance of creating a modern political party and the necessity of formulating a comprehensive programme of action. Although his actual accomplishments fell short of his diverse ambitions, he left behind an intellectual and organizational legacy which continued to inspire future generations and stimulate fresh debates. His example and ideas soon found echoes in neighbouring countries, and led to the emergence of Islamic associations modelled on, or affiliated with, the original organization. This was the case in Syria, Lebanon, Palestine, Jordan, the Sudan and Iraq.

The MBA was essentially an Egyptian movement with a strong Arab dimension. It called for the independence of Egypt and the Sudan and their merger on the basis of the geographical and national unity of the Nile Valley. This was postulated as the first step towards creating a unified Arab world with common historical, linguistic, geographical, religious and cultural characteristics (al-Banna, 1943: 3–4). Islamic unity figured in this scheme as a crowning achievement, composed of sovereign and independent states. Revival of the office of the Caliphate, already discounted by Ibn Badis as a Utopian dream (Ibn Badis, 1968: 410–12), was considered a desirable goal, but not an immediate and obligatory duty.

The economic and political reforms, reiterated by Hasan al-Banna on various occasions, were couched in vague and general terms, such as 'the development of the country's resources', 'the achievement of social equity' and 'a guarantee of adequate opportunity for all'. The MBA exhibited a pronounced opposition to class struggle or active trade unionism. It preferred a corporate state in which all classes and social groups would be placed under the supervision of one single authority. Thus, political parties were deemed divisive elements, hindering the realization of national unity and the operation of a government based on the teachings of the Qur'an. Only foreign influence and domination were attacked, while the entrenched interests of local landowners and capitalists received scant attention. Accordingly, economic exploitation became an issue of ethical implications, and the proposed remedies carried a message of moralistic pronouncements designed to prick the conscience of wealthy Muslims, statesmen and kings (al-Banna, 1938: 3–5, 1945: 9–11).

The members of the MBA were largely drawn from the lower-middle class, such as schoolteachers, clerks, technicians, artisans and shopkeepers, in addition to students. After the outbreak of the Second World War, al-Banna concentrated his efforts on infiltrating the police and armed forces. Moreover, he created a secret 'Special Organization' which trained its members in the use of firearms. He also formed within the Association select groups of Rovers (*Jawwala*) and *Kata'ib*, modelled on the Hitlerite brownshirts and blackshirts. The Special Organization developed its own rules of recruitment and instruction to the extent of becoming a separate entity in its own right. Its leader, 'Abd al-Rahman al-Sindi, often defied the orders of his Supreme Guide, and carried out acts of political assassination on various occasions (Bayyumi, 1979: 118–31; Shadi, 1981: 84–98). The assassination of the Egyptian Prime Minister, Mahmud al-Nuqrashi, in 1948 by one of the Brethren, led in its turn to the dissolution of the MBA and the assassination of Hasan al-Banna on 12 February 1949.

With the disappearance of al-Banna, the MBA entered a period of internal turmoil and struggle. Despite its rehabilitation and re-emergence after the election of Hasan al-Hudaybi as the new Supreme Guide in 1951, it never recovered from the loss of its founder. As early as 1943, British Intelligence reports were increasingly highlighting the pivotal role of al-Banna in the political survival of his organization. A dispatch written in 1946 included this prophetic statement:

> The weakness of the movement however still lies in its leadership. Al-Banna is not only the undisputed leader but the only outstanding personality. The society is believed by the Security authorities in Cairo to be entirely dependent on him, and although he may be dangerous (if his nerve holds) because of the power he can wield, the dependence of the Brotherhood on his leadership may yet be the cause of its downfall. Should he be for any reason removed, the Ikhwan [Brethren] *might* crumble away.
> (Egypt and Sudan, 27 March 1946,
> FO 371/53251/J1324/24/16, Enclosure 'D')

Such an appreciation appears all the more remarkable when it is remembered that the membership of the Brethren was estimated to have reached 500,000, divided into a thousand branches throughout Egypt.

It is generally agreed that every political party, or movement, becomes a viable system of government as a result of three interrelated factors or characteristics. The first concerns the philosophical outlook and political analysis, put forward to diagnose the prevailing conditions and their specific historical features. This diagnosis leads to the level of the particular mechanism by which the analysis, mentioned above, is to be conducted. The third dimension becomes a foregone conclusion centred on the articulation of a political programme geared to the attraction of specific socio-economic groups. These are the three ingredients that constitute the prerequisites for initiating the first steps towards gaining power. No modern political party, be it conservative, socialist, Marxist or Islamist, can aspire to become an influential force without an ideology, a programme and the means of putting theory into practice.

Islamic reformism, as we have seen, did not meet the minimal requirements of a successful political movement. It was in the main a cultural and educational reaction seeking, on the one hand, to reinterpret Islam under the influence of western capitalism, and inject, on the other, the new interpretations into existing political systems. After the First World War, the abolition of the Ottoman Caliphate in 1924 and the rise of various local political parties, the Muslim Brethren endeavoured to make up for these meagre goals by setting up a separate organization. This organization gradually acquired a hierarchical structure and developed a general pro- gramme. However, it never specified the method by means of which it aspired to implement its ideals. Hasan al-Banna did not venture beyond dividing his strategy into three phases: the phase of propaganda, explanation and presentation of the message; that of formation, recruitment, training of followers and their mobilization; and, finally, the phase of implementation, work and creative activity. Moreover, 'faith and work' were the two magic weapons that were supposed to arm his disciples for an eventual victory, the timing of which was left to the discretion of the Supreme Guide.

This open-ended and vague strategy robbed the MBA of the opportunity to follow a consistent policy and formulate a tenable theory. Although it set up a military section, its trained members were never committed to carry out a clear strategy. Nor did it participate wholeheartedly in parliamentary elections. Thus the absence of a clear method led to political paralysis at the centre of the organization, depriving its leadership of taking full advantage of opportunities. This fact became a glaring deficiency in the wake of the assassination of al-Banna in 1949. When the Free Officers launched their *coup d'état* in 1952 and deposed King Faruq, the Muslim Brethren never managed to take a clear-cut stance towards the new regime. As it entered into negotiations with the military Revolutionary Council, its leading politicians and ideologues began to split up into competing factions. Hasan al-Hudaybi, the conservative Supreme Guide, was opposed by 'Abd al-Rahman al-Sindi and Salih 'Ashmawi who represented the militant wing of the MBA. The latter extended their unqualified support to the leader of the Free Officers, Colonel 'Abd al-Nasir (Nasser), while al-Hudaybi could not bring himself to endorse the Revolutionary Council's radical programme of land reform, or forego his insistence on reintroducing the veil for all Muslim women, and shutting down cinemas and theatres (Imam, 1981: 44–6). More importantly, the MBA opposed the existence of all political parties or the creation of new ones, including the Liberation Rally, founded in 1953 by the

Free Officers to establish popular support. It was in the midst of these developments that Sayyid Qutb, the future ideologue of Islamic radicalism, came into prominence as the head of the MBA's propaganda department. He also acted, since the early days of the revolution, as 'a cultural consultant' to the Free Officers. Moreover, he was the only civilian to attend the regular meetings of the Revolutionary Council, sharing with them the same sleeping quarters. It was only after the foundation of the Liberation Rally that Qutb fell out with Nasser and his colleagues. Whereas the Officers wanted to establish a broad-based structure encompassing all shades of opinion, he insisted on an exclusive Islamic party based on the constitution and teachings of the Muslim Brethren (Fadl-Allah, 1978: 91).

In addition to the factions of al-Hudaybi and 'Ashmawi-al-Sindi, a third faction took upon itself the role of an intermediary between the leadership of the MBA and that of the Free Officers. Nasser skilfully played one faction against another until the whole edifice of the Brethren began to disintegrate. This tug of war came to a head when a Muslim Brother attempted to assassinate Nasser on 26 October 1954. The attempt provided Nasser with the opportunity to arrest all the prominent leaders of the Brethren. A week earlier, Nasser had signed the Anglo-Egyptian Agreement with the British government. It ended British sovereignty over the Suez base and stipulated the evacuation of British troops within two years. These events have ever since become part of the Brethren's mythology. Those implicated in the assassination attempt have invariably alluded to their opposition to the Anglo-Egyptian Agreement as the real cause behind their persecution. They particularly single out the clauses that provided for the reactivation of the base should Egypt, Turkey or any Arab state be attacked. However, British diplomatic reports give a totally different account. One report (19 February 1954, F0371/10373/JE 1016/10), confirms that al-Hudaybi and his faction expressed, in the course of a meeting with the British Oriental Counsellor, Trevor Evans, on 7 February 1953, their desire of maintaining a special relationship with Britain. The report goes on to state:

> The existence of a group within the Brotherhood's leaders who were prepared to co-operate with Britain, even if not with the West (they distrusted American influence), and to that extent to abandon the intransigent opposition to all things Western,

probably stems from the increasing middle-class influence in the Brotherhood, compared with the predominantly popular leadership of the movement in the days of Hassan al-Banna.

The disintegration of the MBA revealed the general and vague nature of its political programme, as well as its failure to surmount unexpected difficulties. Hence it was this crisis and its repercussions, rather than the experience of incarceration, that led some of its leaders, such as Sayyid Qutb, to revaluate their whole approach. In other words, the period of imprisonment only served to accentuate an unfolding dilemma and hasten the process of radicalization. The resultant radical response was initially confined to a small circle of intellectuals and students. It was not until the 1970s that what has been dubbed 'Islamic fundamentalism' succeeded in breaking out of its narrow confines.

# Chapter 3

## *Islamic Radicalism: The Prelude*

The reforms, undertaken in the second half of the nineteenth century by either Muslim rulers or European colonial governors, brought into existence new social groups. Concentrated in modern institutions such as bureaucracies, schools, armies and councils, these groups aspired to widen the scope of reforms. Moreover, the achievement of a fairly stable system of public security, the expansion of agriculture and a sustained growth of population, were bound to increase political demands.

Nevertheless, the Muslim world had been gradually integrated into the western economic system. It consequently lost its ability to stage an effective response. The initial reaction, articulated by members of the new middle classes and the intelligentsia, was predominantly political. However, it called into question the inadequate approach of Islamic reformism, precipitating its transcendence. The apparent failure that attended the specific programme of Islamic reformists opened up a new dimension in formulating the perception of Islam, both negatively and positively.

The intervening phase, preceding the emergence of Islamic radicalism, was essentially a struggle for independence from colonial rule. Led and directed by westernized elites, this struggle veered towards patriotic aspirations, the application of parliamentary democracy and the adoption of European legal codes. After 1920 and the final demise of the Ottoman Empire, Islamic reformism lost its association with particular state structures and political institutions. Patriotism asserted itself as a triumphant movement and parliamentary democracy became the magic solution to all outstanding problems. Driven out of the state and the modern economy, Islamic reformism was transformed into Salafism. Advocated by groups of religious students, shopkeepers, traditional artisans and schoolteachers, it soon lost ground to modern forces. Modernist interpretations of the *shari'a*, initially put forward by Islamic reformists, were integrated into the new institutions following the achievement of partial or full independence. Thus, Salafism had lost its *raison d'être*. In this new phase Islam was no longer a political, economic or philosophical system. It ceased to act as a reference or central source of state legislation. This resulted in considering religion a spiritual belief embodied in certain rituals, such as Friday prayers, performing the pilgrimage to Mecca, fasting and undertaking charitable work. In other words, the history of Islam became a cultural heritage to be cherished, drawn upon for literary inspiration and used in its positive implications for the national identities of the various Muslim countries. Even in matters of personal status, such as marriage, divorce and inheritance, the state assumed the ultimate responsibility in deciding the relevance of Islamic laws to the spirit of the age (Coulson, 1978: Ch. 14).

Even Pakistan, a country created to be an exclusive nation-state for Indian Muslims, was pronounced in 1947 by its founder, Muhammad 'Ali Jinnah, to be based on purely secular laws. Addressing the new citizenry, he declared:

> You are free to go to your mosques or to any other place, belong to any religion or caste or creed – that has nothing to do with the business of the state. We are starting with the fundamental principle that we are all citizens and equal citizens of one state. We should keep that in front of us as our ideal and you will find that in the course of time Hindus would cease to be Hindus and Muslims would cease to be Muslims, not in the religious sense because that is the personal faith of an individual, but in the political sense as the citizens of one nation.
>
> (*The Pakistan Times*, 13 August 1947; Munir, 1980: 30)

## Liberalism and Patronage

The drive for a constitutional form of government, guaranteeing the participation of certain sections of the people in the management of their affairs, had become by 1900 a widespread phenomenon in Asia and parts of Africa. Thus, the novel feature of political conceptualization in Muslim countries such as Egypt, Turkey or Indonesia was the assertion of the sovereignty of the people as the ultimate source of legislation. There was nothing distinctly Islamic about such a demand except the fact that some Muslims were involved in this process.

Although Islamic reformists were still arguing for the application of the teachings of Islam, the specific nature of their arguments was coloured by the new political environment. Consequently, the response of Islamic reformism was belated and defensive, rather than anticipatory and innovative. This mood of subordination and tardiness is captured by the way the prominent disciple of Muhammad 'Abduh, Rashid Rida, dealt with the issue of setting up constitutional governments in the Ottoman State, Egypt, Tunisia and Iran. Writing in 1907, he stated:

> The greatest benefit that the peoples of the Orient have derived from the Europeans was to learn how real government ought to be, as well as the assimilation of this knowledge. They thus surged forward in order to substitute restricted rule based on consultation and the law for one based on the absolute will of individuals. Some, such as Japan, have attained their full objectives, others, such as Iran, have embarked on this task; while yet others, as in Egypt and Turkey, are still struggling, by word and pen, to achieve such an end.
>
> This benefit is not a trivial or facile matter. It is a matchless gain, and the height of human development. Those who are content to let a ruler govern them according to his will and desires have to be classed with grazing livestock. This benefit is then ascension from the abyss of bestiality to the apogee of human civility.

Having pinpointed the beneficial aspects of his constitutional theory, Rida tackled the thorny problem of its origins:

> Do not, O Muslim, say that this type of government is one of the basic foundations of our religion, so that we have simply inferred it from the Qur'an and the life stories of the rightly-guided caliphs, and not as a result of associating with the Europeans and being acquainted with the conditions of Westerners. Had you not reflected upon the state of these people, you, or others like you, would not have considered this to be part of Islam. Had it not been so, the 'ulama in Istanbul, Egypt and Morocco, would have outstripped all others in calling for the erection of this pillar.

Most of these 'ulama are still upholders of tyrannical autocracy and are counted amongst its foremost agents [...]

Do you not observe how Morocco, being ignorant of the actual conditions of the Europeans, is staggering in the darkness of its tyranny? No one there utters the word *shura* (consultation), although the Moroccans are amongst those who more frequently recite the Qur'anic *Sura* (chapter) of *al-Shura*, as well as other chapters which command consultation, and delegate the realm of politics to the people of influence and sound judgement.

(Rida, 1907: 279–84)

By the second decade of the twentieth century, the Syrian nationalist and Salafist, Muhammad Kurd 'Ali (1876–1953), was graciously prepared to concede that the Arabs had borrowed all their modern concepts and institutions from the West. He listed, among other things, the meaning of patriotism, parliaments, constitutional governments, the principles of journalism and the publication of periodicals, schools, quarantines and the fundamentals of military service. He concluded by declaring that the Arabs could not attain a favourable position in the world without adopting nationalism, since 'religion by itself would not deliver them from their present predicament' (Kurd 'Ali, 1934–6: 377).

It has already been observed that most Muslim countries, after full or partial independence, adopted liberal constitutions and a parliamentary system of government. However, this democracy was not the result of the ascendancy of the middle classes, or of the pressures exerted by trade unions and the peasantry. Liberalism in Muslim countries such as Egypt, Syria, Iraq, Pakistan and Indonesia was the exclusive domain of absentee landlords, city notables and large merchants, as well as urban lawyers and civil servants tied to commercial interests. Consequently, a system of patronage prevailed whereby the mass of the people were treated as an anonymous conglomeration of clients. According to the rules of patronage, clients were to be grouped into families, quarters, villages, sects and tribes. Independent political, economic and professional bodies were discouraged or frowned upon. Patronage became a vast network of power exercised by political bosses whose accountability largely escaped the stipulations of written constitutions and liberal laws. Such a system, which blurred political and economic struggles by virtue of the personal links binding clients to patrons, militated against the creation of clearly delineated criteria of citizenship and legally protected rights. In a society of patronage, the civil service, the economy and the organs of the state reveal themselves as mere extensions of informal power bases rooted in the daily life of urban quarters, village communities and regional interests. The concrete basis of social structure is thus inverted, forcing the real producer and contributor to act as the grateful recipient of benefits dispensed by a magnanimous protector. The client is drawn towards his patron in the hope of gaining entry to an educational institution, securing a job with a city firm or bank, renewing a farm tenancy, obtaining access to the land for cultivation or contracting a loan from a financial company. In return for services promised or rendered, the patron exacts his own dues. He expects unswerving loyalty, electoral support and abiding gratitude. These are some of the mutual services which create two complementary roles and perpetuate the operation of an open-handed system.

Hence, by the sheer weight of the resources reserved for the exclusive control of the patron, or placed at his behest both on the local and national levels, a relationship of inequality and insidious coercion begins to unfold. The client is invariably trapped in a vicious circle of offering renewable services in expectation of perishable benefits and rewards. These services are political liquid assets invested by the patron in the power game vis-à-vis the state, his colleagues and rivals.

The patronage system entrenched itself in newly-independent societies throughout most of the Muslim world. Since it was vertically structured, it stifled the emergence of class and interest groups. The brokers of exchange, moral support and personal ties were bound to place the state outside the immediate arena of political confrontation or effective participation. The urban centre was normally fragmented into exclusive spheres of influence controlled by absentee landlords, speculators, merchants and veteran politicians. As for the rural areas, patronage ruled with unrivalled supremacy. Tribesmen, cultivators and agricultural workers were in constant need of loans to pay off debts and meet tax demands. It is, however, erroneous to describe such a system as purely feudal, conjuring up the image of European serfdom and fealty. In an unpublished paper entitled 'The political forces in Egypt', commissioned by the Research Department of the British Foreign Office in 1943, the renowned Orientalist Hamilton A. R. Gibb termed the large landowners as 'the real ruling class', and went on to state:

Egypt is still in essentials a feudal society, where wealth is reckoned in arable acreage [...]

It may be said, broadly speaking, that the adoption of a western Constitution and machinery of government has not greatly altered the feudal basis of Egyptian politics and society up to the present time. The owners of medium-sized estates have climbed into power alongside the large landowners, but the activities of Governments of all complexions have still been directed first and foremost to serve the interests of the landed proprietors, whose production of cotton has furnished the staple of Egypt's finances. Even in the growth of political parties the old rivalries of feudal families have played a much greater part than difference of principle. Industrial development has not as yet gone far enough to divert party politics into new channels, for in as much as it is concerned mainly with the processing of local agricultural products it has no interest in raising the standard of life of the fellahin.

(25 February 1943, Foreign Research and Press Service,
FO 371/35530/J1407)

Chapman-Andrews of the British Foreign Office wrote back to Hamilton Gibb with the following query:

Is the feudal basis of Egyptian society rather over-emphasised? The feudal basis of society was of course the tenure of land – but did it not imply a feoff or service by the tenant which among other duties very definitely included that of military service [...] Much wealth in Egypt today is in the hands of brokers, exporters, company promoters, and speculators of all kinds, while merchants, newspaper proprietors, cinematograph owners, insurance and trading agents also do quite well. Unlike a feudal society, most of these gentry are not landowners. The tenants and peasants moreover get precious little but exploitation at the hands of the landowners, and certainly render nothing but labour in the way of feudal service.

(10 April 1943, Foreign Research and Press Service,
FO 371/35530/J1407)

In a revealing policy statement he goes on to say: 'I would not dispute that the basis of Egyptian society is and must remain agrarian'.

Thus a diplomat, unencumbered by the burden of Orientalist analysis, managed to depict the real structure of Egyptian politics without reference to historical continuities. The upshot of the argument was in this case related to the extent of monetization and commercialization in an overwhelmingly agricultural society. The other conclusion had to do with the total cleavage between outmoded political practices and rapid economic changes based on capitalism, or rational calculations of profit-making and investment. However, this was peripheral capitalism serving as an extension of a world order and its western centre.

## Socialism and Militant Nationalism

As the liberal regimes failed to tackle the political, economic, cultural and defensive problems of Muslim societies, parliamentary democracy was discredited in its function as a vehicle of national development. Once faced by a prolonged economic crisis, or an overwhelming military defeat, parliamentary liberalism began to crumble. Its legitimacy became questionable, given the yawning gap between its modernist ideals and meagre results. The mere fact that a perception of such a gap did emerge disclosed the other aspects of this post-independence system: its amorphous and tenuous hold over society, resulting from the nature of patronage relations and formal constitutional arrangements. This made possible the widening of the political space and the emergence of varied parties, associations, clubs and professional institutions. Despite its minimal involvement in promoting the welfare of society at large, it nevertheless undertook to expand the military forces, and build schools and universities. This system, moreover, had to ensure the existence of a relatively efficient bureaucracy and attempt to stimulate industrial growth. These measures led to the emergence of professional army officers, drawn for the first time from the lower middle classes, in addition to teachers, civil servants, doctors, engineers, pharmacists, lawyers, journalists and a nascent working class. It is among these social strata that new ideologies of nationalism and socialism are articulated, or quasi-fascist theories of the state become entrenched. Accordingly, parliamentary democracy is largely bypassed and discounted in its association with economic crises and abysmal military performance.

Political parties, with clear social and economic programmes and hierarchical structures, were consequently formed in most Muslim countries between 1919 and 1950. Professional bodies came into being, and trade unions, straddling artisans and industrial workers, appeared on the scene. More importantly, the armed forces gradually edged their way into the forefront of national politics, dwarfing all other established groups. Built on western models of strict discipline, rationality and professionalism, equipped with advanced technologies and armaments, and drawn from the rural lower middle classes, army officers and their subordinates offered the ideal recruiting ground for ideological-cum-revolutionary parties.

The spectacular rise of Fascism and Nazism in Europe offered to the beleaguered underdeveloped countries of Asia, Africa and Latin America an extremely attractive model. Both Fascism and Nazism seemed the ideal solution to states and social groups still struggling to achieve economic viability and cultural renewal. A new phenomenon began to emerge – the phenomenon of youth movements, built along the lines of paramilitary organizations. In Egypt, for example, all political parties vied with each other in forming their youth organizations in the 1930s. Similar fascist-type movements were to be encountered in the Fertile Crescent, Iran, Pakistan, Indonesia and other Muslim countries. As a matter of fact, the foundation of hierarchical political organizations in the Muslim world is closely bound up with the inter-war period. Turkey, owing to the vigour of its army officers and independently-minded bureaucrats, preceded other Muslim countries by establishing one of the first modern political parties in the early 1920s. In this sense, the MBA was a latecomer when it established its own paramilitary groups in 1940.

The Second World War marked a watershed in the history of the Third World. The decline of traditional colonial powers such as Britain and France sharpened the perceptions of the new political elites. Bedevilled by the legacy of the war and its economic crises, Muslim societies stood on the verge of a new era. Nazism and Fascism suddenly ceased to attract or intrigue. The global influence of the United States and the Soviet Union replaced that of colonial Europe. Two models offered themselves for reconstructing a society, rejuvenating an economy and devising a new political order: American democratic capitalism and Soviet socialism.

In the event, a mild version of socialism was advocated or applied by most Third World governments and political parties, including

Islamic associations. Thus, the leader of the Egyptian Brethren, Hasan al-Banna, derived from certain Qur'anic verses a new Islamic economic system which he dubbed 'reasonable socialism'. This socialism was supposed to combine the best aspects of both capitalism and communism, giving free reign to individual initiative, on the one hand, and affirming the inevitable intervention of the state, on the other (al-Banna, 1957: 157). Even the moderate second Supreme Guide of the Brethren, Hasan al-Hudaybi, could not escape paying lip service to the newly-acclaimed creed. Answering a question put to him in respect of the compatibility of membership in his Association with socialist beliefs, he answered, using an analogy already made by al-Banna:

> We believe in taking what is best from all social movements, from democracy, dictatorship, Communism, and socialism [...] let me use our mosque as an example of what I mean.
>
> There we practice something from all these beliefs. There we practice Communism because a man who comes to pray cannot be removed by another individual from any spot within the mosque he chooses for his devotions. A beggar is the equal of a caliph. In the mosque there is dictatorship when the imam who leads prayers determines when and what postures of worship are to be taken, and all must follow him. There is democracy because any worshipper may interrupt the imam and correct him should he make a mistake in his recitation. And, as I have already told you, there is socialism, because we preach that all citizens should have adequate housing, food, clothing, education, and social justice.
>
> (Peters, 1953: 9)

It must be pointed out, in fairness to al-Banna, that his analogy was put forward as a gesture of light entertainment in the course of delivering one of his lectures (al-Banna, 1957: 9–10). His successor, being a former court judge, turned it into a summation of doctrinal principles and moralistic injunctions.

By 1950 it had become a foregone conclusion that the traditional patriotism of Salafism, along with multi-party parliamentary democracy, was being superseded by socialism and a new type of militant nationalism. Communist parties operating in a number of central Islamic countries, particularly in Indonesia, Iran, Iraq, Syria, Egypt and the Sudan, were showing increasing signs of active involvement in trade unionism, student committees and political demonstrations. Moreover, nationalist organizations, such as the Arab Ba'th Party in Syria, began to highlight the socialist aspects of their programmes. Founded in 1947 by three western-educated schoolteachers – Michel 'Aflaq, Salah al-Din al-Baytar and Zaki al-Arsuzi – the Ba'th merged in 1953 with the Socialist Party of Akram Hawrani, to re-emerge as the Arab Socialist Ba'th Party. Its slogan, 'Unity, Freedom and Socialism', was gradually taken up, in one form or another, by various radical movements in the Arab world. Arab, Indonesian and Iranian nationalisms were inexorably being transformed into an integral part of a general socialist current sweeping the underdeveloped world. Islamic parties and associations were caught up in this wave, and consequently lost both the initiative and the decisive battle for political power. As we saw in our discussion of the absence of clear Islamic policies, strategies and methods of attaining power, these shortcomings were glaringly revealed as national and economic issues interlocked.

Moreover, the majority of Muslim countries were still struggling to achieve full independence, settle border disputes or meet the challenge of neo-colonialist movements. The foundation of Israel in 1948 and its subsequent defeat of the Egyptian, Syrian, Iraqi and Jordanian armies gave Arab nationalism a golden opportunity to discredit the policies of so-called 'corrupt liberalism', 'feudal oppression' and reactionary politicians acting as subordinate agents of western powers. Although the recognition of the state of Israel by the Soviet Union temporarily tarnished the image of communism, the dogged persistence of economic crises and social upheavals ensured its potential appeal to students, workers, the unemployed and members of the intelligentsia. Socialist nationalism and communism were increasingly becoming two rival and dominant ideologies in the Muslim world. The relevance of Islam as a political and economic system seemed to fade into the background as a cultural curiosity.

Even when Islam was vigorously defended, the tone of the argument seemed to carry connotations of conducting a holding operation. Thus, Liyaqat 'Ali Khan, Prime Minister of Pakistan (1947–51), announced in a speech made in 1949:

For us there is only one 'ism – Islamic socialism, which in a nutshell means that every person in this land has equal rights to be provided with food, shelter, clothing, education and medical facilities. Countries which cannot ensure these for their people can never progress. In adopting any reform, the whole matter will be carefully considered in the light of the Shari'at, and before adopting the reform all possible care will be taken to ensure that it is not in any way against any of these sacred laws.

(Symonds, 1950: 178)

As early as 1949 the leader of the autonomous Syrian branch of the original Muslim Brotherhood and member of Parliament, Mustafa al-Siba'i, formed the Islamic Socialist Front to widen the appeal of his party. He also called for close co-operation between the Soviet Union and Syria in order to counterbalance the US and European commitment to the defence of Israel. His suggestion of positive neutrality was another sign of the emerging political configurations throughout the Third World. Under al-Siba'i's leadership, the Socialist Front opposed 'feudalism' in its political and economic manifestations, and stressed the need for social justice, social solidarity and the building of a strong economy (Winder, 1954: 216; 'Abd-Allah, 1983: 115, 156, 169–71). Apart from its adoption of a socialist programme, albeit in a vague and indeterminate manner, the Syrian Brotherhood had a distinctly Arab nationalist orientation. While their Egyptian counterpart displayed an intermittent adherence to the idea of Arab national-ism, the Syrians were more consistent in affirming the para-mountcy of Arab unity. It is true that both saw Islam as the main constituent factor of Arab unity, but al-Siba'i's Arabism was shot through with a nationalist flavour. Thus, when the new military regime under Colonel Adib al-Shishakli embarked on promulgating a new constitution in 1950, al-Siba'i invoked 'Arab nationalism' and 'the national interest' as the sole motives behind his insistence on the adoption of Islam as the official religion of Syria. He declared:

We, the Syrians, champions of Arab unity, consider ourselves to be part of the greater Arab fatherland. Our republic is today a member of the Arab League and will tomorrow, by the grace of God, be part of a single Arab state. According to the lowest estimate the Arabs number seventy million, of whom sixty-eight are Muslims and two are Christians, and all the states of the Arab League (except for Lebanon which has a special position) either specify that the religion of the state is Islam in their constitutions, as is the case with Egypt, Iraq and Jordan; or else their existence is implicitly based on that fact, as is the case with Saudi Arabia and Yemen.

Thus, the specification of Islam as the state religion will be a strong factor for unity between us and our Arab brethren and a formal symbol of the *rapprochement* between the states of the Arab League. Why, therefore, should we neglect the strongest factor – popular and official – for Arab unity?

(Winder, 1954: 220; Mustafa, 1984: 90)

Mustafa al-Siba'i articulated his religious message and political beliefs as a Syrian patriot and an Arab nationalist. While he passionately believed in the national unity of the Arabs, the wider Islamic world represented for him no more than 'a sphere of influence', reserved for the Arabs to foster and cultivate. This modernistic attitude in which religion figured as a nationalistic factor could be seen at work in the intricate field of Islamic law. Thus, he demonstrated the sheer impossibility of applying the Qur'anic punishments in dealing with cases of theft and adultery, by highlighting the strict conditions stipulated for their execution. To him, the verses which alluded to the amputation of a hand, or flogging, were more in the nature of a powerful deterrent, rather than a literal code of law. In other words, the threat of harsh treatment belonged to the category of moral exhortations pronounced to warn and frighten. Moreover, al-Siba'i, not unlike some other Arab nationalists, thought that secularism was a peculiar western invention. He believed that some European states found no difficulty in suppressing Christianity because of its foreign origins. In contrast, the Arabs could never approach Islam in the same spirit of alienation: the emergence of their common identity was bound up with the birth of their religion. Arab nationalism was therefore sustained and strengthened as long as it adhered to its historical roots (Mustafa, 1984: 95).

At first glance, this rejection of European secularism may conjure up the image of a traditionalist Muslim leader advocating the establishment of a theocratic system of government. However, al-Siba'i's stance is almost a faithful echo of intellectual arguments put forward by the co-founder of an Arab nationalist party, normally considered to have embraced since its inception a purely secular ideology. Addressing 'the Arab nation' and 'the Iraqi people' on the forty-second anniversary of the foundation of the Ba'th Party,

Michel 'Aflaq underlined his pioneering discovery of the indissoluble bond between Arab nationalism and Islam as follows:

> Is not faith in the regenerating power of Islam, and its ability to influence the spiritual and cultural destiny of mankind one of the basic tenets of the Ba'th Party? This is equally true of our belief in Islam both as a religion and a civilization for the Arabs, and in its being a vital factor in the modern Arab renaissance, as well as of our perception of its global dimensions in so far as it relates the Muslim peoples to the Arab nation. Hence, it is no wonder that the Ba'th was the first party in the early forties to criticize Western-inspired secularism, and insist upon the irrevocable and organic link between Arabism and Islam.
>
> ('Aflaq, 1989, p. 16)

There is no doubt that the bloody and costly Gulf War (1980–8) between Iraq and the Islamic Republic of Iran occasioned 'Aflaq's renunciation of European secularism. It prompted him, in his capacity as Secretary General of the pro-Iraqi Ba'th Party, to counter Iranian allegations of atheism. By doing so, he simultaneously reasserted the sound religious credentials of the ruling party of Iraq, and underlined its non-western notion of nationalism. It is worth mentioning in this particular respect that fully-fledged secularism has never been adopted by one single Arab state. Furthermore, with the exception of Turkey, all countries with a Muslim majority either apply specific versions of stringent Islamic laws, or espouse reformist and modernistic interpretations of the *shari'a*. 'Aflaq's statement simply confirms this state of affairs, and serves to turn Ataturk's secularism into a daring feat of cultural and social change. The only Arab political organization which made secularism an explicit principle of its ideology was the Syrian Nationalist Party (PPS). Founded in Beirut in 1932 by Antun Sa'adah, an Arab Christian Orthodox Lebanese, it aimed, among other things, at achieving the unity of Greater Syria on a non-religious basis. However, it never managed to harness wide popular support or gain political power. In 1949 its leader staged an abortive revolt against the Lebanese state and consequently lost his life. Betrayed by the first military dictator of Syria, General Husni al-Za'im, to whom he had turned for assistance, he was handed over to the Lebanese authorities, hurriedly tried and executed by a firing squad on 8 July 1949. His execution led to the downfall of al-Za'im, precipitating two successive military coups. The circumstances surrounding his premature death bear striking similarities to those which attended the assassination of Hasan al-Banna. The disappearance of al-Banna and Sa'adah in the same year removed from the political scene two of the most charismatic leaders of quasi-fascist organizations. The hand of King Faruq of Egypt was thought at the time to be behind the tragic fate of both. Others interpreted it as a sign of Anglo-American rivalry, as the United States was seeking to replace an old colonial power. Be that as it may, al-Siba'i's call for positive neutrality appears all the more remarkable in the light of his endeavours to entertain close relations with the Soviet Union. Nevertheless, his particular demand for instituting Islam as the official religion of the state was turned down by almost all major Syrian parties. The struggle for supremacy in Syria seemed to be heading for a final showdown between the Communists and Ba'thists on the one hand, and the Syrian Nationalists, on the other. This became particularly apparent under the third military regime (1949–54), headed by Adib al-Shishakli, a former PPS member. The Muslim Brethren were thus squeezed out in the increasing polarization of Syrian politics.

By 1956 Nasserism had become a major political force throughout the Arab World and beyond. Combining socialism, nationalism and popular democracy based on a one-party system, in addition to a defiant attitude towards both the West and Israel, the Egyptian leader seemed to embody all the positive elements of a new era. To most observers, the message of various Islamic organizations sounded as if it belonged to a bygone age (Mitchell, 1969: vii). Whereas parties such as the Ba'th drew their chief support from members of the rural lower middle class or ex-peasant migrants to cities and towns, Nasserism appealed to the same urban constituencies which constituted the mainstay of the Muslim Brethren. As we have seen, the Egyptian parent organization split into competing factions and virtually ceased to operate for almost a decade. The Syrian 'branch' managed to survive, albeit on a reduced basis, by assimilating the slogans of Nasserism. In 1959 Mustafa al-Siba'i published a book under the title *Islamic Socialism*. One year later he expanded it to run to 260 pages. Nasser immediately adopted the book as 'a major statement of ideology for Egyptian socialism'. When the United Arab Republic was established in 1958 in a merger between Syria and Egypt, al-Siba'i, in compliance with the wishes of Nasser as the new President of both provinces, dissolved his organization along with other Syrian parties. Furthermore, he was one of the few Syrian leaders who opposed the *coup d'état* of 1961 which broke up the Union (Yakan, n.d.: 89; Hanna and Gardner, 1969: 5; Mustafa, 1984: 76–7). By that time al-Siba'i had handed over the leadership of the Brethren to the Damascene high school teacher, 'Isam al-'Attar. In 1963 the Ba'th came to power in Syria, whereby a new phase in the fortunes of the Brethren began to unfold.

## Islam and the Nation-State

Throughout the 1950s the new middle classes and intellectuals in the Islamic world increasingly detached themselves from the old order of city notables, landowners and property speculators. Junior army officers, schoolteachers, civil servants, engineers, doctors, workers and students all joined in working for a new political and economic system. Some succeeded, others failed. Whatever the outcome, there was a perceptible drive towards turning the institutions of the state into a vehicle of development, planning and nation-building. Thus, centralization of political power was the inevitable result. The achievement of political independence or semi-independence shifted the ideological debate to social, economic and military issues. The cultural heritage, the past and religion became the focus of intellectual scrutiny with the aim of evaluating their relevance to societies entering the technological age.

Within two decades (1950–70), all Muslim countries, along with the rest of the Third World, had undergone unprecedented changes in their economic structures, political institutions and cultural systems. These changes were directly related to the growing importance of the state as a central agency of renewal and transformation. Whatever the particular policies, pursued by one state or another, the emphasis on modernization, industrialization, equality and land reforms cut across national frontiers and different political systems. The nation-state with its present boundaries, economy, social configurations and educational establishments, finally emerged as a permanent fact overriding all attempts to sidestep it. Religion was subordinated to nationalism, socialism, popular democracy and a plethora of novel goals. In most of the new national states, traditional landowners and notables gradually lost their position or were co-opted into a wider network of bureaucratic and commercial relations. Pan-movements in Asia, Latin America and Africa, aiming at uniting continents or contiguous countries, ended up by sharpening the distinctive identities of various national entities. Even artificial states survived various separatist revolts and managed to strengthen their central authority, curtailing the secessionist forces in the peripheral regions. The nation-state, growing in confidence and military strength, often managed to defeat the aims of its opponents and force them to redefine their objectives so as to encompass the national territory as a whole. Indonesia, Nigeria and the Sudan, for example, had to contend for years with ethnic, religious and 'national' revolts of separation and dismemberment. After more than a decade of intermittent battles and skirmishes, the Indonesian army crushed the Dar ul-Islam revolt in West Java and the separatist rebellion in Acheh. Secessionist Ibos of Biafra suffered the same fate in Nigeria, while the southern Sudanese, thwarted in their efforts to partition the Sudan, joined other political parties in the North to build a modern, secular state. The secession of East Pakistan in 1971 to form a new sovereign state, Bangladesh, was the exception that proved the rule. A combination of factors – geographical distance, approximate parity in population, naked exploitation of the East by the West and the direct interest of India in weakening a rival power – made the creation of Bangladesh a confirmation of an inevitable trend. In the Arab world, the brief unity between Egypt and Syria (1958–61), brought about by the rising tide of Arab nationalism in addition to fears of a communist takeover in Damascus, marked the final Arab endeavour to effect a complete merger between two independent states.

However, nationalism on its own is neither a political ideology nor a comprehensive programme of socio-economic principles; it merely serves to define a territorial identity with certain cultural and national characteristics. In other words, nationalism may assume a variety of ideological contents, and appeal to a wide spectrum of social classes. In the Muslim world, nationalism entered the political field in conjunction with liberal democracy, socialism, Islamism, secularism and Fascism. To Ataturk, the first President of republican Turkey, populism, nationalism, secularism and *etatisme*, directly derived from European sources, formed an organic unity whose operation depended on the constant preservation of its component parts. He thus abolished the Ottoman Sultanate and Caliphate in 1922 and 1924 respectively, declared Turkey a republic, replaced the *shari'a* in its entirely with secular European laws and used the state to encourage the growth of national industries. Moreover, Sufi orders were proscribed, religious schools closed down, and the equality of men and women was extended to include personal and public rights. All minorities, Jewish, Armenian and Greek, were granted the same rights as the Turkish Muslims. The millet system, introduced under various names since the early days of Islam, was thus swept away (Toprak, 1981: 38–56).

Apart from Saudi Arabia and Afghanistan, Turkey was the only Muslim country which did not fall under direct colonial rule or suffer the consequences of a prolonged foreign occupation. While both Arabia and Afghanistan entered the twentieth century with their tribal structures, primitive economies and traditional political cultures, Turkey inherited the legacy of repeated Ottoman reforms, European capitalist expansion and persistent efforts to build a modern state. By 1920 it was the only Islamic state with a well-trained bureaucracy, a strong army built along European lines and a western-educated intelligentsia unfettered by ties of patronage or landlordism. Between 1914 and 1927, its Greek and Armenian merchants, bankers, farmers and businessmen, in addition to millions of petty traders, artisans and peasants, 'had perished, departed, or been expelled, a number which probably contained 90 per cent of the pre-war bourgeoisie' (Keyder, 1987: 69). These upheavals paved the way for the hegemony of the state under the leadership of its local civil servants and army officers. The patronage system which dominated most other Islamic countries was thus nipped in the bud. The state placed itself at the focal points of society and controlled its policies. Although the Turkish economy in the 1920s was still overwhelmingly agrarian (in 1927 over 4 million adults were engaged in agriculture, while only 300,000 worked in industry, both modern and traditional, and about 257,000 in commercial enterprises), the land was in the main owned by petty producers. This meant the absence of large landlords, except in south-eastern Anatolia, which had a tribal structure composed of a Kurdish majority. The sector of small proprietorship witnessed a steady expansion, growing in a single decade (1950–60) by 30 per cent.

It was in the tribal and semi-feudal areas that 'traditional Islam' made its last stand against the new Turkish order. Led by Shaykh Sa'id, a tribal chief of the Naqshbandi Sufi order, the rebellion of 1925 upheld conflicting demands, ranging from Kurdish separatism to the restoration of the Caliphate. The government, however, succeeded in crushing the movement within two months (Toprak, 1981: 67–9; Davison, 1988: 134). In the wake of these drastic measures and policies, the government launched a concerted and consistent campaign to make Islam a personal creed, bereft of legal, political and economic relevance. The whole apparatus of the state was dominated by the Republican People's Party and its leader, Ataturk. On the other hand, steps were taken to provide wider opportunities for the indigenous commercial class to diversify its activities in co-operation with foreign capital. Self-sufficiency, economic development and industrial production were identified after the Depression of 1929 as the main tasks of the bureaucratic machinery. Hence, a new middle class composed of industrialists, businessmen and merchants came into being as a deliberate creation of the state. A modern bureaucracy, underpinned by the army and a political party, operated an economy of state capitalism which eventually led to the advent of a multi-party system after 1945. Whereas most Muslim countries joined the family of independent states with a traditional government or a liberal type of government dominated by landowners and notables, the Turkish experience was both unprecedented and precursory.

Thus, towards the end of the Second World War, Turkey was witnessing the rapid development and expansion of a private sector. Its representatives voiced their dissatisfaction with a government controlled by rigid bureaucrats and disciplinarian military elements. They pointed out that paternalistic methods and cumbersome practices were incompatible with commercial pursuits and industrial ventures. The state as a whole was subject to severe criticisms for its interference, and its control of economic activities, deemed the prerogative of private enterprise. Accordingly, in 1946, the Democratic Party (DP) was founded to give political expression to the demands of these new interest groups. The parliamentary elections of 1950 brought to power the new party, ending the exclusive rule of the Republican People's Party (RPP). The RPP accepted its own defeat, and stepped down peacefully, letting the DP form its own government. This experiment in pluralistic democracy lasted for almost ten years, whereupon a *coup d'état* took place, and a military regime, with the blessing of the Republican Party, was installed.

The founders of the DP were four prominent personalities in the realm of commerce, industry and landownership: Adnan Menderes, Celal Bayar, Refik Koralton and Fuad Koprulu. In addition to the encouragement of private enterprise, they had a keen interest in attracting foreign capital, particularly American, and opposed the implementation of an agrarian reform put forward by the government (Harputlu, 1974: 166). These demands coincided with the onset of the Soviet-American Cold War, and a shift in Turkish official policy towards the United States. By choosing to align itself with the West, the RPP, led by Ataturk's successor, Ismet Inonu, complied with the wishes of his bourgeois compatriots to lift the restrictions on political parties. From 1947 onwards, the date of the first US economic aid, the Turkish army underwent a noticeable reorientation in its discipline, organization and ideology, thanks to the supervision of US experts. It has, however, continued to act as the guardian and trustee of Ataturk's legacy. On three successive occasions (1960, 1971, 1980) it deliberately and forcefully intervened in the political process, and assumed effective control of the state. Each *coup d'état* was launched against the background of an acute economic crisis, or a rising wave of violence, which threatened the viability of the state. Having accomplished their task, by promulgating a new constitution, enacting new laws and banning certain political parties, the armed forces would once again hand over the reins of power to a democratically-elected government. Consequently, the revival of Islam in Turkey has invariably been *sui generis* in its ultimate causes and results. No Turkish Sayyid Qutb or Mawdudi has appeared on the scene.

A cluster of factors, already alluded to in the context of discussing the emergence of modern Turkey, combined and interacted to create a solid base capable of asserting the paramountcy of the state. Such an equation, composed of interdependent elements, blocked the possibility of reverting to an earlier stage of development. Seen in this light, three achievements stood out for their long-term effects: military professionalism, bureaucratic rationalism and militant nationalism. Each was firmly controlled by a modern political party, imbued with the spirit of state authority, and held to be based on the ultimate sovereignty of the nation. Their gradual maturation formed interconnected channels so that secularism could freely communicate its message to society at large.

Initially confined to urban elites and institutions, this political, legal, administrative and cultural revolution was imposed from above. Hence, the onset of the Great Depression in 1929, coupled with religious and social discontent, revealed the need for more comprehensive policies. *Etatisme*, deemed the only possible solution, widened the scope of the revolution by accentuating the urgency of economic self-sufficiency. In the event, state intervention led to the emergence of a vigorous middle class. Moreover, the countryside,

underdeveloped and hitherto neglected, witnessed a steady penetration of urban activities designed to integrate it into the national
culture and market. By the time of Ataturk's death in 1938, Turkey
had undergone one of the most momentous transformations in its
history.

This process of revolutionary change set in motion by Ottoman
reformers, Young Turks, and Ataturkism, has been punctuated by
phases of severe crises, social upheavals, military coups and violent
clashes. However, modern Turkey has so far managed to weather
the storm: parliamentary democracy, secularism, and nationalism
have become a permanent option of the political system.

The triumph of the DP in the 1950 elections signalled the advent
of free enterprise and market forces. For almost a decade, Turkish
society was dominated by businessmen, entrepreneurs, professionals
and industrialists. The rise to power of the new middle class resulted
in the erosion of the hegemonic authority and material privileges of
three main groups: army officers, bureaucrats and members of the
intelligentsia. On the other hand, the peasantry, constituting the
majority of the electorate, reaped the benefits of policies tailored to
their needs. As roads and irrigation systems were built, credit
facilities made available and mechanization encouraged, the
agricultural sector experienced a steady growth in productivity.
Inevitably, a mild version of Islamic revival emerged in conjunction
with this positive response to rural interests. Secularism, originally
devised by Ataturk to ensure the constant subordination of religion
to state institutions, denoted in the new context a simple
demarcation of two independent spheres of life. In a world of
multi-party politics and electioneering, religion was bound to
become a controversial issue, particularly under a party lacking a
coherent ideology. However, the spectre of reinstating a new Islamic
system, given the irreversible structural changes, remained a remote
possibility.

The 'agrarian revolution' of the 1950s was followed in the 1960s
by a policy of industrial expansion, directly sponsored by the state.
Along with the service and construction sectors, industry was thus
strategically placed to absorb migrants from rural areas, or excess
labour caused by population growth. A diversified economy,
boosted by constant encouragement from successive governments,
became the hallmark of a vigorous middle class. In other words, a
new model of nation-building in which political institutions,
economic structures, culture and social configurations were steadily

adjusted, offered secularism the means to deal with Islam on its own terms.

Perhaps the key to the relative success of Turkey's national experiment resides in a land system dominated by independent small producers. This automatically excluded the entrenchment of a landed aristocracy, sufficiently powerful to turn state institutions into mere extensions of its patronage network. Moreover, the abundant availability of common and state-owned lands, a legacy bequeathed to Anatolia by the central Ottoman establishment, obviated the need to carry out radical land reforms. As a result, landless share-croppers, tenants, families and immigrants were in an ideal position to acquire their own plots of land by a process of gradual reclamation. Land reform became either an official formalization of ownership or a matter of distributing uncultivated state-owned fields (Parvin and Hic, 1984: 222–3; Keyder, 1987: 128–40). Hence, unlike most Islamic countries, including Indonesia, Pakistan, Iran, Egypt and Morocco, there was a noticeable absence of large-scale landlessness. Moreover, the momentum of progressive change escaped the negative aspects of patronage and traditional politics, and established an irreversible trend of developments and events.

In the late 1970s industrial growth and economic expansion, sustained by a policy of import substitution, foreign aid and the remittances of Turkish guest workers in West Germany, entered a period of crisis coinciding with world recession and rising oil prices. Extremist political groups, both of the right and left, became thenceforth more actively involved in violent acts or armed struggle. The escalation of violence, often directed against the state, and encompassing students, workers and minorities, appeared to herald the collapse of the political system as a whole. Fascists, Marxists and radical Islamists vied with each other in attacking democracy, liberal politics and western-inspired models of development. Even the inviolate legacy of Ataturk was for the first time openly questioned. Finally, in September 1980, the army intervened to restore order and initiate a programme of political and economic reforms. The leaders of all political parties and trade unions were arrested, put on trial, convicted of various offences and banned from public life for ten years. A new constitution was drafted and submitted to a referendum in November 1982. It once again reaffirmed the adherence of the Republic to democracy, secularism and 'the nationalism of Ataturk'.

Turkish right-wing radicalism, be it fascist or Islamist, has always maintained an ambivalent attitude towards Ataturk's fundamental principles. The National Salvation Party (renamed the Welfare Party after 1983) was the only significant Islamic organization with a relatively coherent programme. While it rejected secularism as an alien system, nationalism, populism and *etatisme* were implicitly or explicitly incorporated into its general ideology. Its leader, Necmettin Erbakan, repeatedly deplored his country's dependence on the developed world in technological and scientific fields. Being a scientist, educated in Istanbul and West Germany, he stressed 'creativity' rather than 'imitation'. His was a vision of an industrialized society competing on an equal footing with both the East and the West. Whereas Ataturk's nationalism traded Islam for an immemorial and largely mythical past, Erbakan's patriotic drive was infused with the glorious history of Islam and the Ottoman Empire (Toprak, 1981: 98–104). Japan, the model of material progress, as well as spiritual authenticity, inspired his call for a powerful Islamic state. The political vocabulary of Turkish Islamism was thus offered as the shortest and most convenient road to industrial development. Erbakan's fascination with technology and scientific efficiency sums up a modernistic approach anxious to assert a separate and independent path to world civilization. However, in terms of electoral support, this type of ideology has suffered a gradual decline, particularly after the elections of 1987 and the rise to power of the new Motherland Party led by the then Prime Minister, Turgut Ozal, who seemed intent on wooing the religious vote away from extremist circles (*al-Da'wa*, Vol. 26, Nos 12, 15, 16, 1977; Davison, 1988: 180–1). Although its leaders were former members of Erbakan's own party, the present ruling Justice and Development Party, or AKP, which won two successive parliamentary elections in 2002 and 2007, has now discarded most notions related to building an Islamic state and has pledged itself to uphold secularism.

By and large, secularism in Turkey has become an integral part of the modern national culture. It is a challenge to which Islamic radicalism can only respond by accentuating its scientific discourse. Thus, the fortunes of Islam in its Turkish context provide an ideal vantage point to gauge the situation in other Muslim countries.

# Chapter 4

## The Transcendence of Islam

Between 1856 and 1950, Muslim scholars and officials attached to the inherent nature of Islam all the modern labels of rationalism, science, patriotism, democracy and socialism. Islam was thus simultaneously enriched and diluted. Its enrichment held out hope for a new lease of life, while its dilution offered an opportunity to break away from the constraints of textual purity and venture into a new territory of open theoretical frontiers.

To Jamal al-Din al-Afghani, Muhammad 'Abduh and Hasan al-Banna, the plight of the Muslim community, culturally and physically, constituted a problematical paradox that had to be explained and redressed. Hence, the task of reformism consisted in sharpening the Muslims' consciousness of the dynamic character-istics of their faith, and its ability to halt the temporary state of decline. In order to achieve such an end, fatalistic beliefs and traditional practices were combated for their flagrant violation of true Islam and rationalist thought. In other words, reformism aimed at bridging the gap between European supremacy and Islamic culture so as to amalgamate both in one single unit of civilization.

## The New Order

By contrast, Islamic radicalism, operating under different conditions, had to contend with a novel dilemma: the total eclipse of Islam, brought about by the ungodly innovations of secular nation-states. Consequently, the question of rescuing the Muslims from stagnation and ossification became redundant. The reinstatement of Islam, the bedrock of the nation and its unequivocal identity, figured as the most urgent task of a new generation of believers. From being a culture, a code of ethics or a weapon of defence, Islam was henceforth turned into a totalitarian ideology. Furthermore, the circumstances and rules of this unprecedented engagement obliterated the distance between the past and the present, reducing the former to a faithful servant of the latter.

Radical movements of change acquire their fully-fledged growth in societies which have become conscious of their deficient development in a rapidly changing world. This awareness is often accentuated by a nostalgic yearning for past glories and bygone achievements. The reactivation of the past, or its fresh discovery, is governed by a futuristic vision, propelled by the impact of the present. The attempt of overcoming the negativity of the present is, therefore, the decisive factor in the journey towards the past. The historical golden age is used as a springboard for accomplishing a leap into a new world, while the present exerts its overriding influence in illuminating both the past and the future.

Seen in this light, Islamic radicalism is a purely modern, or contemporary, reaction to the emergence of revolutionary nationalism and secular norms of government. Whereas Islamic revivalism was informed by the normative ideals of religious millenarianism, and reformism strove to effect an amalgamation of indigenous and European elements, the ideology of radicalism represents a direct response to the emergence of independent nation-states. Moreover, the militancy, exclusiveness and atavism of Islamic radicalism represent a creative synthesis of both revivalism and reformism. In this sense, it is a violent abrogation of a long line of development, and the last endeavour to rescue the political fortunes of Islam.

Prior to 1970, Islamic radicalism was more of an intellectual current than a political movement. Some of its theoretical principles, such as the exclusive sovereignty of God and the characteristics of *jihad* (holy struggle), were first put forward in British India as a reaction to secular and nationalist ideologies. A number of lectures and tracts, published by al-Mawdudi in the inter-war period, are generally considered to have broken fresh ground, heralding the birth of a new Islamic theory. However, al-Mawdudi's writings, intermittent and haphazard, represented a mere indefinite prototype of radicalism.

It was in Egypt, after the demise of the Muslim Brotherhood and the implementation of Nasser's revolutionary programme, that Islamic radicalism was formulated as a comprehensive and exclusive doctrine. The Muslim Brother Sayyid Qutb (1906–66) has been rightfully credited with the authoritative articulation of this particular ideology, in spite of his obvious reliance on al-Mawdudi in building up a consistent and coherent worldview.

For almost two decades the Qutbist formula was confined to Nasserist Egypt and Ba'thist Syria, while in Iraq Muhammad Baqir al-Sadr (d. 1980) developed his own brand of Shi'ite radicalism. Thus, Islamic radicalism grew out of the peculiar conditions of certain Arab countries. As for Iran, its religious establishment was still engaged in inconclusive debates on the proper role of Islam under an enterprising and modernizing king (Lambton, 1964: 115–35). Even Ayatollah Khumayni, who was sent into exile by the Shah in 1964, had not yet reached definite conclusions as regards his political duties in the absence of the Hidden Imam. The initiation of *jihad*, for example, was considered by him to be the exclusive prerogative of the Awaited Mahdi (Khumayni, 1964: 482).

Egypt, Syria and, to a lesser extent, Iraq, were the breeding ground of Islamic radicalism. How did this come about? What particular circumstances account for such a response? Briefly stated, these were the only Islamic countries which experienced a cluster of interrelated revolutionary changes. These changes included land reforms, industrialization, the assertion of the primacy of nationalism, the adoption of socialism as an inevitable necessity and the imposition of state control over religious institutions, be they courts, mosques or pious foundations (*waqfs*).

These measures and policies, implemented by army officers, technocrats and intellectuals, put an end to the traditional patronage system and swept away the socio-economic basis of an entire class of landowners and their allies. Islam itself became fused with nationalism and consequently lost its universality, except in its spiritual dimensions as a religious creed. Although secularism did not figure as an explicit tenet, the centrality of nationalism subordinated religion to serve secular purposes. Hence a new order came into being in which the state, led by a charismatic leader and directed by a single party, assumed paramount importance.

The land reforms, inasmuch as they liquidated the client-patron system, constituted the most significant structural alteration: they turned the peasants, share-croppers and tenants from clients into citizens whose welfare became the direct responsibility of the state. Moreover, agricultural co-operatives, local councils, credit facilities, clinics, roads, the introduction of tractors and new crops, served to widen the horizons of the rural inhabitants and place them within the multifaceted aspects of the national market. The drift towards the cities by rural migrants took place in a highly fluid context, whereby the new arrivals had already passed the stage of traditionalism. This erosion of old customs, lifestyles and political expectations was further accelerated by the pace of economic, cultural and national institutions of urban centres.

As far as our three countries are concerned, the 1950s and 1960s were decades of construction, sacrifice and the promise of a better future. The common man came to the fore for the first time, emboldened by a benevolent and welfare state. Despite the failure of both agrarian reforms and industrialization to absorb surplus rural labour or meet the consumption demands of a rapidly growing population, social and economic issues seemed, at least for the time being, to have been pre-empted. To Islamic radicalism, wrestling with these conditions, the new problem represented itself in the overwhelming power of the state and its hegemonic monopoly of the political and economic process. While under the *anciens regimes*, Islamism enjoyed a wide margin of manoeuvre; involuntarily vacated by a traditional system of government, the new order appeared to have closed almost all loopholes. Narrow-minded landowners, short-sighted speculators and corrupt politicians could be easily challenged in the name of a moral vision, claiming to be in tune with the downtrodden masses. The army officers and party activists suddenly removed the challenge and offered their own theoretical and practical programme. Furthermore, the language of Islamic reformism was to a large extent made redundant, since these revolutionary states co-opted all its positive elements. In addition to land reform, nationalization and welfare measures, Arab national-ism, irrespective of its denominations and varieties, subsumed in its vocabulary the history of Islam and its heroes. Michel 'Aflaq, co-founder of the Ba'th, spoke of the Prophet Muhammad as the pioneer of Arabism and Arab unity. President Nasser of Egypt was often compared in his personality and exploits to Saladin, the Muslim military genius who unified both Egypt and Syria and scored countless victories against the crusading states. To all intents and purposes no response was viable within the theoretical perimeters traced out by al-Banna or al-Siba'i.

Sayyid Qutb's task consisted of mounting a bold effort to stand outside the entire legacy of Islamic reformism. He perceived that no separate Islamic ideology could demarcate its own space without coming into direct confrontation with socialism, nationalism and the monopoly of political power. Moreover, a new version of Marxism, a much more formidable ideology, was gradually making inroads into the new states. Indeed, Marxism itself can be seen as the immediate progenitor of Islamic radicalism.

Initially, Marxism in its Soviet and Chinese varieties gained the upper hand in the ideological battle. Whereas pro-Soviet communist parties were content to co-operate with the new 'national democratic' states such as Egypt, Syria, Iraq and Algeria, since they were deemed to be charting 'the non-capitalist road' to socialism, Chinese communism, or Maoism, believed in the intensification of the struggle under the political leadership of the vanguard of the masses, the Communist Party. In societies still dominated by agrarian economies, the peasant, rather than the worker, seemed the standard-bearer of the new revolutionary tide. The rhetoric of Maoism, equating in the same breath 'western imperialism' and 'Soviet hegemonism', was bound to find a responsive chord with increasing numbers of Third World intellectuals, students and revolutionaries. In the end this led to the rise of new Marxist parties, as well as factional splits within various communist parties. The examples of the Vietnamese War of liberation against French and later American domination, the Cuban Revolution and the Titoist experiment of independent Communism in Yugoslavia, all made their impact on Asian and African leaders and the western-educated intelligentsia.

In Iraq, the new military regime under 'Abd al-Karim Qasim (1958–63) came to power in close alliance with the Communist Party. Although this alliance was short-lived, it lasted long enough to allow a pronounced communist ascendancy in trade unions, professional associations and student organizations. On the other hand, the the PKI in Indonesia had by the early 1960s come under the influence of Maoism. This suited the policies of President Sukarno, as one of the leaders of the non-aligned movement. However, the massacre of hundreds of thousands of Indonesian communists and their sympathizers by the army and Islamic groups in 1965 signalled the end of such a precarious alliance of convenience. By the time General Suharto replaced President Sukarno in 1967, no land reforms or redistribution had been implemented (Hardjono, 1983: 48). Sukarno's socialism, unlike its Arab counterpart, was limited to confiscating Dutch property and companies, while leaving local capitalist and landowning interests virtually intact. Such a difference of socialist orientations had a direct bearing on the early or late emergence of Islamic radicalism. More importantly, the army in Indonesia had become to a large extent the direct upholder of a multifarious patronage system, a fact which accounted for the shallow radicalization of Islam up to the 1990s.

In Egypt the nationalization decrees of July 1961 marked yet another watershed in Nasser's socialist revolution. Disillusioned with the results of land reforms, particularly their failure to shift priorities to industrial developments, Nasser inaugurated a sweeping programme of industrialization under state supervision. Private banks, insurance companies and industrial plants were nationalized or brought under tighter control. These radical economic measures had a direct effect on the political alliances of the regime. Before 1961, Egyptian communists were either thrown into prison or banned from political life. After the publication of *The National Charter* in 1962, members of the official Communist Party (*Hadtu*) were released from prison and invited, along with other Marxists, to join various state institutions and political organizations. One such was the Vanguard Organization, set up by Nasser in the early 1960s to invigorate and co-ordinate the activities of the newly-established party, the Arab Socialist Union. Egyptian Marxist intellectuals were thus granted extensive facilities to propagate their views in the media, state institutions and universities (Salim, 1982: 61–73). Moreover, the political and ideological pronouncements of Nasser and his associates tended after 1961 to derive their analytical thrust from Marxist notions, be it the nature of imperialism, capitalism or the role of the state in underdeveloped societies. This was clearly displayed in the way *The National Charter*, already alluded to, dealt in its theoretical, historical, political, social and economic sections with various themes and issues.

In Syria, the Ba'th Party witnessed after 1963 a prolonged internal struggle which ended in the triumph of the radical Military Committee. Salah Jadid, an 'Alawi officer, was the rising star of the Committee, and became the strong man of Syria between 1966 and 1970. Under his direction, Syria underwent one of the most extensive programmes of socialist reconstruction. After ousting the traditional leaders of the Party, 'Aflaq and al-Baytar, Jadid sought to rival Nasser as the champion of a comprehensive revolution in the economic, national and cultural fields. His was a new party, dominated by members whose origins were overwhelmingly provincial and lower middle class. While the traditional leadership of the Ba'th thought that nationalism should take priority over socialism, the leftist trend which controlled the army and enjoyed a wide following in the civilian sector advocated the concentration of all efforts on the internal development of Syria. Thus, the intensification of class struggle, and the building of a socialist economy, inspired by Chinese and Cuban models, dominated the activities and political language of the regime. Marxism was implicitly or explicitly encouraged so that a group of intellectuals within the Syrian Ba'th Party called openly for its adoption and Arabization.

However, the 1967 war with Israel dealt a crushing blow to the Syrian army, leading to the downfall of Salah Jadid and his faction in 1970. The coming to power of Anwar Sadat in Egypt and Hafiz al-Asad in Syria reversed the previous trend, and signalled a return to what has been called 'the open-door policy'. In both countries, Islamic radicalism emerged in the early 1960s as a direct response to socialist policies and an apparent shift towards a quasi-Marxist ideology. On the other hand, the brief stupendous growth and increasing influence of the Iraqi Communist Party between 1958 and 1961, along with the 'socialist reforms' of the military regime, resulted in almost similar reactions on the part of Islamist groups. It was in those years that the Shi'ite *al-Da'wah* organization began to operate as a political party, and Muhammad Baqir al-Sadr, its spiritual leader, published a series of works to refute socialism, dialectical and historical materialism. The titles of his two best-known books *Iqtisaduna* (*Our Economics*), and *Falsafatuna* (*Our Philosophy*) indicate his determination to offer Islam as a unique economic and philosophic system, and underline its total rejection of imported ideologies. The Iraqi branch of the Ba'th Party managed to seize power in 1968. By that time, all its rivals, the Communists, Arab Nationalists, Nasserites and other political groups, had either been eliminated or weakened. Unlike its Syrian counterpart, the Iraqi Ba'th was based on a coalition of middle-class urban families led by a strong provincial contingent. It was, moreover, predominantly composed of Sunni members, particularly at the middle level, while its opponents recruited their followers from the ranks of the Shi'ites, who were before the American invasion of Iraq in 2003 the underprivileged community and constituted, according to disputed estimates, about 60 per cent of the population.

In less than a decade, state capitalism in Egypt, Syria and Iraq (until its occupation in 2003) gave rise to a new middle class within the apparatus of bureaucracy. Nevertheless, the state has continued to exercise a commanding position in society, and possesses sufficient resources to pre-empt the emergence of genuine intermediary institutions. The outcome of this process, whereby the private sector was equated with the sham democracy of commercial and landowning interests, manifested itself in the absence of an independent middle class. The detachment of political institutions from their traditional ambience, however, accentuated the distance between the new class, nurtured under state protection, and society at large. Consequently, social confrontations and political opposition were destined to take place between two main camps: the state and the people.

In a second category of Muslim countries, which includes Algeria, Tunisia and Libya, socio-economic policies, political reform and cultural changes did not enmesh in a configuration similar to that of the first category. Whereas in Egypt, Syria and Iraq, the first revolutionary measures tackled the problem of land reform, independent Algeria, vacated by its French settlers who had owned its most fertile lands, was not in dire need of an agrarian revolution. Although self-management and socialism were proclaimed as the twin objectives of a progressive system of government, no land reforms were undertaken until 1971. Their implementation by the new president, Houari Boumedienne (1965–78) occurred as a result of a power struggle launched by the army to undermine the political base of the first president of independent Algeria, Ahmed Ben Bella, particularly his reliance on the only legal party of the state, the Front de Liberation Nationale (FLN). Boumedienne combined a wide-ranging economic programme, financed by oil and gas revenues, with an emphasis on Islamic orientations. About a third of the state budget was spent on education, and the promotion of a new cultural policy of Arabization and Islamization. The regime, moreover, revived the legacy of the Islamic reformist, Ibn Badis, and sought the assistance of Egyptian Muslim Brethren in teaching religious and historical subjects. Thus, by monopolizing the economy and the religious arena, the Algerian government managed to contain political opposition, forcing its Islamic radicalists to act in a diffuse and disorganized fashion. Its mounting economic problems, highlighted by widespread riots in 1981, 1985 and 1988, finally convinced the Algerian leadership, under President Chedli Benjadid, to delete all references to socialism from the new constitution, and the single-party rule, and allow more than a dozen political parties to take part in a new experiment of liberal democracy. But as we shall see, civil war was the unintended consequence.

In neighbouring Tunisia, social and economic development had been largely left to the private sector, except for a brief experimentation with agricultural co-operatives (1964–9). As in Algeria, albeit on a smaller scale, lands vacated after independence by European settlers were taken over by Tunisians who belonged to new provincial elite, closely allied with the ruling party, the Neo-Destour. Whereas the towering figure of President Bourguiba (1956–87) dominated the political process, the economy was largely left in private hands. Even agrarian reforms simply meant administering estates previously owned by religious foundations or former settlers. Thus, the innovations of the Tunisian state, despite the socialist rhetoric of its leader in the 1960s (Hanna and Gardner, 1969: 313–34), were largely political and cultural.

The Tunisian Neo-Destour Party was a rare model in the Arab world, having a clear programme, a hierarchical organization and a legitimate leadership forged in the struggle for independence. In this sense, Tunisia was the only Arab country which had been governed by a mass-supported party, rather than military dynastic rule, or a group of notable families. Hence its political structure bore a striking similarity to that which developed in Turkey in the early period of the republican regime. Nevertheless, despite obvious similarities between the intellectual approaches of Ataturk and Bourguiba, the former's emphatic drive towards European secularism was only matched by an enlightened reformism on the part of the latter. Bourguiba's secular leanings, embodied in the Personal Status Code which he introduced in 1956, stopped short of abolishing the *shari'a*, and opted for a modernized Islamic law. However, by prohibiting polygamy and pronouncing the equality of men and women in matters of divorce and inheritance, the Code stands out as one of the most progressive pieces of legislation ever promulgated in an Islamic country.

Islamic radicalism in Tunisia was initially a cultural reaction, opposed to the priorities and prominent policies of the political system. The transfer of power in 1987 to a new generation of Tunisian leaders, headed by President Zayn al-'Abidin Ben 'Ali, has eventuated in the liberalization of the political process, thereby blunting the instrument of violent opposition.

In Libya the monarchy was abolished by the new military regime in 1969. This measure put an end to a dynasty that had built its political power on tribal and commercial patronage, particularly after the steady increase of oil revenues in the 1960s. The leader of the Libyan revolution, Colonel Mu'ammar al-Qaddafi, initiated a comprehensive programme of socio-economic transformation, and introduced a new ideology, the Third International Theory. His political system, based on local committees and direct democracy, has virtually nationalized all religious institutions and proclaimed its own version of Islam as the only valid and legitimate authority. By applying strict Islamic laws and destroying the material and political bases of his rivals, al-Qaddafi has insured himself against both Marxist and right-wing opponents.

A third category consists of countries in which the patronage system has been incorporated in the modern structures of the state. Such is the case in Indonesia, Pakistan and, to a lesser extent, Bangladesh. A partnership of landowning families, commercial interests and the armed forces has managed to survive a variety of political regimes, ranging from outright military dictatorship to liberal multi-party democracy. In all these countries, no effective land redistribution has ever been implemented, so that the power of landowners has remained virtually intact. Under such circumstances, policies of modernization and industrialization, often financed or supervised by American aid agencies or international firms, have simply consolidated the central authority of the state without effecting a qualitative change in socio-economic relations (Herring, 1979: 519–57; Shahidullah, 1985: 137–61).

Saudi Arabia, Jordan, Morocco, the Sultanate of Brunei, the United Arab Emirates, Kuwait, Oman and Bahrain make up a fourth category with its own characteristics. In these states the patronage system still operates in its full force and ramifications: politics, the economy and national culture interact as legitimate instruments in the hands of a ruling family. Moreover, the strategic position of the royal families, placed at the focal points of their societies, has set the pace of the whole political apparatus, while appearing at the same time to be accessible and within the reach of the ordinary subject. The modalities of the decision-making process, executed without reference to intermediate agencies, arrogate to the royal court the legislative, judicial and executive authority. Even in Morocco where political parties are allowed to compete in regular parliamentary elections, the whole exercise and its outcome have so far been tightly controlled by King Hasan II. Tracing his descent from the Prophet, representing a dynasty that has presided over the fortunes of

Morocco since the seventeenth century, wielding paramount religious authority as the Commander of the Faithful, King Hasan enjoys unprecedented legitimacy in the eyes of his subjects. As chief patron of an evolving polity, he continuously invokes Morocco's national interests, asserts its unsurpassed religious identity and endeavours to play a leading role in Arab and Islamic affairs. His social base, straddling rural and urban notables, ensures a high degree of autonomy combined with the freedom of making free enterprise a royal prerogative conferred on loyal servants of the crown. This patrimonial system, in which the monarch and more than 8,000 large landowners dominate state institutions and patronage networks, has given rise to riots, attempted military coups and a variety of leftist as well as Islamist parties. However, the peculiar position of the royal family and its brand of consummate socio-political manipulation have created ideal conditions conducive to perpetual marginalization of all other social sectors.

Saudi Arabia, a kingdom without a constitution, political parties or trade unions, represents the traditional patronage system in its starkest aspects. A polity built along paternal and patriarchal lines, its oil-rich economy is the exclusive domain of 6,000 members of the royal family. The religious establishment, the bureaucracy and the armed forces have been invariably used to depoliticize society. Professional or interest groups are co-opted into economic and administrative institutions on an individual basis, while the tribal structure of the Kingdom is reproduced at various levels. Hence intensive modernization and patriarchism go hand in hand, thereby deflecting political opposition into messianic outbursts.

In 1979, for example, an armed group of Saudis and other nationals occupied the Grand Mosque in Mecca and declared one of their leaders, Muhammad b. 'Abdallah al-Qahtani, to be the Awaited Mahdi. The state responded by besieging the rebels and using all the military resources at its disposal. It took the authorities more than two weeks to regain control of the Meccan mosque. The Mahdi was killed in the last days of the protracted battle, while the rebels' ideologue, Juhayman b. Sayf al-'Utaybi, was captured and later executed along with the other 62 members. Both leaders were Saudi nationals (al-Mut'ini, 1980: 15–31, 87–129).

All the other states of our fourth category are, by and large, miniature models of Saudi Arabia. Nevertheless, their application of Qur'anic injunctions is often more flexible, and sometimes openly modernistic, as is the case in Jordan.

Politically and sociologically, the Hashemite Kingdom of Jordan shares a cluster of features with a fifth category. Islam in the countries of this category is almost submerged in the interstices of national, sectarian, ethnic or religious differences within one single state. Malaysia, Afghanistan, occupied Palestine, Lebanon, the Sudan and Nigeria make up a cluster of states marked off from the rest of the Islamic world.

In such multiracial or multireligious societies, the interests and culture of each section of the population tend to create a plurality of policies which either cancel each other out, or lead to prolonged civil wars. In both instances Islamic norms are as a rule diluted and reshuffled. Thus in Jordan and Israel, where millions of Palestinians live and work, Palestinian Islamic radicalism figures as an element in the wider ideology of a national liberation movement intent on wresting the right of its people for self-determination and independence. By contrast, indigenous Jordanian politics, centred on the royal court, the armed forces and tribal loyalties, restricts the sphere of Islamic radicalism to particular local and international issues. The Jordanian Muslim Brotherhood, led by 'Abd al-Rahman Khalifa, the Islamic Liberation Party, founded in 1952 by Taqi al-Din al-Nabhani, a Palestinian court judge, as well as other Islamist groups, articulate their political stance in reaction to external events, mainly Israeli occupation, the intermittent confrontations with Syria or the Iranian Revolution. King Husayn has so far succeeded in using Islamic activities to his own advantage. However, once an Islamic group appears to constitute a real or potential threat to the internal stability of the monarchy, it is immediately suppressed (Satloff, 1986: 36–58).

In Lebanon the country's population is almost evenly divided into Muslims and Christians. Each religious community is in turn subdivided into various sects and denominations. Down to the outbreak of the civil war in 1975, the Maronites, the largest Christian sect, monopolized the key positions of the state and determined the direction of an economy based on the services sector – banking, tourism and commerce. The Sunni Muslims, as junior partners, shared power with the Maronites, and were largely the spokesmen of other Muslim sects, particularly the Shi'ites and the Druze. The economic and social changes which occurred in the 1960s and early 1970s resulted, among other things, in the ascendancy of the Shi'ites as the most numerous sect in the country. Islamic radicalism in Lebanon did not emerge until its patronage system began to break down in the late 1970s. The rapid disintegration of the old order was exemplified by the way Sunni urban notables and Shi'ite rural landowners lost their former power and influence under the impact of the civil war, the Palestinian armed presence in Lebanon and the Israeli invasion in 1982. The Shi'ites, being rural or recent migrants to urban centres, developed a more cohesive and militant ideology than their Sunni counterparts. Thus, the main radicalist organization in Lebanon, *Hizb Allah*, or Hizbullah, the Party of God, is an alliance of various Shi'ite factions and groups.

In Afghanistan, the Sudan and Nigeria, sectarian, tribal and national issues are intertwined with economic crises and regional and international spheres of influence. Islamic radicalism in these countries has consequently become an explosive issue that serves to prolong civil wars (Gulbudin Hekmatyar's *Hizb-i Islami* in Afghanistan, and Hasan al- Turabi's Islamic Front in the Sudan). In Nigeria the eastern and western regions, inhabited by the Ibos and Yorubas respectively, are predominantly Christian, while the North constitutes the homeland of the mainly Muslim Fulanis and Hausas. These three regions gained their independence from Britain in 1960 as a federal entity composed of three states, corresponding to a large extent to the three nationalities. The Ibos were better educated, had a relatively large presence in modern professions and dominated the bureaucracy in the capital city, Lagos. The Yorubas tended to pursue purely economic activities as traders and merchants. The Fulanis, led by their traditional Muslim emirs, successors of the Sokoto Caliphate of 'Uthman dan Fodio (see Chapter 1) formed mercantile and landed aristocracies. Since 1966, Nigeria has been the scene of a major civil war instigated by the secessionist movement of the Ibos, as well as a series of *coups d'état*. Despite its oil wealth, the national economy suffers from severe problems. In 1980 the messianic Maitatsine movement, founded by Muhammad Marwa, launched its revolt against corruption and westernization in Lagos, and led to widespread riots before it was suppressed by direct military action.

Islamic movements in Malaysia, a country with sizeable Chinese and Indian minorities, tend to follow a reformist and modernistic political line. The Angkatan Belia Islam Malaysia, like its Indonesian counterpart, the Muhammadiyya, is the most active and popular Muslim organization. Its main activities are primarily social and educational, rather than political. However, marginal groups of radicalists have sprung up over the last decade. The ideology of these groups, be they in Malaysia, Indonesia, Afghanistan or Nigeria, is invariably a local offshoot of Sayyid Qutb's theoretical analysis, or a mixture of Mawdudian and Qutbist formulas.

As a matter of fact, all the major contemporary radicalist movements, particularly the Tunisian Islamic Tendency, led by Rashid Ghannushi, the Egyptian Islamic Jihad organization and the Syrian Muslim Brotherhood, derive their ideological and political programmes from the writings of al-Mawdudi and Sayyid Qutb. On the other hand, moderate reformist movements, such as the Egyptian Muslim Brotherhood under the leadership of its Supreme Guide, Hamid Abu al-Nasr, followed conservative policies that fell short of the teachings of the original Salafist founder, Hasan al-Banna.

Finally, on the eve of its 1979 Islamic Revolution, Iran had characteristics that were common to our five categories, hence its uniqueness in the Islamic world and the success of its revolution. Its patronage system experienced considerable changes under the Shah, but it was never destroyed as in Egypt or Syria. The land reforms, carried out in three separate phases between 1962 and 1968, created a wider group of landowners, without, however, eliminating the influence of the old landowning class. The main outcome of the reforms was the introduction of capitalist relations into the countryside, a development that brought Iranian agriculture into line with that of Egypt in the 1940s. Moreover, agricultural output remained stagnant, while demand increased with the growth of population, precipitating thereby a policy of food imports along with a steady drift towards the cities.

The White Revolution launched by the Shah in 1963, and prompted by the American President John F. Kennedy, resulted in alienating the religious institutions, the traditional merchants of the bazaar and the artisans' guilds. Being foreign-inspired, it failed to win over any substantial allies for the monarchy. The Shah often appeared to stand alone, representing no particular class interests or national causes. When he saw fit, as in 1975, thousands of businessmen were charged with corruption, and made to pay heavy fines or thrown into prison. His political party, *Rastakhiz*, or the National Resurrection Party, was supposed to channel public opinion and mobilize popular support but, in the words of the Shah, it 'failed to achieve the objectives for which it had been conceived: it did not become the channel for the transmission of ideas, needs and desires between the nation and the executive' (Shah,

1979: 22). The Shah looked at Iran as 'a vast workshop' that would produce within a short span of time 'universities, professional institutes, hospitals, roads, railways, dams, power stations, factories, industrial estates, cooperatives, modern villages', as well as one of the best-equipped armed forces in the world. It was to the last that his increasing oil revenues were devoted, swallowing two-thirds of the annual budget. The armed forces and the security services succeeded in alienating additional sections of his subjects: the tribes and non-Persian nationalities that constitute 40 per cent of the population.

By the time Ayatollah Khumayni made up his mind to seek outright political power, the majority of Iranians were already clamouring for fundamental change.

# A Post-Islamic History

The Arab military regimes, particularly in Egypt, Syria, Iraq and Algeria, followed policies which resulted in the nationalization of Islam, along with the vital sectors of the economy. The military state created, or made use of, a wide variety of networks in order to establish its hegemonic position in society at large. These networks, represented by a uniform educational system, bureaucratic machines and the mass media, as well as mosques and other religious institutions, allowed it to establish its own pre-conceptual frame of reference and rules by deploying a steady outflow of inculcation. Culture and the economy were thus being moulded in a modern crucible of post-Islamic engineering.

Hence, an era of limitless progress and open frontiers was for the first time postulated as the destiny of a new Arab nation. This revolutionary prospect was most noticeable in the way Egyptian and Syrian intellectuals interpreted their history at a time when both countries were undergoing unprecedented social transformations. It is true that in the 1920s some Arab scholars and writers, such as Taha Husayn (1889–1973) and 'Ali 'Abd al-Raziq (1888–1966), did challenge long-established interpretations of the formative period of Islam. However, theirs was a private endeavour that failed to withstand the assaults of al-Azhar and its 'ulama, or find a sympathetic response within the official organs of the state. Consequently, Husayn was dismissed from his university post for demythologizing Islamic history and treating the Qur'an as a product of the peculiar circumstances of Arabia, and 'Abd al-Raziq, the Azhar-educated judge, lost his position for turning Islam into a spiritual creed and condemning the Caliphate as an unnecessary and oppressive institution. In the 1960s the transcendence of Islam, both in theory and practice, was explicitly or implicitly carried out as part of an official policy sanctioned by the highest authority of the state. From being a private affair pursued by a handful of individuals, reinterpreting Arab/Islamic history became a public activity and one of crucial national importance. Furthermore, whereas rationalism, Cartesian scepticism and liberalism informed the methodology of Taha Husayn and 'Abd al-Raziq, Marxist analysis and progressive secularism influenced the rewriting of national histories in the second half of the twentieth century.

Modern historical writing in the Arab world has often been an integral part of a more comprehensive and officially-sponsored policy of the governing elites. Arab history is considered an ideological weapon to be possessed, refurbished and brandished in the face of opponents, be they local or foreign. Thus history, or the past, permeates contemporary politics, its facts and themes selected and rearranged in order to preserve or demolish the status quo.

The decade which followed the failure of union between Egypt and Syria in 1961 brings into focus the use of history by Arab regimes in their political and ideological controversies. It is a decade that witnessed various Arab efforts and debates, with the sole aim of expounding and elucidating methods and theories for rewriting the national history of the Arabs. These debates surfaced in the wake of the more radical policies adopted by Nasser in Egypt since 1961, and the accession to power in Syria of a new Ba'thist regime in 1963. While the union of 1958 represented the culmination and heyday of the Arab nationalist movement, the secession of Syria in 1961 was a major setback requiring remedies and prompt responses. New issues came to the fore which engaged both the Egyptians and Syrians in fervent and passionate discussions.

Two particular cases, one Egyptian (1962–6), another Syrian (1964–6), stand out in this respect, as both were official campaigns designed to rewrite and reinterpret the history of each country, or the Islamic past in general. This endeavour accompanied wide-ranging socialist measures which preceded the Syrian secession, and might have precipitated the break-up of the union in September 1961. After that date, the slogan of 'socialism' increasingly dominated all the activities of the Egyptian regime. Egypt was to be totally reconstructed and socialized, so as to act as the new vanguard of the Arab world, and an example of a fully-fledged progressive society to be admired and emulated. Hence a 'National Charter' was proclaimed by Nasser in May 1962. It called for a new 'cultural revolution' in addition to sweeping political, social and economic reforms. The relevant sections of the Charter were widely debated and studied in the press and scholarly journals. It clearly endorsed a reinterpretation of modern Egyptian history as an essential element of the wider revolution (al-Sayyid, 1963a: 87; Mustafa, 1965: 13).

The National Charter, as submitted by President Nasser to the National Congress of the United Arab Republic (UAR), falls into ten chapters, two of which – III and IV – deal specifically with modern Egyptian history, the respective titles being 'The roots of Egyptian struggle' and 'The setback lesson' (see 'Abd al-Nasir, n.d.). It is interesting to note that the Beirut edition uses 'Arab' for 'Egyptian' in the title of Chapter III, while it is clear from the Cairo journals that the title reads: '*Judhur al-nidal al-misri*'.

The Charter itself offers a general sketch of modern Egyptian history. It seeks to recapture the main events of the nineteenth and twentieth centuries which preceded the 1952 revolution and reinterpret them in the light of the new 'socialist concept'. The theoretical analysis of the Charter stresses the socio-economic factors in shaping and determining the modern development of Egypt. It is apparent that the 'new revolution' was trying to highlight the role of popular forces and movements as the makers of historical change. It explicitly expresses strong disapproval of the previous, mainly royalist, approaches which celebrated 'the virtues and achievements' of the Khedives and some national politicians such as Sa'd Zaghlul, who led the '1919 revolution' against British occupation.

The new historical approach operates at two interrelated levels of analysis and exposition. It focuses attention on the positive aspects of the nationalist struggle, perceived as a direct result of the people's aspirations and social conditions, and it pinpoints the various setbacks and failures, attributing their underlying causes to dictatorial, corrupt and opportunistic leadership, or to the colonialist aggression of European powers. Furthermore, it estab-lishes the role of socialism at the centre of modern Egyptian history. The Charter declares:

The socialist solution to the problem of economic and social underdevelopment in Egypt – with a view to achieving progress in a revolutionary way – was never a question of free choice. The socialist solution was a historical inevitability imposed by reality, the broad aspirations of the masses and the changing nature of the world in the second part of the 20th century.

Moreover, it pronounces 'scientific socialism' as 'the suitable style for finding the right method leading to progress' ('Abd al-Nasir, n.d.: 109, 119; Hanna and Gardner, 1969: 358–9).
Scientific socialism reveals the impossibility of repeating a capitalist experiment, on the one hand, and unveils the harmful effects of distorted historical views, on the other. Thus:

The reactionary rulers had to make sure that only those concepts which expressed their own interests reigned supreme. The consequences of such attitudes were imparted into the systems and methods of education, which only recognized defeatist and subversive slogans.
Successive generations of Egyptian youth were taught that their country was neither fit for nor capable of industrialization. In their textbooks they read their national history in distorted versions. Their national heroes were depicted as lost in a mist of doubt and uncertainty, while those who had betrayed the national struggle were glorified and venerated.
('Abd al-Nasir, n.d.: 93; Hanna and Gardner, 1969: 354)

In other words, a new version of history was required: it has to demonstrate to the Egyptian youth their capability of self-government, creative production and industrialization. History itself testifies to the viability of the Egyptian people in building socialism and carrying out the reforms of the government. Moreover, the awakening of the Egyptian people at the beginning of the nineteenth century was not brought about by the French invasion of Egypt in 1798, as some historians claim. As a matter of fact this awakening preceded Napoleon's campaign. It is to be found in the new spirit which imbued the 'ulama of al-Azhar, and the relentless struggle of the Egyptian people against Ottoman rule and oppression, masquerading behind religion and the Caliphate. Before the arrival of Bonaparte, the Egyptians were waging a persistent resistance to the rule of the Mamluks. Nevertheless, it must be admitted that

Bonaparte's invasion did bring with it a 'new revolutionary stimulus'. It acquainted the Egyptians with 'modern science' and scientific knowledge in general, which they had developed earlier, handed over to Europe, and then lost under alien domination. French archaeologists, orientalists, historians, scientists and engineers uncovered the ancient past of Egypt, leading to a new self-confidence of the Egyptians. These discoveries, moreover, opened up 'new horizons before the eager imagination of the people' ('Abd al-Nasir, n.d.: 42–4).

Invigorated and seething with boundless energy, the new popular awakening was the driving force behind the rise of Muhammad 'Ali (1805–48). Although he was the founder of modern Egypt, his personal ambitions and futile adventures wasted and dissipated the energies of the masses. Despising and oppressing the spontaneous revolutionary spirit of the people, he failed to achieve genuine independence or build an 'industrialized society'. His successors accelerated the pace of these reckless adventures and intensified their negligence of the true interests of their country. The outcome of such policies was inevitable 'foreign interference' and widespread corruption. Egypt was turned by international financial monopolies into a 'vast cotton-producing plantation', its sole purpose being the satisfaction of British industry. The Khedives were gradually dominated by foreign powers, and lost their authority completely ('Abd al-Nasir, n.d.: 44–6).

Nevertheless, the spirit of the people was never broken. More importantly, the Charter did not lose sight of the positive aspects of Muhammad 'Ali's dynasty. Culture flourished and developed as thousands of Egyptian youths were sent to Europe to master modern science. Returning home these youths brought 'good seeds' which the fertile revolutionary soil of Egypt 'welcomed and nursed' to produce a flourishing culture on the banks of the Nile ('Abd al-Nasir, n.d.: 46–7). Keeping to its mode of analysis, the Charter asserted that the 'Urabi revolt was the natural climax of the popular tide. Britain had to act swiftly to protect the route to India, to guarantee foreign financial interests and support the authority of the Khedive ('Abd al-Nasir, n.d.: 47–8).

The 1882 occupation, however, did not mean the end of the struggle. New leaders and new forces emerged. As a matter of fact, the period which extends down to 1919 was one of the richest in 'its soul-searching and its mastering anew of revolutionary effort'. Soon after 'Urabi's defeat, Mustafa Kamil (1874–1908) emerged as an uncompromising nationalist leader, Muhammad 'Abduh (1849–1905) exerted untiring efforts to bring about religious reform, Lutfi al-Sayyid (1872–1963) proclaimed the motto: 'Egypt for the Egyptians' and Qasim Amin (1865–1908) called for the emancipation of women ('Abd al-Nasir, n.d.: 49).

The Charter then proceeds to dwell extensively on the 1919 revolution. The reasons for its shortcomings and failures are shown to be those which Nasser's revolution was anxious to avoid, with the benefit of hindsight and the lessons of past experiences. The socialist reforms combined with the wider pan-Arab outlook to ensure the success of the new experiment. Why did 'the revolutionary leadership' of 1919 fail? The answer is clear: the leadership overlooked the demand for 'social change', did not perceive that there was no contradiction whatsoever between Egyptian patriotism (al-wataniyya) and Arab nationalism (al-qawmiyya), and failed to see the danger of the Balfour Declaration which led to the establishment of Israel. Finally, Zaghlul and his colleagues failed to learn from history and their enemy who used devious methods to abort the revolution ('Abd al-Nasir, n.d.: 50–4).

In this manner the Charter goes on to reinterpret Egyptian history up to 1952, endeavouring to present a 'comprehensive analysis' and discover the dialectical nature of social change and political events in accordance with its new 'scientific socialist' conception of reality ('Abd al-Nasir, n.d.: 111).

No sooner had the Charter been published than a torrent of articles and studies began to appear in the press and scholarly journals. A national debate engulfed the universities, research centres, the mass media and all the official organizations of the state. Then Muhammad Anis, Professor of Modern History at Cairo University, seized the initiative and submitted to the government a detailed project for the 'rewriting of Egyptian history'. The Egyptian Ministry of Culture and National Guidance declared its support for the project at a press conference in July 1963. The Egyptian Deputy Minister of Culture, Abu Bakr, outlined in the same conference the general plan of the project and specified the topics that would be studied. He enumerated five major areas: the history of the Egyptian national movement; feudalism; domestic and foreign capitalism; the history of the Egyptian working class; and the history of political, social and cultural thought ('Isa, 1972, p. 40; al-Sayyid et al., 1966, pp. 30-1; Crabbs, 1975, p. 395).

The project was warmly welcomed by various socialist and

Marxist historians and writers, whilst most historians of the old pre-revolutionary school either rejected it outright, or chose to treat it with indifference. The well-known popular historian 'Abd al-Rahman al-Rafi'i (1889-1966) was reported to have stated quite bluntly: 'True [Egyptian] history is already in my books; there is no need to rewrite it'. Nevertheless, a committee was formed of a number of Egyptian historians to study the project and offer its recommendations. The government allocated a budget for this purpose and offered some other facilities to the members. No immediate results were announced for more than two years. Muhammad Anis, who seemed to enjoy the backing of the government, had in the meantime founded 'The Centre of National Historical Studies', and succeeded in obtaining previously unclassified official documents, and the memoirs of two prominent politicians – Sa'd Zaghlul and Muhammad Farid (al-Sayyid, 1963b, pp. 107–8; 'Isa, 1972: 41, 44; Crabbs, 1975: 394–5).

In December 1965 a conference of the Committee, which was enlarged to include new members, was called to discuss the project once again. The agenda of the conference was divided into four topics: political history, economic history, cultural history and social history (Mustafa, 1967: 345). Various charges were levelled against the Committee and its composition. Jalal al-Sayyid, for example, objected to the presence of historians who did not believe in the viability of the project from the outset, while other members 'had nothing to do with the study of history as an academic subject'. Salah 'Isa, a member of the Committee, alluded to the fact that the school of 'socialistic thought was hardly represented'. Most of the members, in his opinion, were university professors who either adhered to the 'old bourgeois school' or were die-hard admirers of the former monarchy. It was obvious that the 'new socialist' trend was encountering varied levels of resistance from the old-established academic community, as the proceedings of the conference reveal (al-Sayyid et al., 1966: 31; 'Isa, 1972: 44).

The historian Muhammad Anis was the main representative of the Nasserite regime at the conference, besides the Minister of Culture, Sulayman Huzayyin, who did not make any significant contribution to the discussions. Anis espoused wholeheartedly a socialist interpretation of history which located the inner dynamics of society in the social and economic infrastructure. He justified 'the re-evaluation of modern Egyptian history' by referring to 'the new transformations in our society', which included political, economic and cultural changes. He further explained that 'this revolutionary theory' did not confine itself to the present or the future, it also extended to the past and 'the nation's heritage' (*turath al-umma*) (Mustafa, 1967: 353; 'Isa 1972: 518).

Anis demanded, with an authoritative tone, a scientific approach that dealt with the people's history, an approach based on facts and documents and the real movement and direction of change. He wanted historians capable of delineating the transition of Egyptian society from 'feudalism' to 'capitalism' and finally to 'socialism'. He conceived this process as an inevitable outcome of the inner economic contradictions and the rise of new social classes in Egypt. Then he asked his audience:

> Where do we find the history of the national movement? The veteran Egyptian historian, al-Rafi'i, does not bother to mention in his works either the relations of production or the forces of production. What has been written so far does not cover the social background of events at all. It is the material background which endows political developments with their proper meaning.

Anis considered the Charter as the most eloquent example of the true 'historical methodology'. It studied the experiences and development of Egyptian society in order to comprehend and plan for the future (Mustafa, 1967: 353; Anis, 1966b: 69–74).

Such views, however, did not appeal to all the members of the conference. Except for one young Marxist historian, Salah 'Isa, no one proclaimed his conversion to the new socialist method. Soon the whole procedure degenerated into random discussions and broad generalizations with no clear objective or theme. Some wanted the government to complete the collection and classification of all the available documents, be they the British *Blue Books*, the French *Les Livres Jaunes* or the official Egyptian diplomatic documents. Ahmad 'Abd al-Rahim Mustafa maintained that no rewriting of national history could possibly be contemplated without the preliminary essential step of proper documentation. Others reiterated similar views as regards their own special fields (Mustafa, 1967: 346–7).

Faruq al-Qadi wondered what the true nature of national history was: was it restricted to the modern period, or did it cover Egyptian history since time immemorial? He ventured to say that the whole purpose of rewriting history was to rectify 'a methodological misinterpretation' whose characteristics were preconceived opinions and 'personal prejudices'. Ahmad 'Izzat 'Abd al-Karim thought that in spite of the elimination of feudalism as a social system in Egypt, it still persisted in its ideological and cultural ramifications. He called for prudence and precision when European stereotypes were used in studying the inner development of an oriental society. Suhayr al-Qalmawi pointed out that cultural history was the most difficult subject to tackle. It had been falsified and distorted by Arab governments and historians so as to serve political or economic interests. As a professor of Arabic literature, she stressed the crucial importance of ideas in changing historical events. It is impossible, she believed, to study the 'Urabi revolt without studying 'Abdallah al-Nadim (1845–96), 'one of 'Urabi's most gifted orators and writers', as he was described by an American professor of history. Naturally enough, S. al-Qalmawi was opposed by Professor Anis who emphasized that the individual was a mere product of his social, material and political circumstances, not vice versa ( Mustafa, 1967: 349–60; Goldschmidt, 1968: 311).

The stumbling block proved to be the periodization of modern Egyptian history. Was it to be dated from the Ottoman invasion of 1517, or should Bonaparte's campaign be preferred as the dawn of modern history? More tantalizing, how could the Egyptian historian determine the precise emergence of capitalist production in his society? Should history, accordingly, be written in terms of broad themes and topics, or should the model for the historian remain the time-honoured narrative, approaching social reality as a record, a sequence of events, no more and no less (Mustafa, 1967: 360–5)?

Thus by a process of elimination the conference ended where it had started. It never reconvened. Muhammad Anis and his disciples devoted themselves to the collection and publication of new documents and political memoirs in the belief of achieving the real purpose of the Charter. This trend secured the full support of the government and was soon to rewrite Egyptian history on the basis of the new approach. Other historians and writers were left to pursue their own idiosyncrasies so long as the living memory of the past, outlined in the Charter, was not tampered with beyond elaboration and further explanation.

The themes and broad generalizations of the Charter emerged as the essential guidelines for any future historical work in Egypt. The 'Urabi revolt of 1882 was re-examined and re-evaluated to the extent that 'Urabi became an Egyptian Cromwell, rebelling against absolute authority, a Muslim Robespierre demanding equality and justice, a radical revolutionary in the best traditions of Third World leaders, asserting the sovereignty and independence of his fatherland. Furthermore, the 'Urabi revolt was interpreted as a natural culmination of new developments in the social structure of Egyptian society. Its leader was depicted as the representative of a broad coalition of social forces and classes, a fully-fledged revolutionary with a political party, a clear programme for action and a new ideology (Anis, 1966a; al-Sa'id, 1967; 'Isa, 1972).

Mustafa Kamil, the founder of the National Party, replaced Sa'd Zaghlul as the genuine Egyptian patriot par excellence and the role of socio-economic factors was brought to bear on the overall changes and transformations of Egyptian society.

The conference of 1965 marked a watershed in Egyptian historiography. It revealed a diversity of opinions and wide differences of approach. Those who expressed their sympathy for the new methods and theories enjoyed the direct patronage and encouragement of the regime, while the lukewarm and the hesitant historians tended to fade gradually, left to pursue their notions and interests in obscure journals and private publications. Muhammad Anis emerged as the dominant figure and scholar under Nasser's regime. He was groomed and fostered so that his authority and expertise soon eclipsed all the other historians. His historical articles started to appear in popular newspapers, journals and magazines such as *al-Akhbar*, *al-Jumhuriyya*, *al-Ahram*, *al-Hilal* and *al-Katib*.

More importantly, the discussions of the 1965 conference revealed the dual identity of Egyptian culture, and the permanent tension between its local and Islamic-Arab past. As a matter of fact almost all the discussions and controversies revolved around the subject of Egyptian history and its periodization. The history of the 'Arab nation', stretching from the Atlantic Ocean to the Gulf, hardly figured at all. The Charter itself, however, lends its broad generalizations to such an interpretation. It never dwells on Arab history per se, except as an illustration of the centrality of Egypt in major Arab or Islamic events and turning-points. Egypt is dealt with throughout the Charter as a self-sufficient cultural unit, a fully developed society with a clear unfolding historical process. It leads other Arab states, enters into union with one Arab country or another, and sympathizes with their problems. Arab nationalism, as the official ideology of Nasser, becomes a crusade with an Egyptian base, character and history. It is a clear indication of Nasser's preoccupations and thoughts, a shift in emphasis to internal reforms and social change. History combines with politics to underline and justify the ideological trends of the day. Egypt was no longer interested in pan-Arab ventures, unless it deemed them worthy of its cause and mission. It was against this background that Syria, Iraq and Egypt entered into a new dialogue in 1963 to reassess the failure of the 1958 Union and attempt to forge a new one. The Cairo negotiations between the three states during March and April 1963 were a complete failure. Egypt was embarking on a course of its own with a view to avoiding the pitfalls of hasty unions and federations.

The trend that was set in motion by the Charter continued to gather momentum, even after Nasser's death. The concept of social history and how it should be applied to the study of Egyptian society established itself as the dominant theme of all new Egyptian historical writing. Just as Shafiq Ghurbal, Muhammad Sabri, 'Abd al-Rahman al-Rafi'i and their colleagues and students monopolized Egyptian historiography up to the 1950s, Muhammad Anis, 'Abd al-'Azim Ramadan, Ahmad Mustafa, Rif'at al-Sa'id and other 'social history' enthusiasts dominated contemporary Egyptian historiography well into the 1980s. These historians, scattered throughout Egyptian and some Arab universities and research centres, pursued the themes and topics of that brief historical sketch of the Charter. They believed that the study of the past should 'produce answers, in the form of concepts and generalizations, to the fundamental problems of historical change in the social activities of men' (Plumb, 1969: 106). Knowledge was not to be gained purely for the sake of knowledge, but as a prelude to political action and fundamental change.

In the wake of the publication of Nasser's National Charter and the subsequent flurry of debates in the Egyptian mass media, the Syrians decided to rise to the occasion. They met the challenge by offering their own view of Arab history, and widened the scope of the discussion to include the Arabs as a whole. By doing so, the Syrian approach reduced the Nasserite version to a mere provincial preoccupation with a limited geographical unit, namely Egypt.

Both Syria and Egypt were engaged at the time in a propaganda campaign. Syrian Nasserites were still pinning their hopes on gaining a firm foothold in Damascus. Soon after the coup of March 1963, which overthrew the separatist regime, Ba'thist and Nasserite officers in the Syrian army started jostling for prominent positions in the government. Nevertheless, the co-founder of the Ba'th, Salah al-Din al-Baytar, was chosen as the new premier, and his supporters dominated the new Cabinet, except for the defence portfolio, which was allocated to General Muhammad al-Sufi, a known supporter of Egyptian policies.

With the failure of the Tripartite Unity Talks in 1963, an open propaganda war broke out, pitting Damascus against Cairo. The Syrian Ba'thists responded by purging the army of prominent Nasserite officers, forcing thereby the resignation of Nasser's followers in the Cabinet. Moreover, street demonstrations became a daily feature in a number of Syrian cities, particularly Aleppo. The Ba'thist Minister of the Interior, Amin al-Hafiz, attempted to stem the tide of popular protests by using the army. This drastic measure, undertaken by al-Hafiz to silence the opposition, inaugurated what was to become a permanent feature of Syrian politics. Almost 20 years later, in 1982, Syrian army units, supported by defence squadrons, turned their awesome firepower against entire residential areas of the city of Hama in order to flush out armed bands of the Syrian Muslim Brotherhood.

By the end of 1964, the Ba'th was locked in almost daily confrontations with a wide coalition of opponents. Various Nasserite organizations, independent politicians, military officers, the followers of the Muslim Brethren led by 'Isam al-'Attar and other Islamic associations contributed to the agitation by combining purely economic grievances with religious issues. The Ba'th itself witnessed an intense internal struggle, which finally crystallized into three main trends:

1  A traditional nationalist wing led by the veteran founders of the party, 'Aflaq and al-Bay tar.
2  The Military Committee (later renamed the Military Bureau and the Officers' Committee), composed of Ba'thist officers who adopted a radical programme of socialist reconstruction.
3  A Marxist and somewhat marginal strand, represented by intellectuals such as Yasin al-Hafiz and George Tarabishi.

Thus, when the Syrian Ministry of Culture and National Guidance decided in 1965 to formulate its own version of rewriting Arab history, it solicited contributions which reflected to a large extent the internal debate of the ruling party. These contributions were first published by the official journal of the ministry, al-Ma'rifa (nos. 41, 42, 43 and 44, 1965), and appeared in a single volume in the following year under the title Kayfa Naktub Tarikhana al-Qawmi

(*How to Write Our National History*). By that time 'Aflaq had stepped down as Secretary General of the party (April 1965), and Salah Jadid, the 'Alawite officer, had emerged as the strong man of Syria (February 1966). In other words, the Regional Command had finally ousted the representatives of the National Command from key positions of authority, leading to long-term changes in Syrian politics and society. Hence, 1966 marked the advent of new social groups whose outlook and policies served to build up the Syrian state as a regional power in its own right.

However, the symposium organized by the official journal *al-Ma'rifa* in 1965 exceeded in its cultural and ideological importance the immediate issues of internal political struggles and the formation of various factions within the Ba'th Party. Its significance resided in the way an official-sponsored debate approached Islam and the history of the Arabs from a detached and totally secular angle.

Three relatively prominent Ba'thist ideologists took part in the symposium: Sulayman al-Khish, a former schoolteacher, poet and journalist, and Minister of Culture and Information in 1964–5; Shibli al'Aysami, a former schoolteacher and a close associate of Michel 'Aflaq, and a member of the Party's National Command; and Zaki al-Arsuzi (1899–1968), who was being groomed by the Regional Command and Jadid's faction as the original founder of the Ba'th. The inclusion of al-Arsuzi was itself a noteworthy event. Born into an 'Alawite family from the province of Alexandretta, he is considered to have brought with him a large contingent of 'Alawites into the Ba'th Party in 1947, including Salah Jadid and Hafiz al-Asad, the present President of Syria (Rouleau, 1967: 56). According to Jalal al-Sayyid, a Syrian veteran member of the Ba'th – not to be confused with his namesake, the Egyptian journalist quoted above – al-Arsuzi had a low opinion of religion, and explained the rise of Islam as a mere indication of the Arab nation's genius. He further asserted that al Arsuzi was a disciple of the French philosopher Henri Bergson, particularly regarding his theory on the primacy of intuition (al-Sayyid, 1973: 35–6).

The journal's editor, Fuad al-Shayib (1911–1980) set the tone of the symposium by stressing the importance of history in the twentieth century as the discipline capable of enhancing 'our knowledge of man'. He pointed out that the existence of conflicting approaches to the study of history was 'a healthy sign' that ought to be encouraged. He went on to say: 'Nowadays we certainly understand our history much better than al-Tabari or Ibn Khaldun ever did. Nay, the educated layman is today able to detect their errors and perceive their deficiencies'. Thus, history could no longer be a recurring event, repeating itself endlessly as if it resembled 'a concatenation of birth, and death, love and hatred, fear and revenge'. Having man as its subject, history had to be the biography of a constant struggle to overcome human nature and change it. In words reminiscent of Nietzsche's *The Use and Abuse of History* (1979: 5), al-Shayib indicated that only the beast had a recurring history, for 'there is nothing new in the life of the elephant, the lion, or the fox'. To write history is, furthermore, akin to 'a pioneering adventure, a conquest, and an illumination'. Seen in this light, human civilization, in its varied spiritual and material aspects, must needs lose its exclusiveness, and become a succession of experiences and their 'cross-fertilization', a mutual mimesis (*taqabus*) of ideas and opinions. Consequently, 'human progress can be seen as a transcendental-dialectical movement in the Hegelian-Marxist sense, full of beauty, righteousness, and promise' (Syrian Ministry of Culture, 1966: 12–13).

The Ba'thist participants were anxious to make the rewriting of Arab history an integral part of their nationalist ideology and their efforts to resurrect the Islamic past in a new form. Religious strife, or sectarianism, Arab unity, as well as the methodology and principles of interpreting historical events, figured as the main themes of the symposium.

Sulayman al-Khish, a close associate of al-Arsuzi, expressed his concern about the way school pupils were taught history. He particularly pointed out the gradual adoption of 'the Marxist methodology' by a large number of schoolteachers. Dialectical materialism and historical materialism were to be rejected in favour of 'a social nationalist perspective'. To al-Khish, this new approach, derived from the specific needs of the Arabs, would enable the historian to be utterly objective and neutral in narrating the religious conflicts that followed the rise of Islam (Syrian Ministry of Culture, 1966: 32–8).

Religious conflict and sectarianism in Islam were discussed in a frank and novel fashion by most contributors. Controversial events, such as the murder of the third Caliph 'Uthman, the subsequent struggle between 'Ali and Mu'awiya, the death of 'Ali's son, al-Husayn, and the Abbasid revolt against the Umayyads, were, however, treated as things of the past. These conflicts, al-Khish explained, had their peculiar character and arose out of particular circumstances. Each camp espoused a certain political principle which in turn constituted a religious stand. The Muslim historians themselves who narrated these conflicts were partisans of one dynasty or another. Although this state of affairs had its justifications at a certain time in the past, it was no longer relevant as far as the modern circumstances of the Arabs were concerned. At present, 'the Arab nation confronts problems other than those related to the Caliphate, the Hashemites, the Umayyads, and the 'Abbasids'. The new questions had to do with 'socialism, democracy, Arab unity, the eviction of imperialist influence, and the destruction of Israel'. All these contemporary issues have replaced the old ones, a fact that makes it incumbent on Arab historians to subject traditional chronicles and narratives to thorough revision and re-examination. By adopting this fresh attitude, al-Khish continues, the Arab historian has to bear in mind that he is writing for the Arabs who live in 'a post-Islamic era' (Syrian Ministry of Culture, 1966: 28).

For all that, many were those who wrote the history of 'post-Islamic Arabs' in an alien and insincere style. In their texts al-Husayn is mourned, or the fortunes of Caliph 'Uthman are lamented, in a manner reminiscent of the old days. Nevertheless, al-Khish affirmed, 'if such practices were natural in bygone times, they are today concocted, artificial, and performed in bad faith' (Syrian Ministry of Culture, 1966: 29).

Zaki al-Arsuzi thought that in composing history books for the youngsters, one should stress the origins of 'our present-day society' and the way it had been constituted. By tracing the underlying causes of a particular development or phenomenon, the future citizens were empowered to determine what was worthy of preservation and what had to be discarded. If, for example, a historian highlighted the factors that led to the emergence of a particular religious sect, stressing at the same time 'the remoteness of these factors from the characteristics of the present historical state, the sap of life which nourishes that sect would dry up, and the fanaticism manifested in its social insularity would disappear' (Syrian Ministry of Culture, 1966: 116–17).

The turning-points of Islamic history are thus deprived of their significance for modern life and contemporary issues. No relevant lessons can be derived from their study other than the necessity of perceiving the historical distance that separates two qualitatively different periods. More importantly, such a historicist perspective paves the way to another, no less momentous, discovery: Islam itself loses its centrality in the historical development of the Arabs and becomes an episode in a sequence of continuous progression.

Hence, for Sulayman al-Khish, his nationalist history is much wider than the history of the Arab race, both in its pre-Islamic and post-Islamic stages. To him, Arabism encompasses in its historical scope all the peoples and races who, over 5,000 years, had inhabited Mesopotamia, Greater Syria, the Nile Valley, North Africa and the Yemen. All the races who settled in those territories descended from the same stock as that of the Peninsula's Arabians, the heroes of Islam. Moreover, they all spoke cognate languages derived from a common mother tongue. The history of Arabism as a result implies a racial, geographical, linguistic and cultural definition. The ancient Egyptians, the Chaldeans, the Assyrians, the Canaanites, the Aramaeans and the Hebrews are 'misleadingly designated as "Semites" by various scholars, and ought to be named "the Arab peoples"', (Syrian Ministry of Culture, 1966: 18–20).

A new definition entails priorities dictated by the needs of a different age. Each element of the definition is constructed within a network of concepts, leading in its turn to a configuration that functions in a modern context. The function of the religious factor assumes in this respect secondary significance: it manages to survive only by association with other objects, such as the nation, the state or the political party and its philosophy. Hence, Zaki al-Arsuzi deliberately avoided the relevance of religion by singling out 'the contributions the Arabs had made to material culture' as a worthy topic to be covered by a new type of history. He gave as an example the Arabs' role in transforming the alphabet from hieroglyphic characters into letters, and the alphabet's dissemination among other people. Moreover, if a nation's culture were found to lack a certain basic characteristic, it became necessary to conduct 'a comparative study' with other cultures in order to make good the deficiency. The Arabs, he pointed out, neglected nature and focused their attention instead on imperative categories of right and wrong. Accordingly, anyone who tended to probe the depths of the human conscience and discover its eternal truths was called 'a Prophet'. By contrast, the Hellenic and Germanic nations devoted their efforts to the study of the physical world and the discovery of cosmic facts. This knowledge was then used in industrial and technological pursuits. The comparative method, al-Arsuzi maintained, disclosed the necessity of co-operation between nations, and made possible the avoidance of 'cultural excesses, deviations, and atrophies' (Syrian Ministry of Culture, 1966: 64–7).

Shibli al-'Aysami reached the same conclusion by deploring the way the culture of pre-Islamic Arabia had been depreciated. To him, the portrayal of life in the period of *jahiliyya* as mere savagery represented an outright distortion of historical evidence. Long before the rise of Islam, he explained, ancient Arabia had made remarkable advances in material and cultural fields. The Yemenite Kingdoms of the South and the Ghassanids of the North provided proof of this (Syrian Ministry of Culture, 1966: 51–2).

It was perhaps the contribution of Yasin al-Hafiz that lent the symposium a distinct flavour. His stricture of ultra-nationalistic interpretations of history stood out as a harbinger of a current of thought that was gaining increasing influence throughout the 1960s. The tone and thrust of his arguments did not spare either religious notions, or the theoretical analysis of Michel 'Aflaq, the Ba'th's principal theoretician. Soon afterwards, al-Hafiz left the Ba'th to form a new organization, the Arab Revolutionary Workers' Party.

He opened his contribution with a well-known Marxist statement: 'the ideas of the ruling class are in every epoch the ruling ideas' (Marx and Engels, 1974: 64). This quotation, stated without attribution, represented to the Syrian intellectual the key to understanding the main features of Arab history. He, therefore, cast doubt on the reliability of all Islamic sources. Written in an invariable annalistic or chronological format, and having the fortunes of successive dynasties as their main subject, these sources offer the historian nothing more than a collection of dead facts, an accumulation of disparate events and items of dispersed information. They thus leave no room for theoretical premises or abstractions (Syrian Ministry of Culture, 1966: 82–3).

As for the modern period, al-Hafiz maintained that two main strands dominated Arab thought and historiography: 'religious McCarthyism' and 'bourgeois nationalism'. Compared with the religious approach, Taha Husayn's Cartesianism, despite its shortcomings, represented a progressive step until he was subjected to intimidation and forced to join the ranks of the old school (see above, p. 00). On the other hand, current history books are shot through with the arbitrary methodology of bourgeois nationalism. Certain episodes of Arab history, such as the struggle between Persians and Arabs under the 'Abbasids, are 'artificially inflated' in order to pinpoint the origins of Arab nationalism. It is, however, futile to deduce the characteristics of a modern ideology from the distant past, or infer the rise of Arab nationalism and socialism from isolated, exceptional events. It is true, al-Hafiz explains, that Islamic history is part of 'the national reality', but the latter, notwithstanding its historical roots, is first and foremost the expression of the needs of modern Arabs and their current situation. Thus:

> The present and the future should claim the attention of the scholar. By doing so, he sheds light on those aspects hitherto neglected by traditional historians. History-writing, from a progressive point of view, is one of the battle fronts one ought to join in order to destroy all the superstructures of the old society. The progressive historian should focus his intellectual efforts on the dialectical contradictions within the movement of history and lay bare the struggle between the old and the new. Historical and dialectical materialism is the most scientific tool for the study of history. It avoids the shortcomings of pragmatism, and eschews the Stalinist attempts to force facts into *a priori* schema.
> (Syrian Ministry of Culture, 1966: 83–8)

These and similar pronouncements moved Abdallah Laroui, the Moroccan political theorist and historian, to issue in 1967 an earnest call to radical Arab leaders to adopt Marxism in an open and creative form as the ideology of their national states (Laroui, 1967, Chs 3, 4; Choueiri, 1989: 168–9).

# Chapter 5

## The Diagnosis: Sayyid Qutb and al-Mawdudi Ignorance and Conspiracy

Although there are ideological and political differences which set radical Islamists apart from other moderate Islamist groups, they both share an implicit a priori methodology. This methodology informs their interpretation of history, politics and society. It is fundamentally an essentialist worldview, or the theory of ascribing permanent and inherent qualities, properties and attributes to individuals as well as their concepts. These immutable properties are used as a tool for analysing and understanding political and religious developments, regardless of time, place or circumstances. Thus, an indispensable substance underlies all phenomena of human existence and its outward appearances. In this sense, a theoretical under-structure, closely related to substantialism or essentialism, dictates the perception of material and cultural change as mere duration within a permanent core of eternal qualities.

To Sayyid Qutb, for example, the war waged by various forces against Islamic countries has always been motivated by one overriding objective – the destruction of Islam and its doctrines. Some writers and scholars, he contends, distort historical facts by imputing to the Crusades materialistic and imperialistic aims. However, modern western imperialism is in fact 'a camouflage concealing the crusading spirit which is no longer capable of appearing in its true colours as it used to during the Middle Ages' (Qutb, 1981/1401: 202).

The assumption of a continual battle launched against Islam by similar movements throughout the ages entails another constant factor: the ever-recurring conspiracy. The organ of the Egyptian Muslim Brethren, al-Daʿwah, seeking to discredit the Baʿth Party, explained its origins by offering the following falsified account:

When it became inevitable for the French to evacuate Syria [in the 1940s], they did not wish to leave before handing over the reins of power to political blocs guided by the same principles as theirs. They, therefore, chose one of the intelligent Syrian students, Michel 'Aflaq. He was brought up and matured in the church under the supervision of the papacy in Rome in order to prepare him for becoming a leading missionary in an unprecedented fashion, as well as to attach Syria to imperialism, and then help him to extend his tentacles outside the country. During a visit made by Michel 'Aflaq to the Vatican, the Pope stood with exceeding respect in front of Michel and said to him: 'What you have done with the Arabs is much more than we did'.

(*Al-Da'wah*, Vol. 25, No. 6, November 1976: 58)

Moreover, this hydra-type conspiracy is considered to have come into being with the foundation of Islam itself. The methods used and the individuals involved may vary from age to age, but the objective has always been the annihilation of the only authentic religion ever preached to mankind. The essentialist conceptual vision unfailingly detects and recognizes the same enemy masquerading under various disguises. Polytheists, hypocrites, the Jews, Christians, secular rulers, communist states and capitalist systems, have all conspired one after another to undermine the foundations of Islam (Qutb, 1981, Vol. II: 924–5). This universal law of confrontation between Islam and all other systems of thought and social organization springs from the fact that two diametrically opposed camps cannot coexist peacefully in the same society. The struggle has always been between belief and unbelief, paganism and godliness, or Islam, as the last and only religion, and all other varieties of erroneous and false doctrines. Judaism, after the birth of Islam, is no longer a religion, but a distorted set of beliefs and practices. Christianity is equally corrupt and untenable, particularly in its Trinitarian dogma which compromises the oneness of God, not to mention its lack of clear temporal regulations as regards government and society. Nationalism, secularism, socialism, communism, democracy and capitalism constitute one single entity which has developed in the West in direct opposition to the message of original Islam. Moreover, Muslim rulers, scholars, 'ulama, writers and journalists have themselves forfeited their right to be called 'Muslims' as they have joined the ranks of the enemy by adopting his laws and way of life. As a matter of fact, Islam no longer exists, and has to be created anew. Islamic societies as a whole, the radicalists argue, have renounced their religion and relapsed to a state of ignorance (*jahiliyya*), not unlike that which flourished before the rise of Islam in Arabia.

*Jahiliyya*, as an Islamic radicalist concept, was first articulated by Muslim Indian writers and political leaders in the 1930s and 1940s. It was initially applied to the Hindus whose religion represented according to Muslim criteria a form of paganism, and then generalized to include all non-Islamic philosophies. In its original meaning, 'religious ignorance' in the Qur'an referred to the conditions and practices prevalent among pagan Arabs. Their ignorance consisted of their refusal to acknowledge the oneness of God, or their awareness of his message and eternal laws. This message was considered to have been handed down to a long chain of prophets, beginning with Adam. Thus, the holy Qur'an considered Islam the common religion of Abraham, Moses and Jesus, culminating in its final form and last stages in the teaching and precepts conveyed by God through his archangel Gabriel to the Seal of the Prophets, Muhammad. The Arabian prophet is consequently judged the most authentic messenger, having as his mission the restoration of Islam to its pure and perfect origins. After the revelation of the Qur'an only the People of the Book – Jews, Christians and Zoroastrians – had the choice of either converting to true Islam or paying the poll-tax as protected second-class citizens in an Islamic state. All other adherents of various beliefs were considered pagans and polytheists (*mushrikun*) living in a state of *jahiliyya* – i.e., unacquainted with the Scriptures.

In 1950 the Indian Abu al-Hasan 'Ali al-Nadawi, Rector of the 'Ulama Institute in Lucknow, published a book in Arabic entitled *What Has the World Lost by the Decline of the Muslims?* It immediately became a best-seller and was warmly received by a great number of Muslim men of letters, particularly in Egypt where it was first printed, before its translation into Urdu in 1954. As its title indicates, the book primarily seeks to explain the decline of Islam by offering a historical account of its rise, expansion and gradual regression. The author's depiction of 'Muslim decadence', which is seen to have taken place under the Ottomans, is followed by a grim description of 'the genealogy of Western civilisation', embracing the Greeks, the Romans, Christianity, materialism, the theory of evolution, nationalism and scientific progress. His verdict is unambiguous: 'Christian Europe' had become in its entire civilization 'pagan and materialistic' (jahiliyya-maddiyya). The Muslims had been forced to join in this mad pursuit of materialism, turning into 'mere passengers' in a train driven by European nations. Nevertheless, al-Nadawi asserts, the Muslims were essentially immune to outright 'pagan materialism', since their spiritual heritage was still 'preserved in its pristine purity' (al-Nadawi, 1977: 279–85, see also 1961: 181).

In 1951 Sayyid Qutb wrote an introduction to al-Nadawi's book in which the term jahiliyya (religious ignorance) as a description of contemporary European civilization is singled out. Ignorance, Qutb explains, has once again prevailed in the world ever since Islam lost its role of leadership. In this sense, 'it is not a particular period of time. It is an intellectual and spiritual temper that becomes preponderant whenever those fundamental values, sanctioned by God for humanity, are replaced by artificial ethics based on temporary whims' (al-Nadawi, 1977: 20). Qutb was at that stage still wavering between two schools of thought: reformist and radicalist. His consequent outright assertion that Islam itself no longer existed outside his own circle did not form part of his ideology until the consolidation of Nasserism, and the entrenchment of Arab nationalism as a popular movement.

In addition to al-Nadawi's book, al-Mawdudi's writings served to heighten Qutb's idea of the exclusive nature of Islam. However, al-Mawdudi never ventured beyond branding modern political ideologies with the stigma of paganism, along with certain politicians, intellectuals and misguided individuals in the Islamic world. Muslims in general were still considered worthy of carrying the name of their religion once its principles were fully explained to them. Hence, although 'ignorance' reared its head during the reign of the third Caliph, 'Uthman (644–56), and gradually overwhelmed the community under the Umayyad (661–750) and the 'Abbasids (750–1258),

it would be wrong to assume that Islam at any time was wholly routed and completely over-powered by this onslaught of 'Ignorance'. As a matter of fact, once a community accepted Islam, the lives of its people ever after bore in some degree the imprint of its reformative influence. It was all due to this imprint of Islam that great tyrants and absolute rulers shuddered, at times, with the fear of God, and were impelled to walk the path of truth and justice [...] On this very account the Muslim people all over the world have always been morally superior to the non-Muslim communities.

(Mawdudi, 1979a: 31–2)

For all the radicalism in his insistence on the inimical relationship between western concepts and Islamic ideology, he never contemplated the possibility of considering his own society nothing more than a conglomeration of pagan beliefs and institutions. Had he done so, he would have undermined the entitlement of Muslim Indians, particularly after the creation of Pakistan, to a separate identity. The peculiar circumstances which accompanied the development of Islamic nationalism in India forced al-Mawdudi to tone down his radicalist approach, so that by the time of his death (1979), his party – Jama'at-i-Islami – had become a mere pressure group funded by entrepreneurs, landowners and conservative Islamic states such as Saudi Arabia (Alavi, 1986: 36). In contrast, Sayyid Qutb's diagnosis was overwhelmingly uncompromising in its condemnation of the new aspects of religious ignorance, with the result that only violent confrontation could ensue between the forces of evil and those of righteousness. This disparity in political attitudes was to a large extent the product of two different historical experiences: the persistence of the patronage system in Pakistan as opposed to its destruction in Nasserist Egypt.

## The Last Gasp of Reformism

In the early 1950s, Sayyid Qutb was still preoccupied with the issues of social justice and economic development. He correctly observed that 'the doctrine of patriotism' lacked the capacity 'to put up any resistance against communism in many regions of the world'. He went on to affirm that the idea of social justice was steadily gaining ground at the expense of the patriotic tendency, particularly in countries which still divided 'its inhabitants into serfs and masters' (Qutb, 1978: 59).

At that juncture (1951), Qutb had not yet joined the Muslim Brotherhood as an active member. He therefore felt no constraints in his condemnation of the abysmal economic conditions of his society, as well as the utter failure of its political system. The opening sentences of his book, *The Battle Between Islam and Capitalism* (*Ma'rakat al-Islam wa al Ra'smaliyya*), published on the eve of the

Egyptian revolution, clearly indicated the pressing need for social change:

> This evil social condition, sustained by the masses in Egypt, cannot last long [...] It is at variance with the nature of things, and glaringly short of all the essential factors of survival. It, moreover, contradicts the real purpose of human civilization [...] the nature of all religious beliefs, and the spirit of the age in all its requirements. More importantly, it is contrary to the most elementary principles of sound economics, a fact that entails the obstruction of economic growth, let alone social and human progress.
>
> (Qutb, 1978: 5)

Qutb was well aware that his advocacy of social and economic reforms would lead certain groups to brand him with the stigma of communism. These groups, spanning 'reactionary 'ulama, corrupt politicians and hired writers, were accordingly castigated for their short-sightedness and complacency. He was certain that the imminent social explosion had to be explained in terms of plain economic factors, rather than revolutionary ideologies or fervent religious beliefs. Accusing social reformers, he warned his detractors, of being 'communists, dissidents, and anarchists', incarcerating them, banning their newspapers, or cutting off their means of living, would only momentarily delay the inevitable collapse of a crumbling system. The voice of the toiling masses, hungry and destitute, would eventually ring out – never to be silenced again. It was, Qutb contended, these masses, totally unaware of communism or other ideologies, who clamoured for change. Thus a revolution was about to break out: leaderless, spontaneous, destructive and solely rooted in material causes (Qutb, 1978: 6–7).

He then proceeded to lay bare the true characteristics of the patronage system: low productivity, wastage, corruption, unemployment, exploitation, mounting poverty coupled with widespread prostitution, and armies of wandering beggars. Under such circumstances, the right to vote, freedom of thought and the declaration of 'the people as the source of sovereign power' had become empty phrases. To Qutb, the death of parliamentary democracy and capitalism was already a foregone conclusion. So much so that the oppressed and ignorant millions only voted or boycotted elections according to 'the will of their masters, employers, and landowners'. Constitutions and parliaments had become 'a topic of humorous talk', totally alien to the discourse of a nation bent on 'an earnest endeavour' (Qutb, 1978: 11–12).

Hence, Egypt was standing at the crossroads, torn between three systems of social organization: socialism, communism or Islam. In this political triad, capitalism hardly figured as a viable alternative. Needless to say, Qutb opted for an Islamic order. His version of Islam, designed to supersede available ideologies, was offered as a new 'synthesis', combining the spiritual dimensions of Christianity and the materialistic aims of communism. Moreover, it preserved the independence and sovereignty of Egypt, unlike imported political philosophies preached by people lacking in true nationalism and awareness of their history as a living entity (Qutb, 1978: 60–1). Thus, Qutb was still entertaining the hope of updating Islam in order to satisfy the requisites of the latest political platform.

It remained for Qutb to convince his readers of the applicability of Islamic law to the complex problems of a modern society. The tone of his arguments resonated with a defensive approach and an apologetic mentality anxious to rebut accusations of anachronism. Having a foot in both camps – reformism and radicalism – his detailed discussion was conducted to refute what he termed 'doubts' or 'misconceptions' (*shubuhat*) about Islam. These misconceptions were listed under six headings:

1. The primitive nature of Islamic government.
2. The domination of Sufi shaykhs and dervishes.
3. The tyranny associated with Islamic rule.
4. The ambiguity of religious texts and provisions.
5. The system of harem.
6. Bigotry towards minorities.

The false notion of the primitiveness of Islam was shown to be the result of confusing the historical formation of Islam with its abstract system and concept. Whereas the first was conditioned by the simple life of the desert, the second was capable of infinite expansion and development. Even Islamic jurisprudence did not cease to evolve over the centuries, creatively responding to novel problems until the decline of the Islamic community sapped its energy. Qutb frankly admitted that Islamic law in its frozen state did not meet the needs of present-day societies: it had to be reinterpreted so as to reflect the modern varieties of human experience. Let the lawyers and judges of

Egypt, Qutb retorted, deride the whole idea! They were more deserving of derision, considering the ignorance, sluggishness and infatuation with an alien civilization prevalent in their midst. The application of the Napoleonic Code by the state for 70 years had not yet succeeded in convincing the Egyptian people of its justice and equity. The rallying of the masses to the cause of law-breakers, idolizing them as heroes, worthy of admiration and encouragement, demonstrated the incongruity of European laws with the character of the people. Only those who were simultaneously aware of modern developments and imbued with the purity of Islam had the ability to satisfy the positive and proper aspects of civilization. In other words, he was suggesting the use of the *shari'a* as a guide for deducing innovative codes of law, while acknowledging at the same time its outdated provisions.

Having rescued Islamic jurisprudence by purifying its history in the purgatory of abstractedness, he turned to other historical corpses. The idea of equating the rule of Islam with that of masters of Sufi orders and dervishes was, Qutb announced, utterly false. Both the theoretical principles of Islam and its concrete application refuted the odious charge. Islam had always stipulated the necessity of merit and qualification for its officers and functionaries. A judge was an official appointed by the state by virtue of his specialization in a branch of knowledge, namely Islamic law. Exactly as a physician or an engineer performed specific tasks, so did a judge. His profession did not render him a member of a clerical body, since Islam was not a church confined to the spiritual realm. Historically, Qutb continued, proficiency in Islamic jurisprudence never qualified a person to be in a position of authority, or occupy posts of leadership and administration. Only competence in a particular profession determined the suitability of a person and his station in society regardless of the level of his jurisprudential knowledge. Not even piety, singled out by Islam as the most sublime criterion for conferring marks of honour, was taken into consideration. A judge in Islam was, therefore, not a clergyman, but merely a Muslim, appointed to carry out well-defined duties for no other reason than his expertise in the *shari'a*.

Other reassuring palliatives were also added to dispel lingering doubts. Authority in Islam, Qutb asserted, was exercised as a result of a process of consultation. The methods and procedural operations were purely technical, and might vary and diverge in gauging the opinion of the entire nation. However, the principle of electing a

Muslim ruler according to the will of the people was firmly established by an explicit text of the Qur'an. In the early days of Islam the tenet of consultation (*shura*) was restricted to the city of Medina. After the death of the Prophet the first Caliph, Abu Bakr, extended this procedure to encompass both Medina and Mecca. Nowadays, the opinion of the masses as a whole had to be consulted. The technical details remained to be worked out in order to put theory into practice. The role of Islam consisted in removing all obstacles which placed the voters at the mercy of landowners, employers or the powers that be. This freedom of choice, Qutb explained, was limited to electing a ruler already committed to the application of the *shari'a* in its updated version. With the exception of theoretical and applied sciences, such as technical skills, the arts of war and the cultivation of land, Islamic law must be paramount, binding ruler and ruled by its injunctions. Obedience to an Islamic ruler was thus contingent on his implementation of the *shari'a*. If he violated its tenets, his obedience was forfeited. Dervishes and Sufi shaykhs were *ipso facto* excluded from an Islamic system of government. Qutb, moreover, affirmed that these 'unemployed and idle sects', living off superstitious beliefs, incessant recitation of God's name and supplicatory litanies, would be made to engage in productive work along with the rest of the nation.

Could such a polity, regulated by a flexible code of laws, governed by a meritocracy and upholding the virtues of productive work, be thought to constitute a menace to intellectual freedom?

Once again, differentiation between historical and normative Islam was posited as a necessary device for reaching an accurate conclusion. Persecution of thinkers, philosophers and scientists, Qutb admitted, had occurred under governments ruling in the name of Islam in a number of countries, but these governments had nothing to do with Islam; their system was based on rife ignorance and intellectual decadence, whereas Islam represented progress, enlightenment and fierce opposition to oppression. It was thus a grave error to demand the removal of Islam from public life on the basis of false deductions. Otherwise, the same accusation would be levelled against parliamentary democracy which was said to prevail in Egypt, Iraq and Jordan. Is it constitutionally democratic when a policeman has the right to arrest any individual on trumped-up charges, and torture him prior to his appearance before a court of law empowered to pronounce his innocence or guilt? There followed harrowing accounts of various methods of torture practised by the government of Ibrahim 'Abd al-Hadi in 1949 against Muslim Brethren accused of assassination attempts and sabotage acts. No less than 4,000 Muslim Brethren were arrested after the murder of the Prime Minister, al-Nuqrashi, and another foiled attack in May 1949, on the Speaker of Parliament, Hamid Jawdah. It was only after the coming to power in January 1950 of the Wafd, the largest political party, that the arrested Muslim Brethren were released from prison. The grisly details of the torture regime installed by Prime Minister 'Abd al-Hadi to extract confessions were widely publicized in the press following his downfall. By quoting these press reports, Qutb sought to discredit the sham democracy of his country, on the one hand, and draw a sharp distinction between the essence of a particular system and its mere distorted application, on the other. He did so not in defence of democracy, but in order to carry the analogy to the territory of Islam, his preferred alternative.

Qutb, in keeping with a traditional stance, judged purely 'scientific subjects' to fall beyond the legal sphere of Islam, while social matters, acts of devotion and 'all that pertains to man's soul and mind' were firmly placed under its jurisdiction. Thus, punishments ordained by the Qur'an, including amputating a thief's hand, flogging an adulterer and whipping a drunkard, had to be carried out. Mitigating circumstances, such as hunger in a case of theft, and irrefutable evidence by trusted witnesses in a case of adultery, were offered as examples of the clemency of Islam and its adaptable legal injunctions.

Furthermore, the stipulations and provisions of the *shari'a* were clear-cut and lucid, leaving no room for ambiguity or abstruseness. Admittedly, Qutb continued, the 'ulama of al-Azhar Mosque were largely responsible for turning Islamic law into a maze of bewildering terms. Writing commentaries on commentaries enamoured of glosses and winding expositions, they obscured the pure origins of Islam. All these religious compilations could be discarded without incurring the slightest loss. As a case in point, he proudly explained how he wrote two books, *Social Justice in Islam* (1949) and *Universal Peace and Islam* (1951), without referring once to these commentaries and glosses.

Two other misconceptions remained to be cleared up: the status of women and that of minorities.

The institution of the harem in Islamic history, Qutb explained, was of Turkish origin, 'and no one could accuse the Turks of being the best discerning Muslims, or of having belonged to the

Companions of the Prophet!' In comparison with pre-Islamic societies, Islam effected a revolutionary leap in the condition of women, to which western civilization had added nothing new save the freedom of licentiousness. What had the virtuous woman, he wondered, to fear from Islam after bestowing on her the loftiest prerogatives? She had been granted the right to own property, earn her livelihood by legal means, marry the man of her choice, come and go as long as she was decently clad. Despite these undeniable advantages, Qutb was totally silent on the absence of political rights for women in the second half of the twentieth century – a point to which we shall return.

The status of minorities in Islam, like that of women, was flaunted as one of exceeding liberty, tolerance and broad-mindedness. Even the Turks, who in another context were said to have 'turned woman into a commodity', and contravened the original teachings of the Qur'an, were unexpectedly paraded as a source of pride. Having denigrated their Islamic credentials in order to absolve Islam of their malpractices, the same 'brutal Turks' were brought back as living witnesses of open-mindedness 'in the dark ages' of Islam. A familiar device, perfected in the heyday of Islamic reformism was resorted to: an extensive passage of a European Orientalist, Thomas Arnold, was quoted as a conclusive answer to an accusation. As in the case of women, Qutb was reluctant to venture beyond generalities and platitudes. The massacre of Armenians by the Turks during the First World War was divested of its religious nature, and explained in purely political terms, since Muslim Arabs in Syria were meted out a similar treatment, albeit on a smaller scale. The persecution of Christian Armenians and Muslim Arabs is furthermore attributed to 'the vilest elements in the Ottoman state which are by their very nature obsessed with bloodshed, brutality and criminal acts, so that both Muslims and non-Muslims were the victims of their crimes and misdeeds'. Whereas Muslims discriminated against minorities either as a result of political reasons, or by contravening the principles of their religion, others always persecuted Muslims for religious motives (Qutb, 1978: 63–92).

However, Qutb's analysis, conducted against the background of acute economic and social problems, disintegrated into contradictory statements as soon as he undertook to prove the permanency of the western crusading spirit. He thus announced that Christianity, from being a religious doctrine, had been turned in Europe and the United States into a nationalist banner. It was merely used as a pretext to whip up chauvinism in all Christian countries. Having simultaneously pronounced the death and resurrection of Christianity in the West, he immediately concluded that 'the crusades have come to an end only in the Islamic world, while in the Christian world they still rage unabatedly' (Qutb, 1978: 94). Both the East (communism) and the West (capitalism) acted in collusion with each other in this conspiracy against Islam. The foundation of Israel in 1948 was given as an irrefutable example: it was a state solely based on religion – since Judaism was not a nationality but a religion encompassing the Russian, German, Polish, American, Egyptian, Yemenite and all other varieties of nationalities – and supported or financed by Great Britain, the United States of America and the Soviet Union. The only explanation of such an enmity towards the indigenous population of Palestine, Qutb believed, was related, on the one hand, to the crusading spirit which underlay colonial policies, and to the dynamic and militant nature of Islam on the other (Qutb, 1978: 95–7).

It was to the masses –the toiling, deprived and oppressed millions of Egyptians – that Qutb looked for the salvation of Islam and the establishment of an Islamic system. And to the masses he announced the bankruptcy of parliamentary democracy, the corruption of all political parties and the utter opposition of their leaders – the representatives of capitalism and landlordism – to the slightest improvement of economic conditions. Moreover, imperialism and local capitalism were natural allies, united by their common interests to control the institutions of the state. Lloyd George, the British Prime Minister, Qutb concluded, saw the 1919 Egyptian revolt against foreign occupation as the direct result of prosperity rather than poverty. Hence, it was the deliberate policy of imperialism and its agents to keep the masses in a state of starvation, so as to prevent the outbreak of a new revolution. This vicious circle of destitution and exploitation was bound to continue 'until the masses take things into their own hands, forming organizations which would enable them to score victories in election campaigns and other fields of struggle' (Qutb, 1978: 113–21). The organization of the masses and the promise of an updated Islam constituted for Qutb the ideal solution to the social crisis of his country. Social justice, rather than communism, was the national answer for a country proud of its unique history and independent character. Ten years later, following the triumph of socialism in Egypt, the functional units of his analysis – poverty, exploitation, social justice, the masses, election campaigns, Islamic modernity and nationalist allegiances – gave way to new notions with their own rules and objects.

In his fresh diagnosis of the characteristics of nationalism, secularism, socialism and democracy, Qutb was to a large extent indebted to al-Nadawi and al-Mawdudi in formulating the new ideology of Islamic radicalism. It is for this reason that his refutations of these concepts and institutions are henceforth discussed in conjunction with those of his Indian forerunners. Points of ideological divergence marking off Qutb's brand of radicalism shall be indicated in the course of our analytical survey.

## Nationalism

As we have seen, modern Islamic radicalism is characterized by its fierce opposition to the concept and movement of nationalism. It perceives the paramountcy of the nation-state in its secular and ideological connotations as a direct threat to the establishment of Muslim norms of loyalty and conduct. Whereas nationalists consider the nation or its institutions the ultimate source of sovereignty and legitimacy, Islamic radicalism asserts the categorical principles of an immutable divine order.

It was perhaps al-Mawdudi who first alerted his fellow Muslims in the 1930s to the dangers of secular nationalism as regards their interests and identity. At a time when the movement of nationalism was sweeping the Indian subcontinent, al-Mawdudi chose to voice his dissent, and attempt to stem the tide which threatened to overwhelm Muslims and Hindus alike.

In an essay published in the early 1930s, he sought to refute secular nationalism by focusing attention on its essential contradiction with the universal tenets of Islam. His speculative notion of history pronounces nationalism to be as old as civilization itself. In this perspective, its origins are deeply rooted in the political cultures of Babylon, ancient Egypt, Persia, Greece and Rome. Its nature is constant, forming a historical continuum. Hence its recent manifestations in countries such as France, Britain and Japan, are based on the same foundations (al-Mawdudi, 1978a: 9–13). Moreover, whether nationalism is built on the unity of race, language or economic interest, it unfailingly leads to wars and aggression, turning one state against another. In other words, it fosters the pre-Islamic solidarity of *jahiliyya* (al-Mawdudi, 1978a: 15).

To al-Mawdudi, the whole conceptual system of nationalism is an irrational approach which destroys deeper bonds between human beings. It divides humanity into racial groups, sets up barriers of languages within one single religious community and demarcates artificial territorial boundaries. By contrast, Islam views the entire planet earth as the abode of humankind, thereby dissolving all these contrived divisions. Its teachings announce the brotherhood of man, God's representative and lieutenant in this world. In order to prove his point, tribal, familial and social conflicts, which were rampant in the Arabian Peninsula before the rise of Islam, are converted by al-Mawdudi into 'nationalist' squabbles. The Prophet is deemed to have initiated his struggle against such loyalties and asserted the overriding unity of poor and rich, slaves and freemen. Thus, the most deadly enemies of Islam are atheism, polytheism and idolatry, along with 'the Satan of racist and national fanaticism'. The latter was combated by Muhammad throughout his prophethood in order to wipe out its deleterious effects (al-Mawdudi, 1978a: 26–36).

Nevertheless, in the wake of destroying various pernicious loyalties, the Prophet put forward a new concept of 'nationalism'. It pertained to the spiritual and intrinsic nature of man, so that materialistic and incidental differences were disregarded. It is a concept closely associated with an innate truth – the truth of worshipping God, performing one's duties and obeying divine commands. Those who profess these beliefs are one nation, while all those who reject them are another. Humanity was thus divided into two nationalisms: that of Islam and belief, and another of unbelief or misguidance. The irreconcilability of these two systems has often led to the migration of believers from the abode of infidelity in order to preserve the integrity of Islam and be in command of their way of life. Accordingly, the loyalty of a 'nationalist Muslim' to a certain spiritual and political system, rather than territory, race or language, is the yardstick which determines his place of settlement and work (al-Mawdudi, 1978a: 39–46).

It is against the background of such ideological attitudes that one may grasp the indifference exhibited by al-Mawdudi and his followers towards the disastrous and tragic migration, be it forced or voluntary, of millions of Muslims from India on the eve of its independence in 1947 to the newly-established republic of Pakistan. This migration has to be seen as the outcome of a modern nationalist movement, aiming at asserting the separate interests of its community. Whereas the Prophet and his followers fled from Mecca in 622 CE on a temporary basis, al-Mawdudi's exhortations for shifting masses of people resulted in creating permanent and irreversible boundaries between two Indian communities. However, al-Mawdudi did not give his unequivocal support to a national entity for Indian Muslims until the foundation of Pakistan had become a fait accompli. Prior to that date, his Jama'at-i-Islami, founded in 1941, was engaged in fierce and bitter campaigns against the Muslim League and its secular leader, Muhammad 'Ali Jinnah. By 1971, particularly after the secession of Bangladesh, al-Mawdudi and his party had become such staunch supporters of their national state that it was no longer possible to delineate the radical strands of their ideology.

In the 1960s, the decade which witnessed the heyday of nationalism in the Third World, al-Mawdudi called for the creation of a bloc of Muslim countries, arguing that the European countries, despite their lack of a common ideology, were moving towards 'the goal of United Europe' by developing common economic and political institutions. The Muslims, facing common internal and external problems, should also unite, since they all believe 'in one God, One Prophet, and One Book'. However, this proposal, addressed to the heads of Muslim states who were planning to convene an Islamic summit at the invitation of Saudi Arabia, was mainly conciliatory in its assessment of nationalism:

> After the Second World War different Muslim countries scattered from East to West were blessed with deliverance from Western colonial rule. The emergence of those nations as separate independent states is the inevitable outcome of a historic movement which cannot be altered. What is regrettable is that all these Muslim countries are following the same doctrine of nationalism that they had imbibed from their Western masters [...] They are not even fully conscious of the revolutionary rule of Islam because of which they are linked to each other, which can unite their Muslim populations into one *ummah*, promote goodwill and cooperation among them [...] [and] turn them into comrades in arms defending each other's territorial independence.
>
> (Mawdudi, 1982a: 19, 34)

Although al-Mawdudi rejected the doctrine of nationalism, he gradually and reluctantly accepted the principle of nationality. So did al-Nadawi who, like millions of Indian Muslims, chose to remain in his original homeland. The need for such an intellectual and practical compromise in the peculiar circumstances of the Indian subcontinent did not arise as far as Qutb was concerned.

To the Egyptian radicalist, having witnessed the disintegration of his mass organization as well as the execution or imprisonment of its leaders, nationalism seemed an abhorrent deviation. No historical or logical theory was therefore necessary to account for its utter aberration. It became simply a matter of stating its untenability in an Islamic divine order. Had the Prophet, Qutb argued, wished to base his message on Arab nationalism, he would have found it infinitely easier to unite the Arabs on such an earthly basis. Descending from the foremost Arab tribe, Quraysh, and its noblest clan, Banu Hashim, and nicknamed 'the trustworthy and the truthful' for his role as an honest arbiter, Muhammad, he went on, could have launched a war of national liberation aimed at freeing the Arab lands from Byzantine domination in the north, and Persian occupation in the south. Having united the Arabs under his leadership and authority, he could have wielded all this enormous power to establish once and for all the doctrine of the oneness of God, and demand their submission to his laws. But God, Qutb explained, directed his messenger to follow a different path: he was instructed to declare publicly that 'there is no deity but God', and endure with the handful of his followers all the hardship that ensued. God decreed that nationalism was not the proper way to implement his eternal laws. A nationalist movement would have freed society from Byzantine and Persian tyranny, only to replace it with Arab tyranny (Qutb, 1981, Vol. II: 1005–6).

Arab nationalism, formerly espoused by Qutb and his colleagues for its positive contribution towards the wider goal of Islamic unity, was suddenly excoriated as a wicked abomination. So intense had Qutb's outrage become that he described it in pejorative and opprobrious terms. Its adherents were compared to 'animals' stranded in a stagnant quagmire. In an oblique reference to Nasserism and Ba'thism, he emphatically pointed out that the sublime nature of the great Islamic society soared above 'the inferior and brutish bonds' of race, colour and language. Such a society, he retorted, was much more than a narrow Arab enclave. Composed of 'Arabs, Persians, Syrians, Egyptians, Turks, Chinese, Indians, Byzantines, Greeks, Indonesians and Africans', it represented the first and only universal community, having based its entire life on the lofty ideals of doctrinal affiliations (Qutb, 1981, Vol. III: 1561–3, Vol. IV: 1888–91).

Prior to the advent of Islam, Qutb reiterated, the Arabs were a worthless conglomeration of tribes, with no national or international standing. Then in an unprecedented historical moment, the message of Muhammad metamorphosed them into an extraordinary nation, charged with leading humanity and laying down its values, way of life and social systems. Thus, Islam became for ever their only 'identity card'. Today, as in former times, the Arabs had one of two options: they could either take up the only mission available to them and gain the respect of the world, or discard it and become once again a negligible quantity. Bereft of their Islamic identity, the Arabs had nothing else to offer other nations. He poignantly referred to the new fields of science, literature, industrial production, economic organization, as well as socio-political philosophies and concluded that the Arabs had unquestionably been overtaken by almost all societies. And for a long time to come they could not remotely hope to add to this impressive array of material culture. Hence, their singular and worthy contribution would *ipso facto* lie in the field of infusing their lives with the eternal flame of Islam. This unique Islamic mission, and not a faint copy of western-inspired nationalism, would secure the Arabs what was once theirs: the leadership of humanity and the concomitant position of deciding its destiny (Qutb, 1981, Vol. I: 511–12).

Qutb's emphasis on the distinctive role of the Arabs in the fortunes of Islam, propounded in a multi-volume commentary on the Qur'an, stands out as a theoretical anomaly in so far as his radicalist ideology is concerned. However, this commentary (*Fi Zilal al-Qur'an*) was written over ten years, particularly during its author's imprisonment (1954–64), and underwent various modifications until it was posthumously brought out in its present revised edition by his brother, Muhammad Qutb. Despite its continuous revision by the author, particularly after his final conversion to radicalism, traces of his reformist or modernistic phase can still be detected throughout the text. For example, in his discussion of the unique function of the Arabs in renewing God's authentic religion, referred to above, he clearly highlights 'their nationalist formation' as being solely a product of Islam. Such a statement is more in line with the standpoint of Islamic reformism, be it that of 'Abduh or al-Banna, rather than a formula of radicalist theorization. While the Indian religious leader, al-Nadawi, whose writings constituted a primary source for Qutb, did expect the Arab world, owing, among other things, to its glorious history, great achievements and strategic position, to shoulder the task of leading the entire Muslim world, al-Mawdudi was completely silent on this particular issue. In this respect, Qutb's radicalist approach was indistinguishable from that of al-Mawdudi. Having finally cut the umbilical cord of his reformist phase, Qutb assigned the leadership of humankind to 'the believers in the oneness of God', irrespective of their nationality or geographical location. Moreover, in this new version the Arabs were held to have become oblivious of their being Arabs, before setting out to conquer vast kingdoms under the banner of Islam (Qutb, 1980: 235–6, 1981, Vol. IV: 2370, Vol. VI: 3980).

## Secularism and Democracy

Secularism and democracy are usually lumped together by Islamic radicalists, since both represent the usurpation of God's sovereignty, and charge human agencies with the task of legislation. In this scheme of things, the validity of Qur'anic principles and injunctions is directly derived from God, whose message was handed down in a perfect and final form to his chosen Prophet, Muhammad. Thus, sovereignty and legitimacy are unassailably placed beyond the realm of human endeavour.

To al-Mawdudi and Qutb, legislators are God's agents and His trusted functionaries; their utterances and decisions should on no account express their free will, or reflect the desires of secular majorities. By devising their own laws without reference to the authentic authority of the Holy Book, deputies and judges engage in blasphemous activities synonymous with the worship of idols or man-made images. In this sense, secular democracy is a deliberate violation of divine laws and a reversion to the days of pagan ignorance (jahiliyya).

In al-Mawdudi's analysis, the whole of modern civilization is based on three principles: secularism, nationalism and democracy. Secularism, or the idea of excluding the Creator from 'intervening' in people's social life, first emerged in the West as a reaction against scholastic theology and its imposition by narrow-minded priests and obscurantist popes. It was, al-Mawdudi explains, gradually trans-formed into 'a separate world view', and became 'the cornerstone of their modern civilization'. The relationship between man and God was deliberately sundered (al-Mawdudi, 1963: 134–5; cf. Qutb, 1981, Vol. VI: 1944). Moreover, secularism, despite its prevalence in contemporary societies, is a foolish and absurd notion. As long as secularists claim that 'religion is a personal relationship between the individual and God', there is no possibility of avoiding the logical consequences of such an admission. The mere recognition of God's existence entails the belief in His sovereignty and rulership. There is, al-Mawdudi asserts, no separation between faith in God and adherence to His social, political and economic injunctions. Only an insane person would venture to think otherwise. Apart from its illogicality, secularism leads to corruption, oppression and treachery. Its application in whatever society has deprived the human being of firm guidance and just rules. Once God's commands are superseded, only whims and fleeting desires alternate in a world of chaos. Secular legislation, being changeable and temporary, lacks the moral sanction to make individuals comply voluntarily with its laws. Consequently, brutal force is resorted to, leading to the disruption of social life (al-Mawdudi, 1963: 254–6). On this score, both Qutb and al-Mawdudi were almost in complete agreement.

To Qutb the fundamentals of the doctrine of Islam and the tenets of its laws are one single whole; the latter is a practical translation of the former. It was only after centuries of 'diabolic machinations' that the legislative exclusiveness (*hakimiyya*) of God became separated from the question of doctrine in the minds of Muslims and non-Muslims alike. Like atheism or immorality, secularism is a mere deviation which perverts the normal course of human nature. With the exception of belief in the God of the Qur'an, conforming as it does to the innate and instinctive inclinations of human beings, all other philosophical or ideological notions serve to erect barriers of artificial and imaginary solutions. Deviation and conspiracy, Qutb was fond of reiterating, could be clearly identified as the two most devastating scourges ever to afflict Islam. Both were the result of a long-term plan hatched by internal and external forces. For a thousand years, Islamic society was governed by the *shari'a*, and became a miraculous occurrence, if it be compared to other societies. Then 'the arrogance of human science', prosperity and material development caused people to search for solutions to satisfy their needs outside the Qur'an. This, Qutb maintained, had been accompanied by 14 centuries of Jewish and Christian intrigues. The outcome of such concerted assaults was particularly apparent in the lands which formerly constituted the abode of Islam: all their inhabitants had ceased to be Muslims and reverted to the Age of Ignorance.

Qutb directed his severest criticisms at Ataturk's secular policies. The Turkish president is repeatedly seen as a mere tool fashioned by world Zionism and Christendom for the sole purpose of destroying the last symbol of Islamic sovereignty – the Caliphate. Contrary to reliable historical evidence, the Allies are presumed to have decided to withdraw their armies from Istanbul in 1922 as a calculated plot:

> When they [world Zionism and Christian nations] decided to destroy 'the Caliphate', and eliminate the last vestige of Islamic authority, 'a hero' was created in Turkey and his praises were sung. The Allied armies which had occupied Istanbul were thus withdrawn before his advancing troops in order to turn him into 'a hero' in the eyes of his countrymen – a hero capable of abolishing the Caliphate, doing away with the Arabic language, separating Turkey from the Muslim world and declaring it a secular state devoid of religion. The fabrication of these false heroic acts is frequently resorted to whenever they intend to deal Islam and the Islamic movements a severe blow in one country or another.
>
> (Qutb, 1981, Vol. VI: 3557–8)

Apart from his obvious revulsion at Ataturk's pronounced secularism, Qutb's strictures were mainly meant to be of direct relevance to Nasser's regime, his immediate enemy. Commenting on a Qur'anic verse related to the practices of the polytheists in Arabia:

> they appoint to God, of the tillage and cattle that He multiplied, a portion, saying, 'This is for God' – so they assert – 'and this is for our associates'. So what is for their associates reaches not God; and what is for God reaches their associates. Evil is their judgment
>
> (Qutb, 1981, Vol. III: 1360)

He declares that this deceitful division of funds, whereby the portions of God and pagan idols are pocketed by their hypocritical worshippers, is the hallmark of contemporary societies. Idols and circumstances, Qutb maintains, may undergo apparent changes, but their underlying substance remains the same. In this sense, modern political leaders, dreading the consequences of revealing their true beliefs, or unable to boast, like the communists, of their atheism, feign respect for, and pretend to derive their laws from, religion. To Qutb, such pretences, in so far as they benumb the surviving, albeit vague, trace of religious sentiment, surpass in wickedness and viciousness the methods of atheistic Marxists. This line of reasoning leads him to draw two main lessons, so that the new generation of Islamic radicalists would not repeat the errors of their reformist predecessors. First, Islamists should not waste their energies on criticizing the trifling details of certain administrative regulations, while the entire constitution of a state is based on non-Islamic premises. Second, as long as the powers that be confine religion to the spiritual sphere, denying thereby its validity as a socio-economic and political system, all their acts and policies ought to be considered grave violations of God's divine order (Qutb, 1981, Vol. III: 1213–20).

These warning signals are designed to alert the prospective disciple against the Janus-faced regimes which, unlike republican Turkey, profess unswerving loyalty to the mission of Islam, on the one hand, and apply secular laws and rules on the other. A case in point was, of course, Nasserite Egypt, Qutb's principal adversary. The same conspiratorial theory, deployed to account for almost all the misfortunes that befell Islam, is used in this context as an heuristic device capable of pinpointing the apparent religiosity of such regimes. The plot, acting under a new guise, he affirms, has never ceased to foment its poisonous ideologies. Although Ataturk succeeded in destroying the Caliphate, his Turkish experiment, being unashamedly secularist, failed to become a model for the rest of the region. Consequently, Christendom and world Zionism, having observed the meagre results of their labour and determined to avoid repeating former mistakes, tried their hands at new political experiments, hoping to achieve the same end by different means. Hence this smokescreen of religious propaganda and the regrettable participation of the 'ulama in its dissemination. By directing their denunciations at minor points, these 'ulama wittingly or unwittingly give the impression that all else is in sound condition. Moreover, Christian and Zionist agencies have now concerted their efforts to endow the Turkish example with novel attributes, judging it to be one of 'the Islamic resurrection movements'. Such a claim, Qutb continues, is made to obscure the fact that Ataturk himself proudly declared his ideology to be pure 'secularism' bent on the complete removal of religion from public life (Qutb, 1981, Vol. III: 1220–1).

Furthermore, by professing their adherence to Islam, the new Arab states represent a deadlier danger than that of Ataturk's irreligious and non-Islamic movement. Aided and abetted by the financial, intellectual and political resources of the Jews, the Christians and the Communists – the sworn enemies of Islam – they deceitfully unfurl the banner of Islam in order to obstruct the emergence of the new movements of Islamic resurrection (*harakat al-ba'th al-islami*). More importantly, 'those simple-minded and so-called Muslims', who still display an unwarranted reluctance to specify the obvious 'polytheist and pagan' character of modern systems are, in Qutb's opinion, more dangerous than the deliberate enemies of Islam (Qutb, 1981, Vol. III: 1648–9). His analysis has thus reached its logical conclusion: reformism in all its intellectual legacy has to be thrown overboard; other, less drastic measures, would only serve the purposes of secularism and pagan nationalism.

This internal debate, launched by Qutb after the debacle of the Muslim Brotherhood in 1954, encompasses in its condemnatory sweep all reformist endeavours aimed at reconciling Islam to the secular environment of modern civilization. He perceived the task of his new Muslim generation as a succession of interrelated battles, fought in order to reverse the trend of events, and force reality to comply with the normative and holistic standards of Islam. The school of 'Abduh and Rida is accordingly attacked for its ceaseless efforts to moderate the tone of certain Qur'anic verses dealing with miraculous happenings, war, the relationship between Muslims and Christians, the actual existence of jinns and a host of other topics.

Qutb's objection to 'Abduh's reformist approach is largely the result of two different views as regards the role of human reason in interpreting religious injunctions, or general historical developments. As far as Qutb was concerned, the faculty of human reasoning must at all times be subordinate to the unequivocal meaning of his revealed text. 'Abduh's statement that the obligation to recognize the mission of a Prophet as divinely given 'does not involve reason in accepting rational impossibilities such as two incompatibles', nor does it preclude the intellect from arriving at the true sense of an apparent contradiction ('Abduh, 1971: 129, 1980b: 108), is, in Qutb's strict judgement, a gross distortion (Qutb, 1980: 21–2). By the sheer fact of equating the function of human reason with that of religious revelation, the former is elevated to the status of an equal rival of the latter. Such an unforgivable error, Qutb believed, denoted the dependence of Islamic reformism on a western rationalist approach which reduces matters of divine origin and metaphysical dimensions to its immediate interest. It also over-looked the whimsicality and volatility of the human mind, as well as its constant need of a higher power capable of restraining its inevitable aberrance. Hence, those who impute to reason a degree of authenticity similar to that of revelation, proceeding from the false premise that both are fashioned by God, rely on propositions advanced by philosophically-minded human beings, and not by a divine agency. Moreover, reason cannot act as a substitute for revelation, simply because God's authoritative evidence is directly derived from His designated Prophets who are well aware of human frailties and inconsistencies. No faculty or institution could share with God the attributes of divinity, lordship and legislative authority. Islam, Qutb explained, meant utter submission to those characteristics as an act of faith and obedience (Qutb, 1981, Vol. II: 888–9, 1098).

Seen in this light, 'Abduh's modest rationalism is dismissed for being a distorted interpretation of Islam occasioned by the peculiar circumstances of its emergence. Confronted with a rigid religious environment, facing widespread superstitious beliefs at a time when 'reason' was being deified in Europe, and having to refute accusations of fatalism levelled against Islam by western Oriental-ists, 'Abduh was forced to highlight the value of the intellect vis-à-vis the revealed text. He thus refuted one distortion by way of producing another. Had he adhered to the Islamic concept and method, Qutb concluded, he would have avoided bestowing on a capricious and limited faculty the attributes of universality and absoluteness (Qutb, 1980: 20–1).

The perils of secularism, being the product of human fallibility and capriciousness, are compounded by democratic notions of popular sovereignty. To al-Mawdudi, democracy originated in the West as a revolt against the authoritarian powers of kings, priests and oppressive landowners. There is no doubt, he maintains, that those who denied the right of one individual, family or class to dominate millions of people were fully justified in their assertion. However, from being a negative rebellion, democracy slowly developed its positive idea of claiming the absolute freedom of the people to legislate their own laws and elect governments accountable to their interests and ambitions. However, once the will of the majority, he asserts, is acknowledged as the ultimate source of law, chaos and corruption become an inevitable result. Whereas secularism detached people from the restraining bonds of religious morality, and nationalism made them intoxicated with arrogant selfishness, democracy opened the floodgates to uncontrollable acts of plunder, aggression and tyranny (al-Mawdudi, 1963: 136, 257). Since legal and political sovereignty belongs to God, those who arrogate to themselves this right contravene the basic authority of the Creator and Ruler of the universe:

> Hence, it is neither for us to decide the aim and purpose of our existence nor to prescribe the limits in our worldly authority, nor is anyone else entitled to make these decisions for us. This right rests only in God who has created us, endowed us with mental and physical faculties, and provided all material provisions for our use. This principle of the Unity of God altogether negates the concept of the legal and political sovereignty of human beings, individually or collectively. Nothing can claim sovereignty be it a human being, a family, a class or group of people, or even the human race in the world as a whole. God alone is the Sovereign and His Commandments are the Law of Islam.
>
> (Mawdudi, 1979b: 37)

Nevertheless, the Qur'an, Mawdudi explains, clearly indicates the real position of man as being God's representative on earth. This vicegerency (*Khilafat*), delegated by God for the sole purpose of executing His injunctions, is the most perfect democracy, and the only political system in which the community as a whole 'enjoys the rights and powers of the Caliphate of God' (Mawdudi, 1979b: 39). This Islamic state, called by Mawdudi a 'theo-democracy', is by necessity based on the will of its Muslim citizens, both male and female. However, the executive authority could only be conferred on a male chief (*Amir*) charged with implementing God's ordinances. The *Amir* is assisted in his task of supreme leadership by a consultative assembly, and both are elected by adult men and women, already committed to 'the fundamentals of the Constitution'. However, pluralism, multiparty politics and equality of all citizens before the law, irrespective of religious or political beliefs, are contrary to the essence of Islam. Since the Islamic state is first and foremost an ideological entity, only those who adhere to its doctrinal principles are to be counted as first-class citizens. All others, as long as they remain 'loyal and obedient', are accorded their particular rights as second-class citizens. Thus, in an Islamic state, two categories of citizen live side by side: the Muslims and the non-Muslims or *dhimmis* (al-Mawdudi, 1983: 16–64). The key posts of the state, be they legislative, executive, judicial or military, are the exclusive preserve of its first category:

> Upon the shoulders of the Muslim citizens of an Islamic state devolves the main burden of running it in accordance with Islam's best traditions, as they alone are supposed to believe in it implicitly. On them alone it enforces its laws as a whole and enjoins them to carry out all its religious, moral, cultural and political directives. It invests them with all its obligations, and demands from them every sacrifice for the defence of its realm. Concurrent with this, it gives them the right to choose the Head of their State and to be the members of its Parliament. It also entitles them to be appointed to the key posts, so that the basic policy of this ideological State remains in conformity with the fundamentals of Islam.
>
> (al-Mawdudi, 1983: 65)

The non-Muslim category is accorded the full protection of the state once its able-bodied male members agree to pay a special poll-tax or *jizya*. This tax is simultaneously a concrete expression of political loyalty and a financial compensation for exemption from military service (al-Mawdudi, 1982b: 22–3). Thus, while distinctions of race, colour, nationality, territory and language are frowned upon as pagan or barbarian allegiances, the classification of human beings according to ideological criteria is extolled as 'the best and most just solution of the unusual complications arising out of the existence of a foreign element in the body politic of a nation or an ideological state' (al-Mawdudi, 1983: 67).

Living in a country whose leaders were frequently engaged in debating the feasibility and exact nature of an Islamic constitution, al-Mawdudi could not resist the temptation to offer a detailed blueprint of his ideal state, or 'Kingdom of God'. His willingness to accept the principle of universal suffrage constitutes the introduction of modern political procedures unknown to historical Islam, while the postulation of 'an ideological state' indicates the direct impact of fascist and communist models to which he repeatedly alluded as justificatory examples. Moreover, other criteria are also added in the allocation of rights and functions. Consequently, a third implicit category of citizenship is firmly established – that of women. This category, stamped with a biological characterization, is differentiated within the Muslim community itself. Since the family is considered 'the foremost and fundamental institution of human society', the role of women in an Islamic state figures within the pivotal position of a wider social unit. In this sense, the family is a microcosm of society, so that the functions of the husband and the head of state are rendered synonymous and interchangeable; both manage and control the affairs of their institutions, ensure that discipline is maintained and provide the necessities of well-being. Although al-Mawdudi allows women the right to vote, this positive gesture is immediately nullified by his enumeration of the duties of a Muslim wife. Stressing the fact that Islamic law specifies 'the home as her special field of work', he demarcates a permanent division of labour, or 'a functional distribution between the sexes', whereby indoor and outdoor duties are clearly and legally assigned within the household (al-Mawdudi, 1980: 163–6). Quoting a Qur'anic verse (4:34) which considers men 'the custodians' or 'guardians' of women because of God's differential choice as well as obvious economic reasons, al-Mawdudi turns it into an absolute political injunction. Nevertheless, the relative generality of the verse left the field open for later generations to lend it a precise and negative connotation. A saying was accordingly attributed to the Prophet making the ruin of a nation the result of its being ruled by a woman. This tradition seals the argument for al-Mawdudi and relieves him of potential controversies (al-Mawdudi, 1983: 60).

Thus, al-Mawdudi's theocracy-cum-democracy is an ideological state in which legislators do not legislate, citizens only vote to reaffirm the permanent applicability of God's laws, women rarely venture outside their homes lest social discipline be disrupted, and non-Muslims are tolerated as foreign elements required to express their loyalty by means of paying a financial levy. However, the ideologue was, whenever political expediency demanded, quite prepared to waive his dogmatic pronouncements. Being temporarily in opposition, al-Mawdudi's party lent its support in 1965 to the candidature of a woman, Fatima Jinnah, sister of Pakistan's founder, to become head of state. This open violation of his irrevocable divine ordinances became an unavoidable necessity in order to stave off the implementation of modernistic interpretations of Islamic law, initiated by Ayub Khan (1958–69), an army general who inaugurated military rule in Pakistan. Just as al-Mawdudi sacrificed his enmity towards nationalism for the sake of preserving the structures of a new Muslim state, he performed a· similar sacrificial act in a different context whereby partial dilution was preferred to wholesale pollution.

Sayyid Qutb was openly hostile to liberalism, multi-party politics and all institutions which derive their legitimacy directly from a sovereign electorate. A true believer, he pointed out, should place his doctrine above all man-made ideologies and avoid falling victim to a temporary whim or fashionable craze. For if the fallible system of democracy be judged part of Islam on the basis of its fashionability, all other socio-political ideologies could be seen in the same light once human capriciousness has changed. By the same method of arbitrary deductions, Qutb argued, one might look favourably at capitalism as it used to be highly regarded by those who were combating feudalism. Absolutism was another system that enjoyed popular acclaim during the struggle for Italian and German unification. As for the future, who can foretell what particular fashion of earthly ideologies shall have an irresistible appeal? More importantly, 'How shall Islam be described then?' (Qutb, 1981, Vol. II: 1082–3).

Democracy is, therefore, the product of immediate needs and transitional conditions. Its early history of high ideals has turned into a nightmare of naked corruption. Having fled from the clutches of a tyrannical and morally bankrupt Church, Qutb explains, the Europeans aspired to protect their newly-won liberties by instituting governments based on freedom, written constitutions, parliamentary democracy, judicial safeguards and majority rule. What were the consequences? There is no need, he continues, to look beyond the absolute domination of 'capitalism' which has rendered all forms of guarantees and safeguards mere labels or sheer illusions. The majority has become docilely enslaved by a tyrannical minority that possesses all financial capital. Consequently, this minority controls parliaments, constitutions and the press. However, this is the fate of all those who think they can safeguard their dignity and interests without God's divine laws (Qutb, 1981, Vol. III: 1754).

The theory and practice of democracy are *ipso facto* forms of polytheism. 'Judgement belongs only to God' (Qur'an, 12:40). His is the only legitimate and viable authority. In an Islamic state, Qutb points out, the entire nation participates in the selection of the Caliph – Amir or Imam – and endows him with the legitimacy of exercising power according to God's *shari'a*. Nevertheless, this right does not mean that the nation is entitled to legislate at will. Muslim scholars, Qutb elaborates, confuse the act of exercising power with that of its source. In other words, people do not possess, nor do they delegate, the right of sovereignty. Rather, they implement what God has legislated in accordance with His exclusive authority (Qutb, 1981, Vol. III: 1413, and Vol. IV: 1990).

Influenced by western notions of democracy, Qutb elaborates, certain Muslim writers indulge in fruitless arguments on the proper procedures to elect representatives to a consultative assembly (*ahl al-hall wa al-'aqd* or *ahl al-shura*), or keep wondering about the exact manner of selecting the Imam of the community. Endless questions are then posed: Is it the common people who select the Imam, or should the representatives nominate him? But if the Imam himself selects these representatives, how can they in turn select the ruler without compromising their integrity? These and similar questions, Qutb retorts, are futile exercises. So long as the prior issue of God's sovereignty is not conclusively settled, any discussion of technical procedures is nothing but a waste of time. Not only procedures of selection, but all other matters pertaining to the administration of an Islamic state should be postponed until Islam as a doctrine has been restituted. The banking system, insurance companies, birth control, tax collection, fiscal and monetary policies, and many other institutional arrangements can only be dealt with under a properly-constituted Islamic system (Qutb, 1981, Vol. IV: 2008–13).

Thus, unless Islam is accepted in its unadulterated substance, and without ascribing to its doctrine characteristics of foreign systems, no true belief could be asserted, be it of an individual or a state. All other known forms of government are the creation of 'blind' minds and 'misguided' options (Qutb, 1981, Vol. IV: 2075–6).

Unlike al-Mawdudi, Qutb was unwilling to entertain even the mere nomenclature of a qualified democracy or theocracy. To him, Islam is self-sufficient, the epitome of perfection and *sui generis*. Moreover, concepts such as democracy, Qutb argues, do not represent neutrally descriptive terms which are confined to administrative procedures. They derive their meaningful functions from a comprehensive theoretical substructure. Being derivative, their exact political identity has to be referred to the original source, and cannot be appropriated on their own as single items of merchandise. The ideological world is thus one single whole, organically interrelated and totally reliant on a philosophical substratum that lends each of its parts a particular significance or function. It is for this reason that 'the Islamic conception' of the universe, man and society must take precedence over matters of administrative and institutional technicalities. The two separate phases of the Prophet's career, the Meccan and the Medinan, are then highlighted as perfect evidence of Qutb's reluctance to discuss the details of his future state. In Mecca the inculcation of doctrinal principles figured as the most fundamental task. Having undergone this basic theoretical training for a period of 13 years, the new community was in an ideal position to enter in Medina into its legislative phase (Qutb, 1981, Vol. IV: 2121–2, 2131–2, 2245).

For all that, Qutb did not shirk the task of elaborating the practical implications of the Qur'anic concept of *shura* (consultation). Mentioned only twice in the Qur'an, this term was seized upon by Islamic reformists to justify demands ranging from a constitutional government to parliamentary democracy. Al-Mawdudi continued this line of argument despite his provisos about God's sovereignty. Qutb, in his turn, contributed a more radical interpretation, but one that can hardly be described as a faithful reading of his revealed text. His repeated stipulation to refrain from discussing administrative details is in this respect waived for the sake of settling a thorny problem of the twentieth century. Nevertheless, the fact that the idea of *shura* is expressed or enjoined in a Meccan verse and a Medinan one (42:38 and 3:159 respectively), the modern phase of restituting Islam fitted its historical precedent almost perfectly.

Qutb saw mutual consultation as one of the most distinguishing features of Islamic society and polity. To him, *shura* did not simply denote a political method devised to conduct state affairs – a view shared by almost all Islamic reformists – but a fundamental tenet of organizing the life of the community as a whole. Referring to the third chapter (*sura*) of the Qur'an in which consultation is expressly enjoined not on the believers, but on the Prophet himself, Qutb takes the opportunity to expound his views on the subject. This chapter partly deals with the ramifications of the battle of Uhud which was fought, in the third year of the Prophet's migration to Medina, between the Muslims and the polytheist Meccans, led by Abu Sufyan, Muhammad's arch-enemy. Although neither party scored a decisive victory, the Prophet himself was wounded during the battle, and most of the Muslim archers abandoned their posts at a crucial phase, causing the other troops to scatter in the face of the advancing cavalry of the Meccans. Shortly before the onset of the polytheists' attack, the Prophet thought that the Muslims should remain within the walls of Medina, so as to pin down the Meccan forces at the entrance of its narrow lanes. But the majority of his advisers insisted on fighting in an open field as far away from the city as possible. In verse 159 of the third chapter the Prophet is said to have decided, despite his contrary view, to abide by the decision of his council of war in order to avoid large-scale desertions in the ranks of his troops. Thus, although he was fully aware of the implications of conducting the battle outside the city fortifications, and in spite of his absolute right to have the final word, the Prophet chose to endorse the decision of the majority. The Qur'anic verse in question reads:

> It was by some mercy of God that thou wast gentle to them; hadst thou been harsh and hard of heart, they would have scattered from about thee. So pardon them, and pray forgiveness for them, and take counsel with them in the affair; and when thou art resolved put thy trust in God; surely God loves those who put their trust.
>
> (111:159)

This unequivocal ordinance, Qutb contends, leaves no doubt as to the perpetual necessity of consultation in Islam, although the particular methods of its implementation are not specified, a fact that reveals God's wisdom in taking into account the changing nature of political and social conditions. Moreover, the ordinance was decreed in the wake of the adverse consequences of consultation. This magnanimous gesture, Qutb elucidates, suggests that Muhammad intended to uphold a fundamental principle and teach his community a basic code of conduct – an objective that far outweighs the mere nuisance of sustaining temporary losses. Hence, instead of repudiating the application of a principle that precipitated divisions at the most crucial moment of a military engagement, he reaffirmed its validity for all time. God, Qutb continues, knew that the best way to prepare 'a nation for the leadership of humanity' is to involve it in the actual procedures of consultation. This is the only way for a community to learn from its mistakes, and take full responsibility for its decisions and actions (Qutb, 1981, Vol. I: 500–2).

However, reputable Muslim scholars have convincingly demonstrated that God in this particular verse did in fact repudiate mutual consultation, except as an advisory procedure (Farrukh, 1980: 919).

Moreover, Qutb's idea of consultation is hard to distinguish from the ordinary principle of majority rule. It is all the more so, since other Qur'anic verses do not lend themselves to the same interpretation. Nevertheless, one may conjecture that Qutb is here making a well-known distinction between technical or administrative procedures and doctrinal tenets or binding religious injunctions. Although such a distinction does exist as a customary practice in historical Islam, Qutb's argument falls outside the same tradition as consultation is declared 'a divine order addressed to His Prophet to be a perpetual and inherent tenet of religion' (Qutb, 1981, Vol. IV: 502). In his commentary on the Meccan verse that deals with the same topic, Qutb adds further complications to his terms of reference. In this verse, consultation is stated in a general context as a pious act, along with prayer and avoidance of sins (42:38). This fact alone deprives it of a precise political or institutional character. But Qutb is once again granted an opportunity to declare *shura* 'a fundamental feature' of the Islamic community in its whole way of life. Since it was revealed in the Meccan phase and thus before the foundation of an 'Islamic state', its early application is said to have paved the way for the emergence of a mature political order. Its significance was so wide-ranging that its implementation permeated the minutest detail of the new community. However, apart from the instance of consultation concerning military tactics, no other concrete practices are persuasively presented. But Qutb ventures to speculate on feasible procedural scenarios of election in his new state. To those who insist on an Islamic tradition that forbids self-nomination and self-canvassing for public office, and yet are bewildered as to its exact implementation in a modern society that takes electioneering for granted, Qutb has a ready answer. In an Islamic society, he declares, the inhabitants of each residential quarter lead a full social life built on mutual acquaintance, closeness and solidarity. It therefore would not be difficult for these close-knit communities to recognize and choose the best-qualified to represent them either in 'a consultative assembly' (*majlis al-shura*) or 'on local councils'. As regards selecting individuals for executive posts, 'this would be the prerogative of the Imam, who is chosen by the nation after being nominated by the consultative assembly' (Qutb, 1981, Vol. IV: 2008–9).

To Qutb, such a discussion was a jurisprudential digression dictated by incessant confusions on the part of Muslims who put the cart before the horse. He only argued that so long as the spirit of

Islamic consultation is inextricably linked with the wider doctrine of faith, the particular methods of application can be safely entrusted to the discretion of the community (Qutb, 1981, Vol. V: 3160–6). Be that as it may, it is worth noting that Qutb unfailingly refrains from using the term 'election' (*intikhab*), and refers instead to 'selection' (*ikhtiyar*).

## Capitalism and Socialism

To al-Mawdudi, the idea of 'social justice' is a stratagem conceived by Satan to intrigue human beings. Its deceitful ramifications are analogous to the original machinations of Satan in Paradise. It was this baneful creature, he continues, that tricked Adam and Eve into disobeying their Lord, and they were summarily banished from Paradise. Social justice is, moreover, the culmination of an erroneous process set in motion by capitalist and liberal systems in the eighteenth century. As these systems exhausted their possibilities by filling the earth with corruption and aggression, Satan dreamt up a new intrigue that became know as 'socialism' (al-Mawdudi, 1962: 867–8).

Nevertheless, despite al-Mawdudi's condemnation of both capitalism and socialism, his strictures have to do with the excesses and ugly face of capitalism, rather than the basic principles of the system. Al-Mawdudi believed in a capitalist economy, based on the principle of free enterprise and competitive ventures. He contended that so long as wealth was earned by 'legal means', the state had no jurisdiction to interfere or deprive the individual of an inherent right of private ownership. These 'legal means' were more or less specified in the Qur'an, and later elaborated by Muslim jurists. The flawed aspects of western capitalism, he believed, resided in excesses which should be eliminated in order to restore the healthy interplay of competition and acquisition according to one's natural means. Private ownership of the means of production, moderate profit earned as a result of investment, as well as the laws of supply and demand, were all essential features and necessary mechanisms of an Islamic economic system (al-Mawdudi, 1979b: 58–67).

In an Islamic way of life, al-Mawdudi explains, the positive or negative nature of an economic policy hinges on the moral qualities which animate those who are in control of its operation. Contrary to the claims of socialists, there is no need to effect a fundamental change in the relations of production in order to arrive at a just and equitable distribution of wealth. The ownership of the means of production by certain individuals to the exclusion of others, he elaborates, is the result of 'natural causes' which govern life and dictate disparities in the economic sphere. Hired labour and capital are accordingly permanent features of society, as well as an inevitable consequence of complex economies. Should exploitation and social injustice arise in spite of the naturalness of private ownership, these undesirable side-effects would be placed in the category of aberrations. Their solution, however, could not be devised by simple economic means:

> Evil in the economic system begins when the natural selfishness of man exceeds the limits of moderation. It develops with the aid of certain other immoral habits and receives further support from an inherently defective political system, especially if the latter has no moral basis.
>
> (al-Mawdudi, 1978b: 13)

'Immoral habits' include extravagant practices and unproductive activities. Capitalism, al-Mawdudi points out, produced in the West a group of people who, owing to their economic wealth, became self-indulgent and oblivious to the needs of other members of the community. For these rich people adultery became a natural way of life, music 'a regular need' and the pleasures of intoxication a daily requirement. Consequently, entire armies were recruited to satisfy these and other wasteful pursuits. Another 'satanic' gratification consisted of a selfish drive to accumulate wealth either by lending money on interest, or investing the accumulated surplus in commercial and industrial projects. These two activities were pursued in order to accumulate further wealth and acquire material means over and above the basic requirements of a moderate mode of living. The inevitable result was the division of society into two classes: a small class of rich and greedy people, and a large class comprising various social strata. The relationship between these two classes was one of conflict and strife. As this class struggle spread, the small class became smaller and the large larger; for the less wealthy lost out in competition with richer rivals, thereby swelling the ranks of the lower strata. Initially confined to its countries of origin, capitalism gradually infected 'all countries and nations so that even after bringing the whole world within its tentacles it still cries for more and more'. Consequently, a system of 'international exchange' came into being whereby 'a handful of bankers, brokers, and industrial and business magnates so completely gather in their clutches all the economic resources of the world that the whole of humanity is reduced to a state of dependence upon them' (al-Mawdudi, 1978b: 14–22).

In a revealing passage, al-Mawdudi singles out certain social groups whose fate concerned him most:

> It has now become well-nigh impossible for any individual independently to undertake any work or business relying merely on his own physical and mental powers in order to secure for himself a portion of the means of living which exist on God's earth. No opportunity is left in these days for small industrialists and agriculturists to earn their livelihood freely. Everyone is compelled to accept the lot of slaves, servants and labourers of these financial princes and captains of industry.
>
> (al-Mawdudi, 1978b: 22–3)

This line of analysis, developed in a lecture delivered by al-Mawdudi in 1941, reflected to a large extent the ambitions of Indian Muslims who, in view of the predominance of their Hindu rivals in the modern sectors of the economy, saw the need of producing their own businessmen and entrepreneurs. This immediate cause, however, occasioned al-Mawdudi's analysis, but would not have determined its particular thrust without the aid of his wider theoretical framework.

While al-Mawdudi voices his objection to certain features of capitalism, condemning monopoly and finance capital as the result of immoral habits, he rejects socialism in its entirety. Being contrary to human nature and the teachings of Islam, he asserts, 'nationalising *all* the means of production in a country' would stifle individuality and lead to 'the retardation of mental, moral, and spiritual development' (al-Mawdudi, 1979b: 66). Moreover, communism is bereft of a sound scientific basis, treating as it does all intellectual, metaphysical and social aspects as subsidiary attributes of economic conditions. By endowing the economic problem with an overriding supremacy, it upsets 'the whole balance of life', disclosing thereby its unnaturalness and artificiality (al-Mawdudi, 1978b: 29).

The collective ownership of the means of production, he argues, may sound like a plausible solution. But communism, like western capitalism, issues in the concentration of economic and political power in the hands of a small minority. After doing away with industrial and financial tycoons, communism entrusts the management of the economy, not to the community, but to 'a small executive body'. It is this body, combining 'the autocracy of a Czar with the absolutism of a Caesar' that enslaves society and distorts the natural growth of human civilization (al-Mawdudi, 1978b: 26–8).

By and large, Qutb's theoretical diagnosis of both systems is ultimately based on similar premises. His interpretation of 'the highest stage of capitalism', however, is shot through with a narrower and more nuanced view of history. To Qutb, each political or economic system has one dominant characteristic that determines the distribution and functions of its other elements. This characteristic is, nevertheless, a mere expression, an outward manifestation of a philosophical substructure which sanctions its existence and potential development. The dominant characteristic of capitalism is usury (*riba*), while that of socialism is common ownership of the means of production. An Islamic economic system, by contrast, is distinguished by its corporate and income tax known as *zakat*. However, both capitalism and socialism are derived from a materialistic view of life. This materialism is subdivided into two branches: secularism in western democracies, and atheism in communist countries. A common substructure gives rise to arrangements that are different in form, but similar in substance or ultimate effects. Thus, the undeniable material prosperity that capitalism has bestowed on certain countries, such as Sweden and the United States, should not be allowed to conceal the concomitance of depravity, religious ignorance and emotional distress. Marxism, on the other hand, treats man as a tool of production, an animal whose horizon does not extend beyond food, drink and lowly material needs. It thus debases the human soul, depriving man of his most precious essence (Qutb, 1980/1400: 82–105; 1981, Vol. IV: 2144–5).

Like Mawdudi, Qutb considered both systems to be against nature, or the instinctive impulse of life (*al-fitra*). It is no wonder, given their artificial origins, that capitalist and socialist promises of a better life have never been fulfilled. Western capitalism, Qutb explains, is not simply a system managed and run by industrialists, financiers and businessmen. In order to grasp its perpetual crises and abysmal nature, one has only to specify a dominant characteristic and its embodiment in certain institutions and individuals. Thus, all the factors of production – capital, labour, land and machinery – are under the direct control of a number of banking institutions and financial houses. Their owners are mostly Jews, for whom usury is the best means of ensuring world domination. These Jewish usurers control all liquid assets, shares, bonds and stock exchange. This gives them absolute discretion in fixing the rate of interest to be levied on loans advanced to landlords, factory owners and workers. The same manipulative principle of profit-seeking by lending money at exorbitant rates is applied in their international transactions. Hence, governments and entire economies fall victim to a vicious circle of mounting debts, spending most of their budgets on servicing loans and contracting new ones (Qutb, 1980/1400: 98–101).

By liberating the economy from usury, Qutb points out, a continual cycle of productive activities, guided by divine laws, would follow. Capital in itself is not the root of the problem; it is, rather, the method and the system which decide its use in usurious transactions. By placing capital within its comprehensive view of life, Islam restores its productive and useful function in society: man becomes a trustee of God delegated to undertake certain activities and refrain from others; interest-earning in all its forms and methods is forbidden in binding Qur'anic injunctions. Usury, like paganism, may vary in outward appearances from age to age, but its nature remains the same. And money, like other products, is conditioned by the way it is used. Its circulation in society must be regulated so as to direct investment towards industrial and commercial projects which are of direct benefit to the community (Qutb, 1981, Vol. I: 318–31, Vol. II: 638).

Productive capitalism, in other words, is encouraged, while parasitic usury is forbidden. It is, moreover, clear that reasons adduced for the harmful effects of interest-earning in a modern economy are, of course, not discussed in the Qur'an. Or, as the Pakistani economist Mufti Muhammad Shafi expressed it: 'Allah, the Exalted, has not enunciated any principle or purpose of the prohibition of interest, but has simply declared trade lawful and interest unlawful, thus making it obligatory for Muslims to abide by this Commandment' (Shafi, 1969: 21). One is, therefore, left with no choice but to seek the genesis of Qutb's nuances in more recent periods or textual evidence. The only source that springs to mind is a well-known current of German economic thought that gained ground in the first quarter of the twentieth century. Its most celebrated representative was the sociologist Werner Sombart (1865–1941). His book, *Die Juden und das Wirtschaftsleben* (*The Jews and Economic Life*), published in Leipzig in 1911, inaugurated the theory of the Jewish origins of parasitic capitalism, culminating in Hitler's diagnosis of Judaism as the originator of both capitalism and Marxism (Hitler, 1969: 289).

While al-Mawdudi did not apparently entangle his criticism of capitalism or socialism in the web of Jewish intrigues, Qutb acted differently. To him, communism is 'one of the Jewish movements, organized to spread atheism' (Qutb, 1981, Vol. II: 1087). Furthermore, *The Protocols of the Wise Men of Zion* represent for Qutb the ultimate aim of the Jews: the destruction of all spiritual values, and consequently human nature as a whole. The dissemination of 'scientific' doctrines is one of the means used to achieve world domination: Darwinism, Freudianism and Marxism are such doctrines, and all serve 'to achieve the terrible Zionist schemes' (Qutb, 1981, Vol. IV: 1959).

In his discussion of the origins of Marxism, Qutb does not neglect to bracket 'scientific socialism' with materialism, thus reminding the Egyptian President of the true nature of his regime. By adopting such phraseology, Qutb meant to say, the 1962 National Charter added a new chapter to *The Protocols of the Wise Men of Zion*. His commentary on the Qur'an, being a germane field of fertile speculation, is fully exploited to hammer the message home (Qutb, 1981, Vol. IV: 1959, 2131–2, 2144–5).

# Chapter 6

## The Doctrine and its Methods

Islamic radicalism is a politico-cultural movement that postulates a qualitative contradiction between western civilization and the religion of Islam. Its emphasis on Islam as a comprehensive and transcendental worldview excludes the validity of all other systems and values, and dictates an apparent restitution of a normative set of beliefs untainted by historical change. The actual unfolding of Islam, possessing its own military institutions, economic organization and schools of law, is thus neutralized and pronounced a gradual corruption of a pristine order.

It is for these dogmatic and theoretical reasons that Sayyid Qutb was quite unequivocal in considering 'the doctrinal foundations' of Islam to have escaped distortion, in spite of all the incessant attacks of numerous opponents. These 'doctrinal foundations' are then assumed to be inherently sound, and conducive to an act of sudden resurrection brought about by 'a new generation' of believers (Qutb, 1983: 39). Nevertheless, Qutb's Islam is offered as a modern ideology capable of absorbing all scientific and technological innovations without being tainted with their philosophical substratum. Such a miraculous achievement is deemed possible by the sheer delineation of a new theory, as well as the necessity of political independence in a 'world of open idolatry'.

Furthermore, Qutb's radicalism is largely a response to Islamic reformism and Arab nationalism. It is a deliberate attempt to demarcate the incongruity between their ideological background and his self-sufficient doctrine. Hence his unrestrained defence of the exclusivity and uniqueness of the Islamic *Weltanschauung*, and his condemnation of all intellectual endeavours to reconcile Islam with other systems of thought. His rapturous depiction of what he dubs 'the characteristics of the Islamic conception' adopts an offensive strategy aimed at recapturing the unadulterated original territory of religion (Qutb, 1980, *passim*). And his rhetorical, poetic and often repetitive style is designed to exhaust rivals, or deal a death blow to their systematic arguments. However, Qutb's aggressiveness is no more than an irredentism that aspires to entrench itself within a purely intellectual vacuum in which the positive elements of materialistic progress are denuded of their distorted spirituality.

Qutb's most radicalist statements were published between 1960 and 1966. Four of his books, *The Characteristics of the Islamic Conception and its Foundations* (1960), *Islam and the Problems of Civilization* (1960), *Signposts along the Road* (1964) and the revised edition of his exegesis, *Under the Auspices of the Qur'an* (1958–66), have acted as the definitive ideological articulation of contemporary Islamic radicalism and provided authoritative guidelines for a variety of Islamist organizations. The first represents a direct refutation of 'Abduh's reformist school, and the philosophical Hegelian trend, inaugurated by the Pakistani modernist, Muhammad Iqbal (1875–1938). The second is an angry denunciation of Nasser's nationalism and socialism, and an anguished effort to offer a viable strategic alternative. The third and the fourth encompass all the theoretical and thematic details of an ideology deemed directly inspired by an intimate and personal reading of the Qur'an.

# God's Sovereignty

Both Qutb and al-Mawdudi considered ideology the engine of other developments in society. Thus, their idea of the oneness of God and of his exclusive transcendental sovereignty is meant to reinstate Islam as a political system. In its revivalist version, the exclusive sovereignty of God served to combat Sufi orders, saint worship and the intercession of human beings on behalf of believers.

The same notion was taken up by radicalists to serve different purposes, aimed at undermining the institutions of the new nation-states and their legitimacy. In other words, the state, rather than Sufi orders, became the target of vilification and condemnation. God's oneness was accordingly perceived to operate in the universe, figuring in its turn as one organic whole, both in its formation and movement. In Qutb's words:

The universe is regulated by one single law which binds all its parts in a harmonious and orderly sequence. This systematic and congruent arrangement is the creation of one will, or the expression of one God. The multiplicity of beings, or essence, leads to a multiplicity of wills, and gives rise to diverse rules and judgements. This will is the manifest expression of an active essence, and law is the aspect of the effective will. For were it not so, the unity which co-ordinates the whole cosmic order, and regularizes its course, direction, and conduct, would disappear, and disorder would follow the disruption of harmony.

(Qutb, 1981, Vol. IV: 2373–4)

This orderly and harmonious universe is monistic in its nature and direction, and the deliberate creation of one single will. God, moreover, has imprinted His signs throughout the universe in order to announce his oneness, authority and Lordship. Man's purpose is to reaffirm this unity by merging his life into the wider organic whole, and submit with reverence to an infinite wisdom. The decisive factor in performing the act of submission is not the mere belief in God's existence; rather, it is the admission of His exclusive authority in determining the moral, political and economic aspects of all societies. Moreover, God created the universe for man's benefit, appointing him as His lieutenant on earth as a sign of His grace. The function of the human being is to receive, respond to, adapt and apply the immutable characteristics of divine rules. These human activities do constitute progress and result in gradual improvements. However, in order to be in accord with God's Lordship and the harmony of the cosmic order, they must take place within 'constant perimeters' and on the basis of a 'fixed axis'. For, as Qutb asserts, the fundamentals, or primary principles, neither change nor evolve: change, be it volitional or compulsory, does not reach beyond the outward manifestations of life and the forms of practical existence. Scientific discoveries, for example, belong to the last category. In other words, the essence of things, their origin and substance remain the same (Qutb, 1980: 85–100).

The permanency of cosmic laws and man's place in the universe, as dictated by God's will, render all earthly developments mere superficial alterations, rather like 'ripples of waves in a vast ocean: they do not change the quality of its water, nor do they affect its underlying currents, being regulated by constant natural factors' (Qutb, 1981, Vol. I: 556). Moreover, the human intellect, no matter how refined, ambitious or scientific, has invariably to 'swim in the sea of the unknown'. It comes across only 'floating islands, and fastens onto them as signposts in a hazardous environment'. Nevertheless, man is often ungrateful, and boasts of being able to discover the laws of nature without God's help. A case in point, Qutb declares, is the title of 'the atheist' Julian Huxley's book, *Man Stands Alone*. It is sheer human arrogance, he continues, when science is made to rival metaphysical knowledge, or affirmed as a more solid substitute. It is equally a degradation of the value of man, who does not become fully human and transcend his animality unless faith in the unknown (*alghayb*) becomes an integral part of his life and thought. Hence, the Islamic mentality, Qutb concludes, is both 'metaphysical and scientific'. It is metaphysical in the sense conveyed by one Qur'anic verse concerning God's knowledge: 'With Him are the keys of the unseen; none knows them but He. He knows what is in land and sea; not a leaf falls, but He knows it' (6:59). It is scientific because it believes in natural laws and only the knowledge of some of their aspects is necessary for human life on earth. Moreover, scientific theories are relative, and liable to perpetual transformations. They could not, therefore, form a reliable basis of a comprehensive doctrine. Science, he scoffs, is built on conjecture and approximate calculations, while absolute truth remains hidden as one of God's secrets. Atheism itself is a whimsical aberration, incapable of being ascertained by scientific proofs. It is a deviation brought about by the oppressive practices of the Christian Church, the Inquisition and distorted religious dogma; the result was the enthronement of human reason as the final arbiter of good and evil. The Jews exploited these historical circumstances, encouraged the Christians to desert their religion, and even invented communism to facilitate their domination of the world. For all that, the Russian people, for instance, yearn in the depths of their instinctive nature to embrace the divine doctrine. Thus, the return to God's message is the only inevitable fact, irrespective of historical or scientific pretensions. Man's innate essence cannot but believe in God and His oneness; all other speculative theories represent an accumulation that is blown away once the true believers assert themselves (Qutb, 1981, Vol. II: 1113–21, 1132, 1087–8, 1164, 1980: 77–84).

To Qutb, man's religious instinct is a reflection of the organic structure of the cosmos and its interrelated components. Hence, his function is not, as western philosophies state, to conquer or subdue nature, but to enter into a harmonious relationship with its elements and gifts. This is the meaning of man's appointment as God's deputy on earth: it simultaneously singles out his unique position in the universe, and reminds him of his comprehensive obligations towards the Creator. And, unlike the god of Greek philosophers, Allah has a positive intercourse with his creatures, relieving them of the onerous task of legislating imperfect and doubtful rules (Qutb, 1980: 66–7, 1981, Vol. IV: 1925–6).

All human activities must, Qutb maintains, reveal themselves as acts of worship, whereby God's purpose is perpetually complied with and renewed. This premise is also most eloquently demonstrated by the fact that the universe is the visible book of God, while the Qur'an is His legible text. Both furnish irrefutable proofs of their creator, and both exist to be active; the universe still moves and operates according to God's will, and the Qur'an has discharged its function towards humanity, but kept its identity intact. The Qur'an is God's message to man whose instinct has essentially remained the same, despite new socio-economic developments or unforeseen circumstances. It is thus still valid, and will be so for ever. Being the final word of God, its nature, like that of the universe, is always active without undergoing alteration. Thus, Qutb concludes:

> If it be ridiculous for one to describe, for example, the sun by saying: 'This is an ancient reactionary star and ought to be replaced by a new progressive star!', or to state: 'Man is an ancient reactionary creature and should be exchanged for another progressive being so that the earth is made a better place', it would be more ridiculous to use the same argument in respect of the Qur'an – the final address of God to man'.
> (Qutb, 1981, Vol. I: 349, Vol. IV: 1937, Vol. VI: 3336–8)

Both Qutb and al-Mawdudi derived similar conclusions from their assertion of the exclusive sovereignty (*hakimiyya*) of God. 'This principle of the unity of God', al-Mawdudi contends, 'altogether negates the concept of the legal and political sovereignty of human beings, individually or collectively [...] God alone is the Sovereign and His Commandments are the Law of Islam' (al-Mawdudi, 1979b: 37). However, Qutb went a step further by linking this assertion to his concept of *jahiliyya* as a pervasive condition simultaneously straddling the Islamic and non-Islamic worlds. So much so that Qutb could be considered the exponent of *jahiliyya* par excellence. Not even his brother, Muhammad Qutb, who wrote a detailed study on the subject, dared to declare the total disappearance of Islam, be it socially or politically. His definition of *jahiliyya* 'as a psychological state which rejects the guidance of God' (1964: 11) does not lead him, as it did his brother, to advance a rigorous classification of all present-day societies. Sayyid Qutb describes this condition thus:

> *Jahiliyya* has the same characteristics, irrespective of time and place. Whenever people's hearts are devoid of a divine doctrine that governs their thought, and concomitant legal rules to regulate their lives, *jahiliyya* is bound to rear its head in one form or another [...] The one in which contemporary societies wallow is not different in its nature from that of ancient Arabia before the rise of Islam [...] Humanity is today living in a large brothel! One has only to take a glance at its press, films, fashion shows, beauty contests, ballrooms, wine bars, and broadcasting stations! Or observe its mad lust for naked flesh, provocative postures, and sick suggestive statements in literature, the arts and the mass media. And add to all this, the system of usury which fuels man's voracity for money and engenders vile methods for its accumulation and investment, in addition to fraud, trickery, and blackmail dressed up in the garb of law.
>
> (Qutb, 1981, Vol. I: 510–11)

Contemporary *jahiliyya* is, however, more sinister than the old one. The adherents of the latter were at least more polite with God, offering gifts to other deities in order to intercede on their behalf with Allah, the most sublime. Nowadays, other deities have been elevated above God, venerating what these deities prescribe, and rejecting out of hand what God had decreed (Qutb, 1981, Vol. III: 1413). Marxism stands out in this context as the most obnoxious usurper of God's authority. Consequently, communist societies, according to Qutb, head the list of modern *jahiliyya*: they flagrantly embrace atheism, make matter the only effective force in the universe, reduce man's actions and his history to a negative reflection of the mode of production, and turn the Party into the sole source of authority. This is the worst case of ignorance, since God is totally and openly absent in words and deeds. This list also includes societies in which heathenism prevails, such as India, Japan, the Philippines and parts of Africa. Although people in those countries, Qutb explains, recognize the existence of a god, they associate with him other deities. They, furthermore, derive their laws from a bewildering variety of sources: priests, magicians, astrologers and secular institutions. Moreover, Qutb asserts that all Jewish and Christian communities have been living in a state of ignorance ever since their Scriptures were distorted, giving rise to false notions of God and his attributes. The Qur'an, he points out, is quite categorical in rebuking the Jews for calling themselves 'the chosen people of God', as well as in its dismissal of the Christian Trinitarian doctrine. More importantly, these communities conduct their affairs by means of representative institutions which enjoy absolute sovereignty, thus excluding the validity of God's commandments (Qutb, 1981/1401: 98–101).

This classification is not political. Nor does it confine itself to certain social groups, such as the intelligentsia, statesmen or religious leaders. It is an unequivocal conviction of entire societies, and a pronouncement of their status as legitimate targets of conquest and subordination. It is, however, a characterization shared with al-Mawdudi, in spite of the more general diagnosis of the Pakistani leader. Qutb's originality and far-reaching radicalism reside in the inclusion of all Muslim societies in his compilation. He readily acknowledges that the Muslim communities still believe in one God and worship Him in their devotional acts. But they relegate the most essential attributes of God – His legislative authority – to others who determine almost all the fundamental issues of their lives. Accordingly, the Muslims join the ranks of the Jews and Christians, becoming latter-day polytheists. Some of these communities compound their errors 'by declaring openly their secularism', while others pay lip-service to Islam, then proceed to violate its social system as a whole, and announce the incompatibility between science and the metaphysical realm. And, in an implicit reference to Arab states, particularly Nasserite Egypt, Qutb points out that in some societies people make their own laws, but do not hesitate to ascribe these human innovations to the *shari'a* of God. Hence, one conclusion imposes itself: all these societies are un-Islamic and illegitimate. The Muslims, in other words, have forfeited their right to be attributed to their religion, and should be deprived of their present appellation (Qutb, 1981/1401: 101–3).

# The Vanguard

Sayyid Qutb postulated the crisis of contemporary societies as a succession of abysmal moral failures. He saw in the corruption and bankruptcy of ethical standards signs of woeful consequences for human life and its natural growth. The western world afforded him with ample illustrations, testifying to his diagnosis. He repeatedly alluded to the steady erosion of liberal values and democratic institutions in the capitalist countries. Such erosion was, moreover, seen to be creating a social vacuum, and leading to the adoption of socialism as a compensatory measure.

Similarly, he predicted a darker future for totalitarian theories, particularly Marxism. For although Marxist ideology attracted at a certain historical period widespread support in the West and the East, it had now lost its appeal, and become an adjunct of the state and its oppressive structures. Moreover, the wretched economic results of communism, he reiterated, had undermined its vestigial ability of survival.

Hence, the leading role of western man in world affairs was coming to an end. Not because the economic and military strength of western civilization had weakened, Qutb explained, but as a result of moral bankruptcy and its devastating effects. In this perspective, all modern developments and theories – the scientific revolution, patriotism, nationalism, liberalism and totalitarianism – had one after the other run their course and reached a dead end. Consequently, the world was desperately searching for new guides to steer its lurching ship into safer waters. This deplorable state of affairs, Qutb concluded, cried out for:

> a leadership that is capable of preserving and developing the present material culture, which was the product of the creative genius of Europe, and also to provide humanity with a fresh stock of high ideals, in addition to an authentic, positive, and realistic way of life. Only Islam possesses these values and this way of life.
>
> (Qutb, 1981/1401: 5–7)

Thus, the present age presented Islam with a golden opportunity to stake its claim for the leadership of the world. It was without doubt the best-qualified system to undertake such a lofty task and salvage the human race from this vicious circle of moral decadence. By welcoming material progress as one of the primary functions of man, as well as 'enjoining the good, and forbidding the evil', Islam solved the eternal riddle of the happy medium. Nevertheless, being both a way of life and a comprehensive political system, Qutb argued, Islam could not perform its reinvigorated role unless it materialized its doctrine in social forms, and became anew an organized community. Its rejuvenation was in this sense contingent on the emergence of 'a dynamic movement', and the restitution of the Muslim nation which had been absent from the stage of history for many centuries. It must be clearly understood, he emphasized, that the Muslim community was neither a piece of territory in which the *shari'a* used to be applied, nor the name of a people whose ancestors once upon a time lived under an Islamic system. Rather, it denoted an association of people whose entire spiritual and material life was perpetually governed by Islam. In this sense, such a nation no longer existed anywhere in the world (Qutb, 1981/1401: 7–8).

A momentous act of restatement and restoration was called for; a surgical operation was required to discover the true essence of Islam; a spiritual and physical resurrection had to be launched by sweeping away the wreckage of pagan beliefs and modern idols. The obligation of bringing about such a surging movement, Qutb underlines, is the prerequisite for the assumption of world leadership. The authentic qualities of Islam, its fundamental characteristics, have to be pinpointed and inculcated. Furthermore, he singles out the fact that each nation has 'a specific mission' in life, a particular skill, and an aptitude to excel in doing certain things. Success is, therefore, proportionate to the ability of discovering one's natural qualifications and carrying out one's vocation. The Muslim's vocation is well known: the doctrine and method of Islam. Material production, science and technology have advanced in the West to the extent that the possibility of catching up is virtually non-existent. It is, thus, a matter of coming to terms with one's options. The Muslims are still able to take up their honourable craft which grants them the facilities to furnish provisions other nations lack, and regain their authentic identity at the same time. The shortage of values in the world market is accordingly the responsibility of one single nation. It is this erstwhile great community, Qutb asserts, that sits unaware on a goldmine of 'moral products'. If it only knew how to reactivate its production lines, the potentialities of sustained growth would be limitless (Qutb, 1981/1401: 8–9).

Qutb thought that the restitution of belief in God's oneness renders the emergence of a corps of believers (*'usba mu'mina*) an inevitable concomitant. For Qutb, this corps, to which he attached the modern and non-Qur'anic name of 'vanguard' (*tali'a*), is the form in which the substance and potency of Islam are actualized. In the light of its crucial importance, the vanguard should be provided with 'signposts' to guide it along the tortuous road towards the ultimate destination. These signposts spell out the exact nature of the struggle, delineate its initial and final stages and clarify the functions of this brave vanguard (Qutb, 1981/1401: 11–13).

Thus, in one of his last statements, Qutb argued the necessity of restoring Islam on the basis of purely pragmatic reasons. His pragmatism, tinged with commercial overtones is, moreover, allied to a paradoxical view of history – a view that explains all modern phenomena against the background of materialistic and worldly motives. To him, contemporary 'so-called Muslims' have to be realistic and level-headed. Their preliminary task consists of making an objective evaluation of their strengths and weaknesses, so as to discover what precise and fruitful function they are able to perform. By conducting a fact-finding study dealing with their capabilities or untapped resources, the Muslims would be in an ideal position to chart a long-term course of action, and put the results of their survey into immediate use.

What does such a survey tell the Muslim activist, or the potential recruit for a new vanguard? It tells him, unquestionably and irrefutably, that the whole world is living in a state of religious ignorance (*jahiliyya*) and wallowing in a sink of iniquity. This is an essential fad that has to be grasped and kept in mind at each interval of the journey. A true believer cannot fail to see that all societies are governed by persons who devise their own laws, and in this way transgress God's legislative authority, His most exclusive attribute and prerogative. This universal transgression is the underlying reason for moral degeneration, and which manifests itself in psychological dilemmas, personal misery and spiritual vacousness. One has only, Qutb is fond of reiterating, to survey the available statistics in western societies on divorce, illicit sexual relationships, illegitimate children, homosexuality, promiscuity, drunkenness, gambling and suicide, to appreciate the depraved nature of such a civilization. As a result, it is destined to a grim fate. A true Islamic society is, by contrast, a superior haven of moral values and clean, healthy relationships (Qutb, 1980/1400: 120–62, 1981/1401: 124–6).

# The Family

The Islamic activist, Qutb elucidates, is able to gauge the exact nature of a society by studying its family system, the division of labour between husband and wife, the relationship between the sexes and the manner in which children are brought up. This criterion is bound to yield the best results because the family forms the principal basis of society. Consequently, all other norms and institutions pass or fail the test in proportion to their attitude towards the family, as well as the respective functions of its constituent parts. Unlike al-Mawdudi, Qutb, who remained a bachelor throughout his life, refrains from quoting sayings attributed to the Prophet in order to demonstrate the evil character of women. His is a biological and functional argument, buttressed by quotations from conservative, mainly western, sources. One favourite author repeatedly quoted by him was the French surgeon biologist and Nobel prize winner, Alexis Carrel (1873–1944). For example, Qutb cites at length a statement by Carrel which asserts the differences between man and woman to be the direct result of the structure of the tissues and specific chemical substances, in addition to dissimilarities in the nervous systems of the male and female (Qutb, 1980/14000: 132–4). These biological differences entail differences of functions, sensitivity, passivity or positivity. A woman fulfils her function by being a wife and mother, while that of a man is to be the undisputed authority, the breadwinner and the active member in public life (Carrel, 1935: 103–6; Qutb, 1980/1400: 13–5).

The significance and role of marriage and the family unit are exalted by Qutb far beyond the way historical Islam considered both as down-to-earth civil contracts. In accordance with conservative theories of motherhood and education, he speaks in glowing terms of the family as 'the nursery of the future', breeding 'precious human products' under the guardianship of woman. He furthermore celebrates the holy bond of pure love between a man and a woman, who both voluntarily enter into a relationship of marriage as two equal partners, each discharging functions assigned by nature and biology. Qutb highlights the fact that Islam paid more attention to the organization of the family than almost any other institution. The sheer number of Qur'anic verses dealing with family life attests to the pivotal importance of this institution. The whole Islamic social system, he continues, is an extended family system, pertaining to a divine order and set up in conformity with human instincts, needs and requirements. Not only human beings are created to form families, but all living beings and organisms are fashioned in couples. More importantly, the Qur'an, in marked contrast to the Bible, states that God created both Adam and Eve of the same matter and 'of a single soul' (4:1, 7:189).

However, the natural existence of pairs as ordained by God does not presuppose monogamy or eternal union. Divorce becomes inevitable when one or both partner can no longer be reconciled, and after the prescribed Qur'anic procedures have been exhausted. Polygamy has its roots in biological factors as well as divine wisdom. Biological factors, Qutb explains, dictate that while a woman can become pregnant only once at a time, and as a result of the agency of one man, the latter can in the meantime make three additional women procreate. For Islam allows a man up to a maximum of four wives. Moreover, the fertility of a man extends to the age of 70 or beyond, whereas that of a woman ceases at the age of 50 or thereabouts. There are at average 25 years of reproductive potential in the life of a man unparalleled in that of a woman.

The divine wisdom in assigning biologically-based functions within the family and society at large manifests itself at various levels. One such, and the most relevant for an activist, is related to the initiation and conduct of *jihad*, or struggle in the path of God. Qutb indicates that God did not specify in his Book the exact role of woman in *jihad*: she was neither commanded nor forbidden to perform this religious duty. There were many instances during the early Islamic conquests, and as a result of certain exigencies, when a number of women did participate as combatants, and not as nurses or carriers of provisions. But these were exceptional and rare cases, and should not, he adds, form the basis of a general rule. 'Be that as it may, God did not prescribe *jihad* for woman as he did for man'. The reason is not hard to find:

> *Jihad* was not prescribed for woman because she begets the men who fight in the cause of God. Her entire organic and physiological formation is shaped to procreate men and prepare them for both *jihad* and life. She is in this field better equipped and more useful: better equipped because each of her cells is physiologically and psychologically made to perform this function [...] and more useful as far as the long-term interests of the community are concerned. In the wake of war whereby men are mowed down and women left untouched, the latter would fill the

gap by becoming centres of procreation. The same result would not be feasible if war destroyed both women and men, or only women. In an Islamic state, one single man, acting within the limits of religion and his capabilities, can have up to four child-bearing women, and thus make up fairly quickly for the loss caused by war. On the other hand, one thousand men cannot make one woman conceive more than she would from a single man.

(Qutb, 1981, Vol. I: 234–6, 580, Vol. II: 644, 1980/1400: 120)

Qutb took pains to offer some plausible and rational explanations for the division of labour in an institution that is essentially an immutable structure ordained by God into existence. Hence, he tries to highlight a range of beneficial possibilities, and select those which appear of direct relevance to the internal organization of his vanguard, as well as its future state. General Qur'anic rules are then supplemented by medical evidence and biological statements. The strict demarcation in functions, rights and duties finally emerges into daylight armed with scientific substantiation, on the one hand, and divine infinite wisdom, on the other. Thus, in a Muslim community, Qutb expounds, feminist or liberal demands for woman's liberation become meaningless. Accorded rights and duties in conformity with her biological, mental and emotional constitution, a woman is bound to be content in discharging a sacred task that is utterly an outward manifestation of her innermost being. The battle of the sexes was pre-empted at an early stage, while the underlying factors for rebellion, organizing women's associations and agitating for parliamentary membership are made redundant or unnecessary (Qutb, 1981, Vol. II: 643, 645).

Marriage is thus highly recommended. All true believers should endeavour as far as possible to marry at an early age. By doing so, they fulfil a religious obligation and strengthen their resistance to corruption and depravity, the hallmarks of all contemporary societies. However, marriage, being a 'holy bond' and 'a sanctity directly linked to God', must not be taken lightly. The selection of a partner, particularly in a situation of prevalent idolatry, is one of the utmost importance. Qutb concedes that although the Qur'an forbade a Muslim male to marry 'idolatresses', it gave him permission to enter into wedlock with a Jewish or Christian woman. However, the contemporary blatant corruption of Christianity and Judaism is bound to have disastrous effects as far as the future of the household is concerned. 'It is undoubtedly true', Qutb asserts, 'that a Jewish, Christian, or non-religious, wife colours her home and children with her character, and brings up a generation completely removed from Islam'. A Muslim mother is, therefore, a sine qua non to stem the tide of infidelity and safeguard the nation's youth. The members of the new vanguard, Qutb emphasizes, should devote their attention to the formation of the Muslim female so that she would raise a proper Muslim family. Unless these recommendations are adhered to, 'the construction of the Islamic community shall be delayed for a long time' (Qutb, 1981, Vol. I: 240–1, Vol. VI: 3096, 3619).

Such a novel interpretation, whereby a general Qur'anic rule (5:5) is abruptly suspended, corresponds with what Qutb calls 'the dynamic nature' of Islamic jurisprudence. It is a creativity closely related to the essence of a doctrine that unfolds its full connotations in the open field of ceaseless struggle. Consequently, the activist is the only person who is qualified to interpret the details of legal rules. Those who sit behind their desks, peruse old books and attempt to offer a comprehensive itemization of religious laws and regulations are bound to fail, producing an abstract version of a living, exuberant entity. In other words, the emergence of an Islamic community precedes the meticulous works of jurists and scholars, and determines the particular issues that have to be tackled (Qutb, 1981, Vol. III: 1734–6, Vol. IV: 2008–13).

## Historical and Prophetic Lineages

The question of choosing the opportune moment to discuss jurisprudential reform is one aspect of a wider domain. Since jurisprudence itself developed as a response to historical circumstances and changing needs, the history of Islamic societies must be put in perspective. An Islamist, sworn to bring about a radical political transformation, should judge this history in the light of the original blueprint, and not vice versa. Immoral practices, slavery, concubinage, despotism and treachery, Qutb acknowledges, did prevail in some Muslim societies at one period or another. However, Islam and the history of Muslims are two different entities: one is impeccable and divine, the other fallible and human. The first should not, therefore, be judged by the shortcomings of the second. It is not simply a logical measure of correlation worked out between two variables; the blame for the frequency of such immoral acts lies with the Muslims who departed from the straight path (Qutb, 1981, Vol. I: 533, 544).

However, this depreciation of Islamic history does not imply that Islam never existed except as a theoretical hypothesis. To Qutb, Islam had a golden age that has never been rivalled, be it in ancient or modern times. During the Prophethood of Muhammad, when God was in direct communication with His chosen community, and under the rule of the rightly-guided Caliphs, Islam became identical with its society. All the members of the new nation turned Islam into a living presence, so much so that its principles and injunctions were easily and effortlessly implemented. Being the expression of an immutable essence, addressing a community which was still innately sound, embraced by a unique generation of men, the teachings of Islam, Qutb explains, struck their roots in the most suitable and fertile soil. Moreover, Islam did not emerge in response to socio-economic needs, political factors or geographic necessities. Its rise and expansion, he affirms, defy all materialistic and historical explanations. It was God's magnanimity which opened up all the factors and possibilities: 'He honoured His creatures by selecting one of them to be the confluence of His divine light, the depository of His wisdom, the cradle of His words, and the representative of His predetermination on this earth.' Thenceforth, the march of history turned to flow in a new direction. This momentous event, and the subsequent 23 years of Muhammad's career, witnessed the erection of indelible signposts that guide humanity along its road towards God. As long as faith in God's message remained solid and unadulterated, the believers were never vanquished. Defeat is the result of a breach in the faith, causing a person to falter either in his morale or deeds. Nevertheless, losing one battle cannot mean the end of the war, provided the spirit is sufficiently sound to be rekindled and stimulated for another round. Once the prerequisites of faith are marshalled, Qutb continues, the complementary material requirements would instantly become a foregone conclusion. These are the lessons of Muhammad's biography and those of all true believers (Qutb, 1981, Vol. II: 782–1046, Vol. VI: 3936–8).

To Qutb, an Islamic activist, engaged in embodying a divine mission, places this unique ideal beyond history, time and place. Seen in this light, Islam can never be reduced to 'a historical event', or an occurrence that took place a long time ago, and may thus be studied as a cold academic subject. Rather it is 'a constant encounter' that humanity has to face until the last Day of Judgment (Qutb, 1981, Vol. IV: 1255). Islam possesses as a result an independent existence over and above the actual conditions of its adherents (Qutb, 1981, Vol. I: 584).

Qutb's Islam, towering above history and man, is repeatedly defined as being simultaneously a doctrine and a method, an organic unity of theory and practice. Its doctrine was revealed in Mecca over 13 years. This relatively long and gradual process was a deliberate decision of the Creator, wisely taken in order to inculcate the fundamental principles of Islam. The absence of legally enforced injunctions during the Meccan phase was a matter of choice as well as meticulous differentiation of priorities. No firm basis could have been built, Qutb argues, without the prior assertion of the exact attributes of God – His oneness, Lordship, exclusive sovereignty and divinity. It had to be clearly stated and grasped that He was the creator, the sustainer of the universe in all its beings, phenomena and things. Then the mysteries of life and death, man's function on earth and the ultimate significance of human existence had to be positively established. Having laid out its foundations, God through the medium of His Prophet moved to the next stage. In Medina, Islam materialized its doctrine in a way of life, a process of political, socio-economic, military and spiritual construction. The distinct complementarity of these two phases forms the quintessence of Islam as a comprehensive movement. An Islamic activist has thus to envision the unfolding events of that sublime moment, conjuring in his depths its priorities, phases and triumphant climax. History has turned full circle, Qutb points out, and a similar task challenges the vanguards of Islam. Today, as in that distant past, the absolute paramountcy of affirming the fundamental principles of Islam overrides all other activities. One cannot undertake to build a state, delineating all the minute details of its laws, while the preliminary obligation of re-enacting a new Meccan phase is obscured or neglected (Qutb, 1981, Vol. I: 22–6, 305–6, 348–50, Vol. II: 701–2, 1010–14, Vol. VI: 3619).

Qutb thought that those Islamists who insisted on discussing the finer points of an Islamic constitution were victims of naive sincerity or an orchestrated campaign. An activist has to be aware of such traps, since their only purpose is to sidetrack the vanguard from the right path. Drafting constitutions or electing consultative assemblies amount to mere technicalities. The particular procedure of electing a nation's representatives falls into the category of forms. These forms spring into life once the contents have been assembled and reactivated. Moreover, these demands for endless discussions and studies on the merits of technical procedures, he says, arise from a well-known misconception. Some misguided persons believe that Islamic rules and laws, and in spite of some obvious violations, are still operative in their society. They then proceed to draft detailed solutions, so that what is considered an essentially sound base would emerge fully repaired. But this is an illusion. All societies, including the Islamic world, have banished 'true religion' from their lives, and turned their institutions into ultimate sources of authority. In other words, humanity has once more reverted to 'polytheism' (Qutb, 1981, Vol. II: 94–50, 1015, 1106, Vol. III: 1735–6).

Thus in the terminology of contemporary Islamic radicalism, polytheism (*shirk*) has become the essence of all non-Qur'anic, or rather non-Qutbist, approaches to politics, economics and ethics. According to Qutb, polytheism may assume many forms and functions at different levels. It is, therefore, not that simplistic description which confines its manifestations to acts of worshipping pagan idols and stones, or trees and stars. These were practices of ancient heathenism, he explains, and have been replaced by more sinister and intricate ones. Moreover, the mere recognition of God's existence does not exclude polytheist violations, unless this belief is accompanied by an unequivocal admission of His absolute authority in all aspects of life (Qutb, 1981, Vol. II: 1063–4, 1083–4, 1083–5). Belief in God, His angels, books and messengers, as well as the Day of Judgement and predetermination, is as much an integral part of Islam as His legal rules. Acts of worship and those of worldly affairs are one seamless garment woven by God to enwrap man's entire being (Qutb, 1981, Vol. IV: 1042, Vol. VI: 3609).

More importantly, acceptance of the oneness of God entails faith in the uniform teachings of His messengers and prophets who were sent whenever the human race had relapsed into a state of religious ignorance. An Islamic activist, Qutb contends, belongs to a noble lineage, deeply rooted in the recesses of time. He is a participant in that 'majestic procession' that had at its head an honourable galaxy of leaders: Noah, Abraham, Ismael, Isaac, Jacob, Joseph, Moses, Jesus and the Seal of the Prophets, Muhammad. Although there were 'outward differences' in the geographical locations and racial origins of their communities, all the prophets faced and endured similar situations and experiences. Their careers, as narrated in the Qur'an, furnish ample illustrations of the way an ideal shapes the course of history. They also show that a divine message does not achieve its purpose by the mere acts of revelation and verbal communication; it becomes a living and vibrant reality when 'a group believes in it wholeheartedly, adopts it as a way of life, and strives to enlist recruits for its cause' (Qutb, 1981, Vol. I: 12, 528, Vol. IV: 1866).

Hence, history moves in successive cycles, carried along by a chain of messengers. Each link duplicates its antecedents, so that all subsequent prophetic missions are repeat performances of the original one. However, whereas Islam abjures racial discrimination, its continuous chain, extending from Abraham to Muhammad, is firmly connected by direct descent from one patriarch. Thus Muhammad is descended from Ismael, Abraham's first-born son. His mission restored Islam to its Abrahamic purity, closed the circle and sealed the last two links of the chain. Nevertheless, the linkage has snapped under the gnawing impact of European civilization. In accordance with this line of exposition, Qutb says this rupture coincided with Napoleon's invasion of Egypt in 1798. It was only after that foreign intrusion that 'God's attributes of exclusive sovereignty and lordship were appropriated by human beings, and large numbers of Muslims started to desert the teachings of their religion' (Qutb, Vol. IV: 842, 1130, 1144, 1134, Vol. V: 3184–5).

If all the prophets preached the same message and taught one single doctrine, including its legal branches, why should the Qur'an be the sole source of Islamic radicalism? Two main reasons are advanced. First, all other religious books, particularly the Bible, have undergone a long process of distortion and interpolation. The existing versions, as a result, are not the direct, unadulterated word of God, but a jumbled mixture of late reports and edited accounts. The Qur'an, on the other hand, is the only authentic Book, revealed by God to His messenger at certain intervals in the form of verses. These were immediately communicated by Muhammad to his community, written down, recited, and instantly memorized by his close companions. Contrary to common belief, Qutb contends, the division of the Qur'an into chapters and its collection in one final version were the work of Muhammad himself. It has thus been preserved, sound and unaltered, as God's divine revelation. Second, despite the uniformity of their message, not all prophets addressed humanity at large. As a matter of fact, with the exception of Muhammad, all other messengers were sent to a particular people or locality. These restrictive factors often resulted in constraining the full development of the universality and comprehensiveness of the message. Muhammad's Islam, being both universal and comprehensive, spelt out God's final word. Hence, all divine revelation after Muhammad's death came to an end (Qutb, 1981, Vol. I: 216, 282–3, Vol. II: 842–3, 1138–47, 1168; cf. Mawdudi, 1980: 10712).

Although this line of analysis is certainly a restatement of a large number of Qur'anic verses, its main purpose is directed at Muhammad 'Abduh's modernistic interpretation of some of these verses, as well as the theory of evolution, particularly in its application to the study of religion. According to 'Abduh, 'distortion of the Bible does not necessarily presuppose a corruption of the text as such: it can also be brought about "by attributing to an expression a meaning other than the one which was originally intended"' (Asad, 1964: 105, Note 60). If such liberal views were entertained, Qutb's argument for conducting a concerted assault on 'polytheism' as a worldwide phenomenon would lose much of its pugnacity. Similarly, evolutionary notions had to be discarded, since they implied progression from lower to higher forms. A study on 'the concept of God' throughout the ages by 'Abbas Mahmud al-'Aqqad, an Egyptian writer and one of Qutb's mentors in his early career as a literary critic, is strongly rejected on the grounds of its comparative approach. Since al-'Aqqad postulated Islam as the culmination of a long line of polytheist and henotheist beliefs, he reduced monotheism, in Qutb's eyes, to a projection of human needs, making it subject to 'speculation, experimentation and scientific knowledge'. Apart from these grave consequences, such an evolutionary theory would leave the door open to all sorts of persons to pass laws in conformity with their stage of development. God's exclusive sovereignty, Islam's cornerstone, is thus compromised (Qutb, 1981, Vol. IV: 1096, 1882–5).

However, Qutb's apparent regressiveness is limited to religious and moral issues and does not prevent him from conceding, or indeed welcoming, 'the results of science', its evolution and progress. Consequently, members of his vanguard are encouraged to study all the available scientific and experimental disciplines, such as chemistry, physics, biology, astronomy, medicine, industry, agriculture, administrative techniques, warfare methods and other related sciences. These subjects can be acquired under the direction of Muslims and non-Muslims alike, but matters of faith, morality and all that pertains to the organization of society have to be derived from God, or learnt from a true believer (Qutb, 1981/1401: 138–40).

By dividing knowledge into two separate domains, one change-able and the other immutable, he was treading in the footsteps of a wide 'galaxy' of fellow radicalists, be they of the right or left. Furthermore, like his reformist predecessors, he was utterly convinced that the 'experimental' or 'empirical' method, which underlies the emergence of modern industry in the West, was borrowed by Europe from Islamic universities during the Middle Ages (Qutb, 1981/1401: 142).

## *Jihad* in the Path of God

Having armed himself with these tools of analysis and articles of faith, a vanguardist is strategically placed to tackle the resultant practical steps. However, the struggle for restoring Islam, Qutb warns, is bound to be an arduous and protracted task. It involves strict adherence to a time-honoured plan of action, invariably applied whenever the message of Islam has to be resurrected. This process is initially set in motion by a single individual. He is then followed by a vanguard that proceeds to wage relentless battles against the symbols of ignorance. Tribulations, momentary setbacks and persecutions are bound to occur. Some weak-minded activists may desert their 'compact group', defect to the enemy or plunge into an engagement without due preparation. As for those who persevere, infused with unshakeable faith, yet not prone to adventurous miscalculations, 'God shall pronounce judgement in their favour', and open the gates of one idolatrous state after another to His victorious soldiers. Once political power has been seized, the masses, after standing on the sidelines while the dust of the battle filled the air, 'shall enter God's religion in throngs'. This scenario is a faithful re-enactment of the Meccan period, and requires, according to Qutb, a leader and an elite no less gifted or steadfast than the Prophet and his Companions (Qutb, 1981, Vol. IV: 2013).

This constant appeal to recall the early events of Muhammad's mission, however, is governed by the power of imagination, on the one hand, and the new circumstances of contemporary life, on the other. Qutb was well aware of both. His appeal for freeing jurisprudence from the dead weight of past generations is a case in point. Moreover, he insisted that there was 'similarity' rather than complete congruence between the conditions of ancient Arabia and present-day societies (Qutb, 1981, Vol. IV: 2122). This similarity allows the believer to look at the past from his current position, and paves the way for a creative approach to modern techniques and technologies. Thus, Qutb steps into the shoes of a new prophet, and science reclaims its rightful place in Islamic universities.

By the late 1950s Qutb, along with some members of the dissolved Muslim Brotherhood, became convinced that mass organizations, such as theirs in former times, were irredeemably unsuitable for the novel task of confronting centralized systems of state which were dominated in their key institutions by army officers. As for the common people, he believed they were basically unreliable and easily swayed by demagogues, particularly in the age of the mass media. There was, therefore, an obvious need to think of a creative solution commensurate with the specific conditions of the day. In early 1960 Qutb published a book on *Islam and the Problems of Civilization*. Towards the end of his study, he puts forward for the first time in his career the necessity of organizing 'a body of believers' (*'usba mu'mina*), called into existence by the faith of one man (Qutb, 1980/1400: 193). Instead of opening its arms to all and sundry, this new corps would be confined to 'the chosen elite' (*al-safwa al-mukhtara*), the vanguard of professional revolutionaries who dedicate their whole life to one purpose. Well-disciplined, highly organized and imbued with the spirit of a new era in the long march of Islam, they cannot fail to win (Qutb 1981, Vol. IV: 2036–7).

This compact group is, moreover, directly modelled on the physical and political structures of its enemy. As contemporary paganism, Qutb argues, is not simply a theoretical formula, but a dynamic movement in command of a society, which constitutes an organic whole, Islam itself must be embodied in a dynamic association of its own, surpassing its rivals ideologically and structurally. This is the only way to possess the capability of obliterating a new cycle of ignorance. Being dynamic like a living organism, the vanguard has to demarcate its own spatial boundaries by asserting its unequivocal independence. It cannot, therefore, allow political expediencies to impinge on its ultimate aim the seizure of political power. All other issues – parliamentary elections, amending the constitution or expounding the details of an exhaustive programme – become futile exercises in casuistry. Exclusively built on doctrinal allegiances, the vanguard shuns the lower forms of earthly loyalties (Qutb, 1981, Vol. I: 216–17, Vol. III: 1556–62, Vol. IV: 1946).

Thus, the battle lines are clearly drawn: two antagonistic forces face each other in a life and death fight. The inevitability of a violent encounter between two irreconcilable entities necessitates an immediate dissociation and separation from the battleground of the enemy. Each side is then instantly recognized by its organization and leadership, titles and labels, ideology, loyalty and way of life. This declaration of war entails at the practical level the withdrawal into a new society which rejects all the laws of the old one. However, it is an internal withdrawal within one's own country, and takes place as a policy of non-cooperation at the political, educational and administrative levels. The idea of migration from the land of unbelief to settle in that of belief is 'creatively' reinterpreted so that only the form is modified (Qutb, 1981, Vol. IV: 1947, 2101–2, 2438). Hence, various contemporary radicalist movements have, as an expression of dissociation, resorted to building separate mosques, clinics and schools, or creating networks of financial institutions which ban usurious transactions. It is often the case that some acts are deliberately undertaken as calculated violations of existing laws, in order to demonstrate the illegal nature of state legislation. As Qutb declares, 'the summoners to God must be distinct and a community unto themselves'. Severance of relations is then carried to its logical conclusion: all manoeuvres to bring about a gradual penetration of existing political establishments must be abandoned; collaboration, no matter how limited, always leads to subordination, followed by loss of identity; amorphousness is a sign of inertia, while Islam is motion, vitality and the proclamation of self-liberation. Moreover, blurring a clearly defined message means an indefinite suspension of its essential aims, culminating in abject surrender. Consequently, dissimulation is to be avoided under all circumstances, and the truth should go out in its entirety, without flattery or sycophancy, so that people are made to realize the falsehood of their beliefs. No victory is possible, Qutb points out, unless this total dissociation is applied daily by the chosen elite in its confrontation with the state. The history of all prophetic missions confirms this deduction: one particular way of life must stand diametrically opposed to another. More importantly, this was the significance of the Meccan period. In it one can clearly discern how doctrine, movement and organization were inextricably linked. The Meccan experience also indicates, Qutb adds, that dissociation is not to be confused with total isolation; radicalism in proclaiming the truth goes hand in hand with a courteous style of presentation. A maximalist attitude does not preclude 'mingling with unbelievers', provided the sole purpose is admonition and rectification of corrupt concepts. If a believer associates with 'the godless', but overlooks their sinful deeds as a way of engaging in dissembling, he is conclusively forbidden to do so. In other words, a studied and purposeful interaction is allowed and encouraged, but social intercourse with infidels for mere pleasure or aimless amusement amounts to an evil innovation (*bid'a*), with consequences graver than praying in a church or a synagogue (Qutb, 1981, Vol. II: 941, 1013–14, 1125, 1128–30, Vol. IV: 2030–5).

Qutb's insistence on fully-fledged dissociation (*mufasala*) as well as the synchronization of theory and practice, results in a society split into two warring camps. The believers, represented by God's select group, are thus continually locked in conflict with the unbelievers, whose earthly falsehood spans both society and the state. It is, moreover, a confrontation of doctrines, overriding all distinctions of class, nationality or language. Whereas all other political ideologies base their struggle on socio-economic interests or narrow issues of worldly values, Islam conducts its combat in the cause of God. Hence, the faithful elite shun the comforts of life, and despise immediate gains and losses, fix their sights on a sublime mission of utter devotion to divine ideals. *Jihad* is then the continuation of God's politics by other means. It is an obligation that becomes incumbent on the believers whenever the tenets and legal rules of Islam are violated or neglected. In this sense, *jihad* is a form of political struggle designed, as Qutb argues, to disarm the enemy so that Islam is allowed to apply its *shari'a* unhindered by the oppressive power of idolatrous tyrannies. By the mere removal of the political obstacle, the central aim of revolutionary struggle is accomplished, a fact which refutes the charge of forcible conversion. This is, for example, the correct meaning of the Qur'anic statement: 'there is no compulsion in religion'. Contrary to the opinion of liberal-minded Muslims, this Qur'anic verse, Qutb explains, presupposes the hegemony of Islam in society, thereby freeing individuals from the political domination of non-Muslim rulers. Once political power is in the hands of the new Islamic elite, and its divine laws are firmly established, the subjects of the state are given the choice either to embrace Islam or persist in practising their inherited religions and beliefs. However, this tolerance is a conditional agreement concluded between a victorious party and vanquished subjects (Qutb, 1981/1401: 71–5).

Both al-Mawdudi and Qutb made painstaking efforts to place *jihad* at the forefront of religious obligations. They argued that it was a duty incumbent on all Muslim men, particularly at a time when their religion was under concerted attack. Consequently, its neglect or absence amounted in their eyes to sedition and a deliberate perpetration of a serious sin. There was thus a strident emphasis on the intimate connection between the use of force and the nature of Islam as a dynamic movement. Reformist and nationalist Muslims who confined *jihad* to defensive purposes, or restricted its scope to Islamic territories, were severely reprimanded and accused of abdicating a sacred duty under the pressure of western influences.

Although al-Mawdudi preceded Qutb by more than 20 years in putting forward the obligation of *jihad* as the golden rule of Islam, his was a general argument that eschewed the specific circumstances that accompanied the revelation of Qur'anic verses enjoining struggle in the path of God. He accordingly called Islam 'an ideological movement' or 'a revolutionary ideology', and compared it to Marxism, Fascism and Nazism. This meant that Islam shared with these sister movements the same ambition of wresting power by all means, but differed in its ultimate aims (al-Mawdudi, 1981/1401: 42–3, 1977: 19). Qutb, on the other hand, exhibited a distinct reluctance to compare Islam to, or associate it with, other known ideologies. Nevertheless, he showed no hesitation in reproducing extensive excerpts from one of al-Mawdudi's lectures on '*jihad* in Islam', so as to underline the basic similarities of their approach (Qutb, 1981, Vol. III: 1444–52).

In this lecture, which was delivered in 1939, al-Mawdudi rejects western views of *jihad*, particularly its depiction as a 'holy war' waged by religious zealots in order to convert infidels by force of arms. He also reproaches those Muslims who, in their anxiety to rebut the accusation, adopt a diametrically opposite view, declaring *jihad* an instrument of self-defence. By doing so, they go to great extremes to demonstrate the peaceful and pacifist characteristics of their religion. Thus, both camps misconstrue the real meaning of Islam by basing their arguments on two false premises. First, Islam is looked at as 'a conventional religion' similar in all respects to other systems of faith and spiritual worship. Second, the Muslims are consequently thought to be 'a nation' in the modern sense of the term. Hence, by confining Islam to the private realm of the individual, and the Muslims to a delimited territory, *jihad* is logically excluded as a means of spreading a worldwide message. However, al-Mawdudi is not oblivious to the fact that modern nation-states often resort to the use of arms, not only in self-defence, but to 'deprive other people of their rights' as well. This type of war is summarily dismissed as blatant aggression, unleashed for the sake of worldly gains (al-Mawdudi, 1976: 1–5).

Western depictions and Muslim apologia are in this way the result of a secular culture that reduces all theoretical constructions to its relative purview. Al-Mawdudi redresses the balance by endowing Islam with a thoroughly modern definition, which in its turn paves the way for an equally updated notion of the Muslims. Being a non-conventional religion, he argues, Islam is 'a revolutionary ideology' and its adherents are as a result an 'international revolutionary party'. Being simultaneously revolutionary and internationalist, this party has as its main aim a worldwide revolution that transcends artificial boundaries and national territories. *Jihad* is then the process of 'revolutionary struggle', initiated in order to achieve the objectives of Islam. It, moreover, encompasses a wide spectrum of activities, such as writing an article in a newspaper, making a speech at street corners or donating funds and provisions. Nevertheless, its highest form remains the use of force as part of a general strategy (al-Mawdudi, 1976: 5–7).

According to al-Mawdudi, this type of political and armed struggle is not carried out on behalf of particular social groups, nor is it restricted to certain races and nationalities. It addresses itself to all human beings – even to kings, noblemen, oppressors and exploiters – and urges them to join the ranks of the faithful. Having the service of humanity as its main aim, 'the revolutionary party' concentrates all its efforts on seizing political power as the focus of other aspects of life. Hence, the immediate and central aim is to disarm one's opponent and transfer power into the hands of 'the functionaries of God'. Political power, not forcible conversion, is the consummation of *jihad* and its *raison d'être*. Although geographical boundaries are not taken into account in theory, the inescapable division of the world into nation-states forces al-Mawdudi to limit 'the initial stages' of the revolution to one particular territory, carried out by one particular group. Nevertheless, an Islamic state is bound by the sheer characteristics of its ideology to burst out of its temporary borders. This outward drive consists in the main of a series of appeals to 'the citizens of other countries to embrace the faith' of Islam. However, al-Mawdudi does not rule out, resources permitting, the use of force to topple the governments of neighbouring or distant countries (al-Mawdudi, 1976: 6–33).

Stripped of its revolutionary rhetoric, Mawdudi's concept of *jihad* amounts to a well-planned *putsch* launched to replace one government with another. Having arrogated divine sovereignty as an exclusive domain of its ideology, the stuff of political life renders 'struggle in the cause of God' an affair of extreme human fallibility, perpetually renewed in the creative interpretations of its functionaries.

As al-Mawdudi's argument for the inevitability of *jihad* is based on an analogy with other internationalist ideologies, the intricate question of its relevance to the formative period of Islam is conveniently obscured. However, he never pretended to be resurrecting an Islam that had become extinct as a social force. This was the heavy burden that Qutb thought he was destined to shoulder. Consequently, it fell to him to map out a strategy that appeared not to depart in its broad outline from the Meccan and Medinan phases of the Prophet's career.

Two main features that accompanied the formation of Islam were instantly noticed by Qutb, and seemed to nullify his justification for armed force as the only method to rebuild an Islamic community. The first was the absence of proper state structures and their attendant institutions of coercion in central and western Arabia on the eve of the rise of Islam. This condition, Qutb thought, made tribal solidarity an overriding factor in social relations, and thus afforded the Prophet in his first years with a minimum degree of protection. These peculiar circumstances were, moreover, one of the reasons for God's choice of Arabia as the cradle of His divine message. Given these two characteristics – absence of political authority and tribal solidarity – he argued that the need for *jihad* did not arise. Hence the silence of all Meccan verses on the use of armed force. This logical outcome was the result of the inexpediency of *jihad* (Qutb, 1981/1401: 77–83, 1981, Vol. II: 714–15).

The second feature had to do with the Prophet's emigration in 622 CE to Medina and the immediate political consequences that flowed from it. In the course of Qutb's discussion of this episode, 'the new Muslim state', as he put it, emerges into the daylight of history without one sword being drawn, or a single Qur'anic verse on *jihad* having been revealed. Once again, the non-existence of political authority in Medina is put forward as a satisfactory explanation. However, upon reaching this point, Qutb instantly senses a more congenial atmosphere as far as his particular topic is concerned: he revels in demonstrating how immediately thereafter 'raiding parties' were organized by the newly-established state in order to intercept Meccan caravans, or subdue the recalcitrant Jews of Medina. Relevant Qur'anic verses are then profusely quoted, so that the new recruit is left in no doubt about the use of armed force as a divine injunction to stamp out sedition (Qutb, 1981, Vol. III: 1439–44).

Nevertheless, this rather delayed action is bound to be an anticlimax, given the fact that the eager reader, having been kept in suspense, had in the meantime witnessed an eminently peaceful foundation of the first Islamic state.

Looked at from a different perspective, the two phases of Mecca and Medina, considered by Qutb to be conspicuously distinct, seem to merge into each other, forming a single unit. Their unity is conjoined by the emergence of the first Islamic state in history as the result of a non-violent process of political ingenuity. It is also noticeable in the consequent practice of *jihad* as being an official policy undertaken by the head of an established state. Moreover, it is worthy of note that the 'raiding parties' alluded to, as well as their Qur'anic seal of approval, targeted communities of polytheists and Jews who were in their turn bereft of state institutions, a fact that adds further complications to Qutb's definitions of both *jihad* and *jahiliyya*. In other words, Qutb's postulation of armed force as the only means to topple an infidel government represents, as he would have put it, a 'creative re-enactment' of the early period of Islam, and a 'dynamic interpretation' of the Prophet's career.

If Qutb's idea of both the vanguard and its violent methods of seizing political power was not directly modelled on the formative phase of the Prophet's Islamic state, where did it come from?

It has been customary for a number of scholars to cite the writings of certain 'radical' jurists, such as Ibn Taymiyya (1268–1328), or the experiences of rebellious Muslim groups, particularly the Kharijites' opposition to the fourth Caliph, 'Ali b. Abi Talib, as direct sources of influence. However, Qutb himself in singling out Napoleon's invasion of Egypt (see above, p. 00) as a qualitatively unique event in Islamic history (a view that accords with the diagnosis of the Egyptian chronicler, al-Jabarti, discussed in Chapter 1), has already relieved us of such comparative speculations. Put differently, as far as Qutb was concerned, the pervading state of religious ignorance did not come into being before the nineteenth century. Despite his allusions to 'similarities' and the 'permanent essence' of *jahiliyya*, he was quite aware of wrestling with problems that did not offer themselves to an Ibn Taymiyya or a Kharijite. His differentiation between resemblance or similarity (*shibh*) and complete likeness or correspondence (*mithl, tamathul*) allowed him the possibility of postulating a new cycle of Islamic renewal that surpassed in its scope all the previous ones. Hence, Muhammad's confrontation with polytheism and distorted beliefs of the People of the Book, Ibn Taymiyya's condemnation of the Mongols as unbelievers in spite of their profession of Islam, and the Kharijites' revolts against impious Muslim rulers, became much less troublesome tasks than the one he had in hand. One is therefore forced at Qutb's own insistence to search for modern explanations of a modern phenomenon.

## The Unknown Man

Several possibilities of inspiration, derivation and direct influence may suggest themselves. These varieties, however, have to be situated within the modern cultural and social conditions of Egypt and the Islamic world. This framework, already sketched in broad outline, has to take account of the subject as a representative figure of a wider social group whose outlook was closely tied up with the advent of a revolutionary system of government, i.e. Nasserism. In the case of Qutb, two main factors, both of intellectual and political dimensions, may have inclined him towards his radicalist Islamism.

First, the failure of the Muslim Brotherhood as a mass movement to gain power, and its rapid disintegration in the wake of a badly managed confrontation with the Free Officers.

Second, Qutb's own political and cultural career in the 1930s and 1940s had predisposed him to lay stress on the creative power of the imagination, the spontaneous and the unpredictable. He was a man of letters who read and wrote romantic novels. As a literary critic, he developed his style under the intellectual patronage of the Egyptian liberal author and member of the semi-secular Wafd party, Mahmud 'Abbas al-'Aqqad. His political sympathies were directed towards fascist-type youth organizations which sprang up in Egypt in the inter-war period. Unlike other Egyptians who joined the Muslim Brethren at an early age, Qutb became a member only as a mature middle-aged intellectual with an independent frame of mind. Ever since he began to write on Islamic issues in the late 1940s his approach indicated a consistent reluctance to associate Islam and

Islamic notions of authority or socio-economic life with other current ideologies. Thus he always rejected the idea of attaching the label of 'socialism' to the theory of social justice in Islam. He did so because he had already come to believe that economic and political concepts are ultimately based on a comprehensive worldview, a *Weltanschauung* that authorized and conditioned the details of its embodiment in concrete institutions. Moreover, the organization he joined in the early 1950s had at its helm Hasan al-Hudaybi, a court judge whose low-key style of politics and aristocratic demeanour were in marked contrast to the fiery and charismatic leadership of its founder, Hasan al-Banna. Although Qutb did not immerse himself in the factional disputes of his organization, he always stood for clear-cut policies based on ideological principles. These character-istics set him on a collision course with Nasser as soon as he was approached to become the revolution ideologue. Nasser, a pragmatic man who dealt with ideology as a series of practical policies, and Qutb, an ideologue who placed dogmatic issues above all other considerations, broke off their tense sessions of negotiations within six months. Sent to prison, along with a number of his colleagues, Qutb embarked on a search for a more radical, watertight solution. By the time he was released in 1964, Egypt and his ideological approach had undergone fundamental transformations.

One is reminded at this point of Rashid Rida's statement, quoted in Chapter 3, as regards the way Muslim intellectuals began to read new interpretations into the Qur'anic notion of consultation. It was, he said, under the impact of modern European culture and way of life that such an Islamic concept was suddenly discovered to mean 'limited government' and electoral democracy. Qutb's abrupt discovery, upon rereading the Qur'an, of the vanguard, its characteristics and method of struggle, and the role of elites throughout history, is a familiar occurrence in political and ideological theorization. This familiarity, however, is not to be understood as a peculiar trait of modern Islamic culture: the English Puritans adopted the Bible as their guide and blueprint in building a new commonwealth; the French Jacobins evoked the vivid ambience of Greek culture and Roman statesmanship; and Hitler conjured up visions of the Middle Ages and their martial and agrarian values. Qutb's cultural background, his political experiences and his distinct approach to Islam inclined him to accept certain ideological theories and reject others. His modern outlook, like that of fellow radicalists, is often obscured by perpetual references to past events and primeval origins. Hence, the massive concentration of Qur'anic verses and traditions that dots almost every page of Qutb's writings has often served to conceal the contours of his own landscape. It is by reducing this overgrowth to its minimal significance that one is able to gain a foothold within a modern design fully draped in holy relics.

For all that, the transference of cultural influences is a complicated affair, and takes place under conditions of selection, reordering and local pride. Vehement strictures of Western civilization do not always imply wholesale rejection of its material benefits. On the other hand, a reverse tendency, whereby complete adoption of modernity is espoused, may take on board a paraphernalia of folkloric tales and legends. It has often been observed that experimental science had its origins in alchemy, the most fruitless and speculative branch of medieval philosophy. Be that as it may, this digressive discussion has at least served its purpose by pointing out the dangers of simplifying cultural influences and intellectual derivation.

As has been observed, Qutb's case is made all the more difficult by his constant references to Qur'anic verses and 'the sound sayings' of the Prophet. However, one of his books, already referred to, offers the reader a unique opportunity to come to terms with a line of argument that keeps shuffling between the seventh and the twentieth centuries. This book, entitled *al-Islam wa Mushkilat al-Hadara* (*Islam and the Problems of Civilization*) is virtually built on a series of long quotations from an Arabic translation of a French work published in Paris in 1935. It is also unique in another sense. Out of all the European and American historians, scientists and scholars quoted by Qutb, it is the author of this particular French work who is conspicuously singled out for praise, and the only one who is considered worthy of a biographical notice. This was Alexis Carrel, the author of *L'homme, cet inconnu* (1935). His book was translated into English in the same year, under the title, *Man, the Unknown*, and became a best-seller in the 1930s and 1940s.

In the West, Carrel is hardly a household name. However, in Islamic radicalist literature his views on modern civilization, morality and human knowledge are quoted and requoted, but often at second hand. It was perhaps the Indian religious scholar, al-Nadawi, who first brought Carrel's book to the notice of a wide Muslim audience in the 1950s. But al-Nadawi offered only a glimpse of Carrel's broad vision (al-Nadawi, 1977: 241–2). It was thus Qutb, in his preoccupation with the intricate problem of power, who extracted from Carrel's views and recommendations a radicalist theory of politics.

Before Carrel's book is discussed, it is necessary for reasons connected with his ideas to present a brief outline of his career. Carrel was educated at the University of Lyon where, after graduation with an MD degree in 1900, he taught anatomy. He later moved to the Hull Physiological Laboratory of the University of Chicago. Then, in 1906, he became a Member and Fellow of the Rockefeller Institute of Medical Research in New York City. It was there that he developed what became known as 'the Carrel suture' for stitching blood vessels. This achievement earned him the Nobel prize in medicine in 1912. He also served during the First World War as a major in the French army medical corps. In 1919 he returned to the Rockefeller Institute. There, in collaboration with Colonel Charles Lindbergh, he announced the development of the first mechanical heart. These items of information are more or less what the reader is told by Qutb about his favourite author (Qutb, 1980/ 1400: 9). However, when the Second World War broke out, Carrel returned to France and joined the French Ministry of Public Health. In 1940 the Nazi-dominated Vichy government appointed him director of the Fondation pour l'Etude des Problemes Humains (Foundation for the Study of Human Problems). Thus he was finally able to put his programme of reconstructing the mental and physical aspects of mankind into practice. It was a programme he had already expounded in his book, *Man, the Unknown*. The liberation of Paris by the Allies in 1944 brought his career to an end: he was charged with Nazi collaboration and dismissed from his post. He died in the same year (Sourkes, 1967: 74–5).

It seems that Sayyid Qutb, upon reading Carrel's book in 1959 or 1960, felt as if all the pieces of the puzzle had begun to fall into place. And for a while Carrel's views and Qur'anic verses appeared to speak the same language, conveying similar messages. Carrel, for example, underlines the deficient nature of the study of human beings by declaring: 'It is quite evident that the accomplishments of all the sciences having man as an object remain insufficient, and that our knowledge of ourselves is still most rudimentary' (Carrel, 1935: 6). Qutb quotes in his turn the relevant Qur'anic verses to confirm the opinion of an eminent scientist. There are three entire pages adorned with Qutb's substantiating evidence. Two short verses, however, may suffice for our purpose: 'But most men do not know it. They know an outward part of the present life' (30:6–7); and

'They will question thee concerning the Spirit. Say: "The Spirit is of the bidding of my Lord. You have been given of knowledge nothing except a little'" (17:85; Qutb, 1980/1400: 21–31).

Carrel painted in his book a gloomy picture of western civilization. In it he highlighted the destructive effects of material progress on the individual and his psychological well-being. He directed his strongest attacks at the men of science, whose discoveries paved the way for an industrial world in which 'the body and consciousness' of the individual were left out. He thought that the study of the human being was built on 'mere logical constructs' that did not apply to the actual constitution of its object. Each scientific discipline concentrated on one single aspect, whereas 'man is an indivisible whole of extreme complexity'. This dichotomy of seeing things in isolation – separating man into two different entities, turning nature into an object of conquest, and reducing the intricate structure of the universe to mathematical calculations and hypotheses – has resulted in the most devastating mode of life. Thus, from a wholesome being, imbued with religious, spiritual and intellectual yearnings for the unknown, man has been turned into an animal and a machine. The pattern of work in industrial factories and bureaucratic institutions has made individuals cogs in huge, monstrous machines. Carrel pointed out that 'the laws of nature' had been repeatedly violated ever since the Renaissance. Morality and intelligence had accordingly witnessed a steady erosion. Matter and mind, body and soul had been torn asunder.

The dualism of Descartes, Carrel argues, lies at the root of this dilemma:

> The error of Descartes was to believe in the reality of these abstractions and to consider the material and the mental as heterogeneous, as two different things. This dualism has weighed heavily upon the entire history of our knowledge of man. For it has engendered the false problem of the relations of the soul and the body.
>
> (Carrel, 1935: 137–8)

This fundamental error led to the slow degradation of man by concentrating all attention on organic structures or physiological mechanisms. The study of 'thought, pleasure, sorrow, and beauty' was thus excluded.

Galileo, Descartes, Newton and Lavoisier all share the responsibility of building up a system of abstract thought that gave birth to science, industry and technology. Hence, modern civilization was born out of an intellectual error and an ignorance of man as a complex being. The transformations brought about by scientific discoveries were particularly harmful in their applications to political and socio-economic problems. The principles of the French Revolution, the Utopian visions of Marx and Lenin and egalitarian democracy, all announced the advent of a false dawn. The division of the population of a particular country into different classes, Carrel explains, has a profound biological base, and is dependent on the physiological and mental properties of each individual. 'The myth of egalitarianism', particularly in its implications for political and family life, is ridiculed and dismissed as an aberration that was no longer viable. Thus:

> The dogma is now breaking down under the blows of the experience of nations. It is, therefore, unnecessary to insist upon its falseness. But its success has been astonishingly long. How could humanity accept such faith for so many years? The democratic creed does not take account of the constitution of our body and of our consciousness. It does not apply to the concrete fact which the individual is. Indeed, human beings are equal. But individuals are not. The equality of their rights is an illusion. The feeble-minded and the man of genius should not be equal before the law. The stupid, the unintelligent, those who are dispersed, incapable of attention, of effort, have no right to a higher education. It is absurd to give them the same electoral power as the fully developed individuals. Sexes are not equal. To disregard all these inequalities is very dangerous. The democratic principle has contributed to the collapse of civilization in opposing the development of an elite.
>
> (Carrel, 1935: 328)

The French surgeon's criticism of modern civilization encompassed liberal democracy, Marxism, the equality of man and woman, the mediocrity of education, art and literature, the chaotic nature of technology and the harmful effects of drugs and alcohol. His diagnosis amounts to a theory of western life as a new type of *jahiliyya*. He termed it *'la barbarie'* (Carrel, 1935: 32).

Carrel called for a moral and social revolution in order to create an equilibrium between the material and the spiritual forces of society. He abhorred complacency, laziness and cowardice, and extolled instead the discipline of martial arts, sacrifice and devotion to duty. His most radical suggestion resides in the creation of a new elite that would restore humanity to the right path, and arrest its degeneration towards barbarism. This elite would weed out the feeble-minded, the unintelligent, the weak and the unfit. The laws of natural selection, brutally suspended in favour of uniformity and standardization, would be restored to play their vital part. Two techniques are indispensable 'for the perpetuation of the strong': eugenics and euthanasia. Eugenics is necessary because 'a great race must propagate its best elements'. Euthanasia ensures the gradual disappearance of creatures who infect the body politic with terminal diseases:

> Those who have murdered, robbed while armed with automatic pistol or machine gun, kidnapped children, despoiled the poor of their savings, misled the public in important matters, should be humanely and economically disposed of in small euthanasic institutions supplied with proper gases. A similar treatment could be advantageously applied to the insane, guilty of criminal acts.
>
> (Carrel, 1935: 365, 388)

Carrel, a man with a clear scientific differentiation of the abstract equality of all human beings and the concrete disparity of individuals, has an equally distinct fondness of the unknown and the unseen. He believed that mysticism, telepathy, clairvoyance, intuition, asceticism, spiritual illumination and the search for God were expressions of a constant endeavour to reach 'the ultimate truth'. These phenomena, he declares, are real experiences that have to be investigated and accorded their rightful place in a new science of man (Carrel, 1935: 143–7, 157–60, 319–20, 322–5).

Such an appreciation of metaphysical phenomena, in addition to a strict moralistic and medical diagnosis of a degenerate civilization, earned Carrel an unprecedented commendation from an Islamic radicalist not known for gratuitous appraisals. He was thus said to be 'a man of wide knowledge, high sensitivity, extreme sincerity, and liberal mindedness. A dissenting rebel against industrial civilization' (Qutb, 1980/1400: 167).

Carrel's use of biological terminology to analyse social phenomena struck a responsive chord with Qutb; both looked at society as a living organism that is constantly attacked by vicious microbes and foreign viruses. More importantly, Carrel's practical proposals for bringing about a new social revolution seemed to solve one of the most difficult questions Qutb had to tackle. How does an elite come into being in a society that is bent on the destruction of all creative minorities? What characteristics are required of its members? Is there a past model that could be copied in an imaginative manner so as to be commensurate with new conditions?

These, and other questions, were answered by Carrel in a succinct style and confident manner. It remained for Qutb to lend them an unmistakable Islamic flavour, and insist on Islam instead of Carrel's new 'science of man' as the final solution to all human problems.

Carrel believed that 'relative isolation and discipline' were the key that unlocked the secret behind the inner strength and success of a variety of elites. His favourite examples, however, were derived from the social history of the Middle Ages. The organization, codes of conduct and way of life of three particular social institutions figured in his positive exposition. These were the monastic orders, the orders of chivalry and the guilds of artisans. The religious orders, he explained, submitted to a strict physiological and mental discipline; the knights had regulations that varied according to the different orders, but they were all prepared to sacrifice their lives for a higher cause; the artisans regulated their relations with the public by meticulous rules, and each guild had its customs, ceremonies and religious festivals. By and large, these men set themselves apart from society and renounced the ordinary mode of life. A question was then asked: 'Are we not capable of repeating, in a different form, the accomplishments of the monks, the Knights, and the artisans of the Middle Ages?' (Carrel, 1935: 357).

Carrel believed, and Qutb agreed, that modern 'barbarism', with its soulless technology, shallow but popular mass media and cheap inducements, was much harder to resist than previous states of moral degeneration. The French surgeon, therefore, laid down a strict code of conduct for the future member of his elite. An individual who desired change should immediately adopt a new style of life, create his exclusive and proper environment in the midst of 'the unthinking crowd' and impose on himself a specific physical and mental discipline. Complete isolation, Carrel thought, was neither desirable nor feasible. In order to fight successfully against one's material and cultural surroundings, one had to join forces with individuals having the same ideal (Carrel, 1935: 356). A small group slowly emerges animated by the same spirit of revolt and organized on the basis of mutual support. Its members adhere to a clear set of rules and regulations, derived from those of military or monastic discipline. The 'baneful' influence of a corrupt society is thus gradually neutralized. To depart from traditional norms, or follow codes of behaviour that run counter to the common customs of one's community, has been a common practice throughout the ages. It was thanks to small groups of this type that European civilization of the Middle Ages developed and flourished. The renovation of man in modern societies must proceed at parallel levels of intellectual, moral and religious activities. Carrel suggested that one important step would be to set up separate schools and other educational institutions, so that the elite's children would be instructed in disciplines befitting a new world. Dissociation, one of Qutb's seminal ideas in Islamic radicalist circles, could thus be accomplished by various means. Each individual, Carrel explained, had the power of selecting particular friends and avoiding the company of others. The theatre and cinema could be boycotted, as well as certain schools, newspapers and radio programmes (Carrel, 1935: 356–7).

Moreover, such a group does not have to be composed of large numbers. It is discipline, continuously upheld by a compact elite, that counts. The masses, driven by 'the herd instinct', have always followed a determined leadership. Thus the seizure of power is spontaneously associated with the emergence of such a dynamic movement. The use of violence is also taken for granted:

> It is a well-established fact that discipline gives great strength to men. An ascetic and mystic minority would rapidly acquire an irresistible power over the dissolute and degraded majority. Such a minority would be in a position to impose, by persuasion or perhaps by force, other ways of life upon the majority.
>
> (Carrel, 1935: 358)

One final feature of this 'remarkable' plan of action is the refusal of its author to enter into discussion of the details of his programme. This aversion to discuss concrete policies, often described as 'futile arguments about mere technicalities', has become the hallmark of contemporary Islamic radicalism. The role played by Qutb's negative approach in this respect was undoubtedly the most decisive factor (Qutb, 1980/1400: 185–92). Carrel insisted that the urgency of radical change did not entail the delineation of a programme. For a programme 'would stifle living reality in a rigid armour. It would prevent the natural effusion of the unpredictable, and imprison the future within the limits of our mind' (Carrel, 1935: 392).

Hence, a configuration of conceptual elements coalesces to form an identifiable paradigm: a vanguard, discipline, moral, intellectual and religious codes of conduct, dissociation from barbarism, aversion to concrete policies, persuasion and force, and the inevitability of triumph – the list is too long to be a mere coincidence. It must, however, be pointed out that Qutb did not directly indicate his indebtedness to Carrel and his description of the new elite. Moreover, Carrel's social models and Qutb' s 'creative' use of his proposals bring us face to face with certain political and intellectual traits that are common to a wide number of Islamists.

An Islamic radicalist combines in his attitude and outlook many of the characteristics alluded to in Carrel's three orders – the monks, the knights and the artisans, rolled into one. An Islamic radicalist is a monk in his devotion and passionate belief in an omnipotent power. Day after day the intrinsic authenticity of his scriptures is confirmed and made immutable. To him, God's signs are implanted in animate and inanimate things and beings. At regular intervals, his gaze glides off the pages of the scripture and is entranced by the majesty of nature's manuscripts, written by God without letters or words. He is a knight whose whole being is pervaded by a moralistic code of conduct: courteous and honest, yet gallant and heroic. His is the duty of a paladin whose martial valour protects the structure of an ideal society. To him falls the honour to repulse the onslaught of barbarian invasions. Behind his armour he shields the weak, the deprived, women and children. His foes are treated with generosity but firm justice. Finally, he is an artisan who considers his craft an integral part of his being. He deals with his hand-made products not as mere objects, but as works of art, a tangible exaltation of beauty and God. No artificial skill, mechanical trickery or defiance of divine grace are involved.

Thus, three social types, thoroughly medieval in their attributes, stepped onto the stage of the twentieth century, gesturing and speaking the language of biological sciences and political elites. A spectacle of moral and scientific imperatives whipped up the faint images of ideal types, and refashioned their characters in a creative mood of revolutionary activity. While Qutb's 'signposts' pointed in the direction of Arabia, Carrel's 'super-science' remained faithful to Catholicism as an eternal institution of man and God.

Qutb's book, as already indicated, consists of a series of long quotations from an Arabic translation of Carrel's work. These quotations are then augmented by adding passages from other references, but which tend to reinforce the argument of the master text. Qutb's personal experiences during his two-year sojourn in the United States are also included for the benefit of his vanguard. As an officer of the Egyptian Ministry of Education, he spent 1948–50 in California and Washington, studying modern pedagogic methods, and came back to Cairo with impressions of decadence and depravity that Carrel's analysis seemed to confirm. The inevitable Qur'anic verses punctuate the text at appropriate intervals. By doing so, Qutb appropriates two original texts – the Qur'an and the medical diagnosis of an eminent scientist – turning both into living witnesses of a sordid state of affairs. What Qutb fails to inform his vanguard, however, is that the code of conduct he subsequently elaborated in his 'commentary' on the Qur'an matches that of Carrel much more than Muhammad's own Traditions.

However, Qutb was a sincere Muslim, and no attempt is being made to cast doubt on his belief in the Qur'an as the final word of God. The issue of one's sincerity, national or religious pride, is in this context neither relevant nor essential. A political ideology, articulated in the second half of the twentieth century, is bound to be saturated with the available intellectual currents. By a process of elimination Qutb ruled out Marxism/socialism and capitalism/democracy. He was thus saddled with a Third World version of fascism. Carrel's book acted as a stimulus, a focus, and an opportunity for crystallization. He vehemently protested against Carrel's racist exaltation of the white race and its scientific discoveries, but he went on to assert the priority of the Islamic world in developing the methods of scientific experimentation. He thus adopted one of the most prominent aspects of European culture, and strengthened his religious pride at the same time. Carrel's view of religion as an exclusively spiritual experience was rejected out of hand. To Qutb, Islam in its resurrection at his hands and those of a new elite represented an inexhaustible source that encompassed all aspects of life. Nevertheless, it was an Islam that overreached itself, so that its interchangeability with a modern model rather than a distant one paraded itself in transparent clarity. Not wishing to be outdone, and as a result of defective rendering into Arabic by his translator, Qutb thought that the French surgeon intended to destroy industry and technology altogether. He accordingly protests in the strongest terms, considering 'industrial civilization' a natural development of a long process, and an integral part of human society and its basic needs (Qutb, 1980/1400: 163–81).

One of the most paradoxical aspects of Carrel's book is its conspicuous silence on Adolf Hitler and Nazi Germany, except in one or two passing references to national socialism. Only Benito Mussolini is spoken of in the most reverent terms. He is alternately called a man of genius, a builder of a great nation and a leader whose personality grew beyond human stature (Carrel, 1935: 72, 264, 316). Nor is the domination of international finance by Jews, a favourite topic and scapegoat of Hitler, mentioned by Carrel. As a matter of fact, the Jews, be it as individuals, a religious community or a race, are totally absent from his book. Perhaps the city of New York with its sizeable Jewish population, and where Carrel was working when he published his best-seller, holds the key to the deceptive mystery. Be that as it may, Qutb volunteered to fill this glaringly wide gap. He explains that capitalism in the West is a system built in its entirety on usurious transactions. All the principal classes – workers, industrialists, businessmen, managers of factories, landlords and landowners – work as hired labour for the benefit of bankers. By controlling share issues, deposits and liquid assets, credit banks determine the amount lent to these social groups and interest rates to be charged. Consequently, the most sinister aspect of capitalism is not merely the way international finance exploits entire nations and governments, but 'the specific class' which orchestrates the whole operation. This class, Qutb continues, is usually concealed from the public by sophisticated economic theories, propaganda campaigns and great institutes of education. It is this class of usurers that spreads corruption, encourages pornography in films and plays, and promotes prostitution, alcohol and drugs. Moral depravity and dissolute life are thus an inevitable outcome of these usurers whose only aim is to make the maximum profit in the shortest time. The majority of bankers and financiers in the world, Qutb points out, are Jews. Furthermore, one has only to read *The Protocols of the Wise Men of Zion* to be convinced of their multifaceted schemes to dominate the world (Qutb, 1980/1400: 98–102, 147–9, 179–80).

This view of capitalism, in which echoes of Hitler's *Mein Kampf* are clearly discernible (Hitler, 1969: 272–96), does not disturb Qutb's special intellectual relationship with Carrel. On the contrary, it reinforces its individuality. Qutb's endorsement of Carrel's diagnosis stopped short of allowing 'Islam' to suffer the same fate as Christianity. He therefore accentuates the sin of modern civilization by laying stress on its rejection of religion as a way of life. Thus, Carrel's concept of sin was related to 'the violation of the laws of nature', but Qutb modifies this to become 'the laws of instinct (*fitra*), implanted by God in his creatures' (Qutb, 1980/1400: 124). In this sense, Islam can effortlessly appropriate any 'science of man', and yet remains self-sufficient in its unique sublimation of humanity. Consequently, a dichotomy of ultimate aims opens up: whereas Nazism depreciates man's present accomplishments to the extent of wishing to replace him with a superman, Islamic radicalism exalts him to a degree that he is left suspended in mid-air between religion and science.

# Chapter 7

## National Dilemmas and Failures

In 1964, Sayyid Qutb published his *Signposts* as a direct response to the socialist ideology of Nasserism. He had in the meantime been released from prison, and continued his endeavours to win disciples as potential recruits in a new organization. In August 1966 he was condemned to death after the Egyptian authorities had uncovered an underground network of militant cells, whose aim consisted of carrying out a series of sabotage acts, such as blowing up power stations, vital economic installations and bridges. These acts, coupled with a plan to assassinate President Nasser, his Prime Minister, and a number of intelligence officers, were intended to paralyse ordinary life in the main Egyptian cities and thus pave the way for a swift seizure of political power.

In his affidavit Qutb defended the acquisition of arms and the training of young recruits in their use as mere defensive measures, designed to avoid the repetition of the 1954 events. He considered his new organization to be an instrument forged to meet the inevitable confrontation with a state bent on the destruction of Islamic radicalists.

The Syrian Marwan Hadid, one of Qutb's disciples, was implicated in the same plot, but managed to escape arrest and fled to Syria towards the end of 1965. Just as his mentor decided to forego the traditional methods of the Muslim Brethren in Egypt, so he bypassed the equally traditional line of 'Isam al-'Attar, the Syrian Brethren's leader. Armed struggle, rather than peaceful means, became Hadid's central task as he set about recruiting select groups of holy fighters in order to wage war against 'the secular and ungodly' Ba'thist state. His idea of armed struggle, however, was mainly aimed at assassinating prominent personalities of the regime. By 1971 his old organization was split between two factions, the

Damascene wing led by al-'Attar, which opposed the adventurous ideas of Hadid, and a radical one concentrated in the north of the country under the leadership of Sa'id Hawwa and 'Adnan Sa'd al-Din (Abdallah, 1983: 101–8). In 1975 Hadid was finally captured by the authorities and died the following year in his prison cell. Six years later militant members of the Brethren in the city of Hama, Hadid's main centre of operations, staged an armed revolt against the regime and gained control of popular residential areas, particularly the central quarters inhabited in the main by artisans and shopkeepers. It took the special squadrons of the Syrian army almost a month to regain control of the city. In the process large sections of the city were razed to the ground. However, a few years later the entire city was rebuilt with wider avenues and improved facilities.

Despite Qutb's absence, his new ideology continued to attract followers inside and outside Egypt. The defeat of the Egyptian, Syrian and Jordanian armies by Israel in the June war of 1967 had far-reaching consequences in a number of ways. The most important of these was the humiliation of two socialist states – Egypt and Syria – and their failure to meet the challenge of the Israeli army. Having been discredited, ideologically and militarily, they were unable to contain the shockwaves which swept through the popular masses across the Islamic world.

The political vacuum was first filled to a certain extent by the activities of various Palestinian organizations, which had been waging an armed struggle against Israeli targets since 1959. However, this was a short-lived political reaction that did not last beyond the Arab–Israeli war of 1973. In the meantime, Nasser had been replaced by Anwar al-Sadat and Salah Jadid by Hafiz al-Asad. Both pursued a more moderate policy than their predecessors, internally and externally. But it was Sadat who carried the moderate approach to its logical conclusion.

By achieving considerable military successes in the initial stages of the war, and despite the reverses the Egyptian armed forces were to suffer in its closing phase, Sadat took the opportunity to effect a large-scale retreat on both the domestic and international fronts. Moreover, the stupendous rise in oil prices in tandem with the 1973 war gave him the opportunity to claim a direct share in the new wealth of the oil-producing countries. The shift towards an open-door policy dictated closer links with the United States and an abrupt rupture of relations with the Soviet Union. Whereas the

Syrian President inherited the legacy of a state that was being regimented along an austere line of revolutionary measures and rhetoric, the Egyptian President governed a state that was already relaxing its grip on the economy and political life in general. Consequently, al-Asad's moderation was restricted by the concrete conditions created by his predecessors, while Sadat's eagerness for a complete accommodation with the United States and Israel could rely on a prior basis of support. Nevertheless, al-Asad had behind him the various organs of the Ba'th party in addition to the armed forces, so that popular legitimacy appeared easier to channel or marshal. Sadat, on the other hand, found himself opposed by the majority of Nasser's political organization, the Arab Socialist Union. His aim, contrary to that of his Syrian counterpart, consisted of dismantling the single party of the regime and building an alternative instrument of mobilization. This he did by falling back on the only available, and relatively coherent, political grouping: the Muslim Brethren. Between 1970 and 1975 their leaders and cadres were released from prison and accorded unprecedented facilities in the mass media to propagate their ideas. Islamic student unions in universities and colleges throughout Egypt seemed to mushroom in ever-increasing numbers, having as their aim the elimination of foreign ideologies, i.e., Nasserism, Arab nationalism and Marxism.

Sadat set in motion forces which were destined to turn against his policies, given the intractable economic problems of Egypt and the intricate nature of according Israel full recognition in the face of mounting Arab opposition. It was at this juncture, after he had made his 'historic visit' to Jerusalem in 1977 and signed the Camp David agreements a year later, that Sayyid Qutb's original circle widened its activities and came forward with the idea of launching holy war against an infidel ruler. In October 1981 Sadat was assassinated during a military parade celebrating the anniversary of the 1973 war. His assassins belonged to an organization called al-Jihad. Its ideologue, 'Abd al-Salam Faraj, had already circulated an internal document to his cells of activists, setting out the merits and inevitability of armed force against contemporary paganism. Entitled *The Absent Obligation* (*al-Farida al-Gha'iba*), it argued the necessity of launching immediate warfare in order to restore the Caliphate as the only legitimate form of government (Faraj, 1982: 6–7). Although this document received wide publicity, and was acclaimed as one of the most creative tracts of Islamic radicalism, it was merely a rehash of Qutb's main theoretical principles, and a restatement of the diagnosis of military regimes by Sa'id Hawwa, the new ideologue of the Syrian Muslim Brotherhood. Both Hawwa and Faraj put forward the idea that most Islamic countries were in a state of religious apostasy, brought about by army officers and nationalist parties. This sinful violation of God's laws was in its turn said to have been preceded by two similar episodes in Islamic history. The first occurred immediately after the death of Muhammad in 632 CE and consisted of the refusal of Arab tribes to continue the payment of religious taxes to the Prophet's successor, Abu Bakr. The first Caliph therefore responded by launching sustained military campaigns against apostate tribes. By the time of his death in 634, he had subdued the entire Arabian peninsula and restored the supremacy of Islam. This was Hawwa's favourite analogy. As for Faraj, he chose to dwell on the Mongols of the fourteenth century who, despite their conversion to Islam, were considered by the Hanbalite jurist Ibn Taymiyya (d. 1328) to be living in a state of apostasy. Ibn Taymiyya's legal opinion singled out the adherence of the Mongols to their customary laws, known as the *Yasa* of Genghis Khan, as proof of their polytheism and apostasy. His disciple Ibn Kathir (d. 1372/3) repeated the same argument, and both concluded that it was a religious obligation to fight the Mongols until they agreed to abide by the explicit tenets and injunctions of the *shari'a* (Hawwa, 1977: 511; Faraj, 1982: 8–13).

Both analogies, however, suffer from apparent theoretical weaknesses. Whereas in Abu Bakr's case *jihad* was fought against subjects who had renounced their allegiance to a legitimate authority, and Ibn Taymiyya's response was made in the name of an Islamic state, i.e., the Mamluk Sultanate, Hawwa's and Faraj's diagnosis bore the stamp of a rebellious group seeking to overthrow established governments. Moreover, their legal arguments on the nature of apostasy in Islam were designed to justify acts of assassination as an authentic religious duty sanctioned by a pious Caliph and a renowned theologian.

Faraj's analogical deductions are also governed by a selective methodology and a tendency to recast the Prophet's early career in Mecca in a totally fabricated form. For example, he passes over one of the main recommendations of Ibn Taymiyya's religious ruling, namely emigration (*hijra*) from the abode of disbelief as a personal duty incumbent on a believer (Faraj, 1982: 12). As a matter of fact, Faraj emphatically rejects the whole concept of emigrating to another territory, considering it 'an impossible task' that had to be avoided at all costs. Furthermore, he ridicules this duty as 'a strange idea' that is alien to the proper methods of conducting armed struggle (Faraj, 1982: 16). His scathing remarks are apparently directed at another radicalist Islamic group that espoused such ideas. This group, originally called Jama'at al-Muslimin, and led by a former MBA member, Shukri Mustafa, was dubbed by the Egyptian authorities 'The organization of ex-communication and emigration' (al-takfir wa al-hijra). It first came into prominence in 1977, after having kidnapped and murdered a moderate 'alim and former Minister of Religious Affairs, Shaykh Muhammad al-Dhahabi. Shukri Mustafa was consequently put on trial and executed in 1978. Mustafa's failure to dent the legitimacy of the Egyptian state became for Faraj an index of the obsolescence of the revivalist notion of migration. 'Our foremost duty', he declares, 'resides in establishing the rule of God's laws [...] and the extermination of those infidel leaders' who paved the way for the supremacy of imperialism in the lands of Islam (Faraj, 1982: 18).

The priority of fighting the internal enemy is deduced from a fabricated saying of the Prophet, said to have been uttered before his emigration to Medina in 622. The Prophet is alternatively quoted as having addressed members of his tribe Quraysh as follows: 'I bring you slaughter', or 'I bring you the sword' (Faraj, 1982: 6). In this respect, Faraj's innovation surpasses that of Sayyid Qutb, his original master.

As for Mustafa's concept of emigration, it consisted of setting up new communities of believers in the Egyptian desert, away from the iniquitous paganism of his society (Abu al-Khayr, 1980: 104–5). However, this organized withdrawal did not prevent the leader, along with other cells of activists, from living in furnished apartments in Cairo in order to kidnap a former Cabinet minister, or liquidate 'defectors' in their residential areas (Abu al-Khayr, 1980: 49, 65–66, 75). In other words, the new Islamic nation-state, with its networks of modern institutions, technology and bureaucratic control, has finally annulled the possibility or validity of repeating the revivalist sequence of migration and jihad.

Furthermore, whereas Faraj was relatively consistent in his diagnosis of contemporary Islamic countries, the Syrian Sa'id Hawwa seems to offer a more flexible scheme of gradation. He therefore refused to pronounce a wholesale condemnation, as Qutb did in his diagnosis (Hawwa, 1977: 10). This apparent flexibility is, nevertheless, dictated by political and logistic considerations. Given the fact that most leaders of the Syrian Muslim Brotherhood (SMB) have lived in exile since the 1960s, their need for a base of operation makes ideological rigidity a suicidal affair. Thus, between 1979 and 1985 the SMB enjoyed the direct patronage of the Jordanian monarch. Being temporarily at odds with the Syrian government over the peace process with Israel and other issues, King Husayn offered the Syrian President's most vehement opponents his unqualified support as a political lever. Upon patching up his differences with Damascus towards the end of 1985, the Syrian Brethren, as well as their Jordanian variety, were suddenly out of royal favour. Consequently, the SMB moved its headquarters to Iraq, another neighbouring country that is a more reliable ally in its enmity towards the Syrian government.

Qutb's original blueprint underwent further modifications as it entered the Tunisian scene. Rashid Ghannushi, the leader of the Islamic Tendency Movement (MTI), fell under the influence of Qutb's ideology while studying philosophy at Damascus University in 1966. Up to that time, he had been an adherent of Nasserism espousing Arab nationalism as a theory that did not seem to clash with his Islamic upbringing. According to his account, Islam was simply ignored within his ideological framework, so that no discussions were raised dealing with its validity in a modern state. His contacts with Islamic activists, however, began to change his outlook; he suddenly discovered a new world that had been completely overlooked by a whole generation of Arab youth. His adoption of Islamic radicalism was thus a conversion to a set of beliefs under specific conditions. For Ghannushi, the most decisive factor that precipitated his conversion was the way nationalists in Syria considered Arab Christians and Jews to be equal in all respects to their fellow Muslims. To someone whose country, as he argued, had fought Christian colonialists to gain its independence, this seemed an illogical attitude (Ghannushi, 1988, no. 441: 30–3). Whatever the immediate cause of Ghannushi's conversion, there is no doubt that his Islam became a comprehensive world view that helped him to perceive the situation of his country in a new light.

The organization he established in 1981, after a period of intensive political and ideological debates, looked at Tunisia's socio-economic problems as the result of its single-party system. This diagnosis led it to stress the role of the mosque as a place of worship and popular mobilization. Between 1970 and 1981, Ghannushi's main activities were confined to cultural and political issues, such as the contradictions between the secular laws of the state and the tenets of the *shariʻa*. As the Tunisian President attempted to implement his open-door policy, social and economic problems claimed the attention of all political groups. From being a cultural association, the MTI was transformed after 1982 into an organized militant party that concentrated its ideological arguments on the rights of the workers, and the necessity of dealing with the problems of women outside the superficial issue of wearing the veil (Ghannushi, 1984: 184–6). Moreover, *jihad* to Ghannushi has become a non-violent activity that has a purely political and social character. As is the case in Turkey, Egypt, Syria, Iraq and Indonesia, the Tunisian government has so far refused to grant official recognition to an organization that bases its ideology on religion. This open rejection of religious parties on the part of Islamic states explains to a great extent the nature of Ghannushi's conversion. (Hence, Ghannushi's organization has now adopted a more neutral name: *al-Nahda* or the 'Renaissance'.) It clearly indicates that Islamic radicalism, rather than being a simple transposition of traditional values, is a totally new experience for the majority of Muslim youth. The 1979 Iranian Revolution was another concrete example of this novel phenomenon.

# Khumayni's Government

While Qutb and al-Mawdudi were primarily concerned with articulating a comprehensive ideology based on their concept of God's sovereignty, Khumayni's main task consisted of positing the clergy as a viable political elite. Accordingly, his ideological world envisaged a theocracy in which a priestly order, hierarchically organized, exercises absolute political power.

Unlike the two founders of Sunni radicalism, who were both laymen with a secular education, Khumayni was a cleric with a distinct rank and defined functions. As for his education, it involved a familiar set of subjects: Arabic, Qur'anic exegesis, jurisprudence, Islamic philosophy and Greek logic. Moreover, he worked and moved within the framework and ambience of a religious institution with its formal or informal hierarchies, properties, seminaries and schools. A *mujtahid*, well versed in the intricacies of Islamic law, he represented a counterbalance to the secular state, particularly its educational and judicial systems. His status grew in proportion to its fumbling policies and the increasing aloofness of a monarch who placed himself above all social groups and finally became their most hated enemy.

Sayyid Ruhollah al-Musawi al-Khumayni (1900–89) represented to the ordinary Iranian all that the Shah lacked: perseverance, devotion to a single cause, independence of will, as well as that rare ability to abuse opponents, sound sincere, while simultaneously conveying an air of reverence without having to stage grandiose ceremonies.

The Shah in Iran never managed to establish the unquestioned legitimacy of his rule or dynasty. There were always question marks, rumours and innuendoes about the manner his father usurped power in collaboration with the British. His own return from temporary exile in 1953, as a result of a *coup d'état* engineered by the American Central Intelligence Agency, only served to widen the rift between the Pahlavi dynasty and its doubting subjects. Consequently, question marks became hard facts, stubbornly resisting refutation.

As the Shah's policies of seeking the aid of American advisers, technicians and investors unravelled, so did his downward slide towards the embodiment of all western intrigues. Each new economic or social measure contributed to the alienation of one more social group, in addition to stirring up riots and even sowing dissension within the ranks of his own successive governments. Land reforms and distribution of villages to landless peasants disturbed a long relationship of mutual trust between the Shah and the landowners. Although they managed to hold onto most of their fertile farms, and received adequate financial incentives to engage in industrial ventures, their grievances assumed direct political connotations as they sought a more adequate arrangement in running the affairs of the state. Facing a monarch who seemed to espouse the cause of his peasants, the landowners exerted all their influence to evade redistribution of villages and farms, strengthening in the process their demands for proper political representation. The new owners, who were required to join co-operatives set up by the state, resented the presence of police forces and army units, deployed to secure law and order. Agribusiness farming, a model imported from the United States, added another grievance, and its mechanized methods swelled the ranks of the unemployed. The enclosed cycle of village life was thus shattered, and its fortunes tied to the fluctuations of the national and international market.

The clergy, numbering about 60,000 according to the Shah's own estimate (Shah, 1979: 26), felt all the more threatened as a social group with certain privileges and functions. Having been deprived of their erstwhile dominant role in the judicial and educational institutions, they now stood to lose what they had left of their properties and pious foundations. The religious institution was thus being reduced to a shadow of its former self.

The drift towards the cities by landless peasants and a young generation looking for better opportunities was fuelled by a spiralling birth rate and a falling standard of living. Once settled in an urban environment, the new rural migrants eked out a living as occasional workers on construction sites, or as porters, taxi-drivers, street vendors or workers in small workshops specializing in industries such as textiles, leather and food processing. Within a decade (1966–76) the population of the capital Tehran had almost doubled, rising from 2.719 million to 4.496 million (Hooglund, 1982: 115–20). These migrants lived in a world of their own. Having no desire to reclaim the harsh realities of rural life, they however never managed to integrate their lives into an urban centre, with its inflationary economy, high rents and increasing cost of living. The economic shock was compounded by a political straitjacket that allowed only a selective number of official unions. Political organizations, other than the Shah's stillborn National Resurrection Party, were frowned upon as instruments of divisiveness. Hence, the Shah found himself surrounded by a disparate collection of office-hunters, contractors, speculators or mere opportunists. Nevertheless, two old-established parties, the National Front and the *Tudeh* had survived into the 1960s and 1970s, one representing the aspirations of a new middle class of technocrats, and the other increasingly under attack as a tool of Soviet policy. Out of the ranks of the first a new group split off and founded an urban guerrilla organization, the Mujahidin-i Khalq. It professed to believe in class struggle, socialism and Islamic values at the same time. Combining a Maoist reverence for popular customs with a Gramscian emphasis on the role of the intelligentsia, it tended to draw its political inspiration from the writings of the Iranian sociologist, 'Ali Shari'ati (1933–77). The lectures he delivered between 1968 and 1972 to student audiences concentrated on his twin concepts of religious forms and modern contents. He was eventually arrested and spent almost two years in prison before managing to escape to London, where he died under mysterious circumstances. His line of thought and that of the Mujahidin-i Khalq were labelled by their rivals, or enemies, 'Islamic Marxism', a fitting description despite its paradoxical construction. As a matter of fact, Shari'ati's novel approach to Islamic history gained wide influence in Iran at a time when Khumayni was still formulating his ideas to a chosen circle of religious students in his Iraqi exile. Thus a French-educated layman, with a distinct hostility towards the clergy and their role in society, postulated Islam as a social revolution, directly concerned with the needs of the working people. Consequently, he used Islamic terminology as a mere form and injected it with new notions of class struggle and national self-determination. His hopes of rejuvenating Iran bypassed the theological debates of the clergy, and were pinned on a new elite that would emerge from the intelligentsia.

Another urban guerrilla organization, Fida'yan-i Khalq, was founded by members of the *Tudeh* Party as a reaction to its traditional style of political struggle (trade unionism and pamphleteering). It was more elitist and secretive than its counterpart, and offered itself as the only vanguard of the masses.

These two new organizations launched lightning raids on police stations and other state targets, attempted to assassinate prominent politicians and intelligence officers and constantly called for the downfall of the monarchy. However, theirs was an underground struggle, often confined to students and a handful of die-hard revolutionaries. The traditional networks of veteran politicians, merchants and clergymen proved in the long run much more efficient in confronting the coercive arms of the state, particularly its intelligence and security services.

The bazaar, with its traders, shopkeepers and merchants, saw in the Shah's White Revolution a direct threat to its traditional source of livelihood. It feared the onrush of modern stores, the growing role of governmental agencies and a coterie of businessmen importing consumer goods. These new economic measures bypassed old established channels, reducing the bazaar to a dispenser of decreasing local goods in a rapidly shrinking market. Thus, old-time allies – traditional merchants, religious dignitaries and artisans – were forced to renew their bonds of mutual support on a more solid basis. The rural migrants, the middle class and those tidal waves of young men and women comprising more than 60 per cent of the population, joined hands with financial patrons and mullahs. Social classes and political organizations which formerly led separate ways of social and economic life were henceforth brought together by one overriding, but negative, issue.

This broad and disparate front articulated demands with a

deliberate concentration on the most glaring faults and failures of the imperial regime. Accordingly, land reform came under attack for its deleterious effects – reduction of agricultural production, flight from the land and farms being under the control of foreigners. The decision to grant women the vote, allow them to enter government employment or gain access to higher education, received indirect disapproval by means of highlighting the prevalence of social malaise and moral decadence. Industrialization was depicted as yet another convenient ruse to enrich the Shah's friends, rob the workers of their rights and allow the foreigners to gain full control of the economy. The steady rise in oil revenues, which led the Shah to triple and quadruple his budget within a few years and build up one of the most formidable arsenals of American arms, was shown to be a miserable saga of corruption and megalomania.

These issues found their crowning grievance when the Shah decided to replace the Islamic calendar with a new one based on Persian imperial history. He, moreover, turned overnight into a rabble-rouser, lashing out at his religious and secular opponents with abusive language. The gulf between the monarch and his subjects had become unbridgeable.

Khumayni, living in the Shi'ite holy city of Najaf in Iraq, had in the meantime convinced himself, as well as a number of colleagues and disciples, that the jurists rather than secular politicians were the natural rulers in an Islamic polity. Being experts in interpreting the *shari'a*, he argued, it was their duty to supervise the proper application of its injunctions. The Qur'an and the corpus of jurisprudential writings left behind by learned Shi'ite scholars were thus pre-eminently comprehensive and wide-ranging in dealing with all profane and sacred rights and duties. Hence, government in Islam did not imply competence in legislation, since it was adequately provided for, but an ability to implement set rules and regulations. Muslims in general, and the ordinary Shi'ites in particular, should therefore imitate their source of religious knowledge (*marja' al-taqlid*) in all matters of life, relegating to him the ultimate judicial and executive power (Khumayni, 1981: 40–54, 79–125).

To Khumayni, not all jurists were equal in rank or function. One, the most learned, just and pious, would be recognized as such by the masses, and declared the Supreme Guide. He would thus be entrusted with the highest office of a religious government ordained by God: the guardianship of the jurisconsult (*wilayat al-faqih*). His selection would amount to a spontaneous act dictated by divine ordinances, so that the authority wielded by him had to be derived from one unbroken chain, embodied in the lives and careers of the designated and infallible Imams. Hence, the twelfth Imam, while still in occultation, had to be represented in his absence by a deputy whose reputable credentials entitled him to assume this responsibility. Ever since the Greater Occultation, Khumayni explained, Twelver Shi'ites were required to manage their spiritual and mundane affairs under the leadership of such a deputy. All other forms of government, under which Shi'ites were forced to live or serve, ought to be considered illegitimate. Islam did not recognize kingship, nor did it condone despotic tyrannies (*tag hut*). Accordingly, the state set up by the Pahlavi dynasty in Iran was a flagrant usurpation and a violation of binding divine ordinances. It had, therefore, to be uprooted and consigned to the dustbin of history. The abhorrent policies of the Shah, in other words, were the direct result of a perennial illegitimacy. If the people, Khumayni stressed, grasped this simple fact and acted accordingly, the whole imperial structure would fall to the ground (Khumayni, 1981: 31–9).

Khumayni thought that the absence of a true Islamic government in Iran resulted from plans hatched by imperialist powers, 'three or four centuries ago', and carried out by their local lackeys such as the Shah. In order to put an end to western plots and imperialist machinations, the clergy should engage in direct political activities. Their task was not simply to pray or peruse old texts, but to consider themselves the vanguard of society, an elite appointed by God to establish His government on earth. It did not require, he maintained, armed struggle, urban or rural warfare, or a new political organization to bring about the desired transformations in Iran. Let the religious leaders speak out in their mosques, seminaries, homes, schools and wherever possible. Let them denounce an idolatrous state and point out its illegitimate nature. Once this programme of direct action was put into effect, eventual triumph would become a matter of time (Khumayni, 1981: 114–18, 126–49).

This line of analysis, first developed by Khumayni in 1971, constituted a revolutionary rupture with the traditions of Shi'ite theology (see Chapter 1 under 'The Hidden Imam', p. 00). By claiming the political leadership of society to be the rightful and exclusive domain of the clergy, Khumayni nullified in theory and practice the validity of awaiting the return of the Twelfth Imam. To his followers, he consummated a promise that had been awaiting to be fulfilled for more than a thousand years. After his return from exile in 1979, following the departure of the Shah, Khumayni's official position became that of the deputy of the Absent Imam, Master of the Age. Nevertheless, his disciples and large sections of the people discarded such technicalities and called him simply 'The Imam'. Absence was thus abrogated and his presence filled a void long left gaping in despair: the Imam had returned, borne by a modern aeroplane that took off from Paris and landed in Tehran. Without the required white horse, or the sharp sword, as predicted in innumerable traditions, he arrived to establish a theocracy led by a high priest of impeccable credentials. Politics was once again the domain of moral values and divine injunctions.

However, it must be pointed out that not all Twelver Shi'ite jurists accept Khumayni's creative interpretation of the role of clergy. Iranian, Iraqi and Lebanese Shi'ite religious leaders have thus expressed their misgivings about these deductive arguments. Muhammad Jawad Mughniyya, for example, published a book in 1979 to refute Khumayni's theory of 'the rulership of the jurist'. Mughniyya, a highly respected Shi'ite theologian and court judge, based his refutation of Khumayni's thesis on the classical sources of Twelver Shi'ism. He simply showed that only the Twelve designated Imams were entitled to assume the absolute authority envisaged by Khumayni for a jurist whose only function could not encompass other than the issuance of legal rulings and dispensation of justice (Mughniyya, 1979b: 57–66).

Truth, according to Khumayni, is obscured by successive veils – lust, vainglory, arrogance, love of power, selfishness. Once these veils are removed, the light of God will shine within the soul of a believer. The act of removing these veils, or deadly sins, is called 'the greater *jihad*'. Its consummation opens the way for a fruitful engagement in worldly affairs. This engagement consists of cleansing society of decadence, corruption and tyrannical govern-ments. The performance of these and similar tasks constitutes the parameters of the 'lesser *jihad*'. However, society cannot but be divided into two unequal sections: teachers and students. All the people stand in constant need of instruction that is provided by religious specialists, the 'ulama. Thus, whereas men are in charge of women, the 'ulama are the paramount guardians of both as well as their children (Khumayni, 1979: 57–9, 80–2, 1982, Vol. II: 127–9, Vol. III: 35–41).

In this scheme of things, political participation as an inherent right of sovereign citizens is excluded and considered to be another veil that obscures divine truth. Consequently, it was inevitable that all former allies of Khumayni's broad coalition dropped out, or were liquidated for the sake of preserving the original aims of the revolution. The Iran–Iraq War (1980–8) afforded his followers a golden opportunity to insist on absolute political control. By the time of his death in 1989, active political involvement has become the preserve of two factions within the institutions of the state. However, in 1997, Muhammad Khatami, the former modernist Minister of Culture, was elected president of Iran with an overwhelming majority. His victory signalled a genuine desire to curtail the influence of the conservative religious establishment.

Moreover, the Iraq–Iran Gulf War and its destructive effects on Iran's economic structures and social fabric dampened the early revolutionary zeal and robbed die-hard radicalists of displaying their achievements as a model for others to follow. The war also brought to the surface the specific grievances of Arab Shi'ite communities as a potential source of exploitation by the Iranian government. Hence, governments of Arab countries with sizeable Shi'ite communities, such as Iraq and Saudi Arabia, implemented wide-ranging economic and social programmes designed to remove underlying causes of unrest.

Apart from Khumayni's innovative contribution to a Shi'ite theory of government, his conceptual frame of reference accords almost in all other aspects with that of Sunni radicalism. As regards his legal system, Twelver Shi'ism was declared by the 1979 Constitution (Principle 12) to be the official school of jurisprudence. While some differences in applying the law of inheritance, or contracting short-term marriage (*zawaj al-mut'a*) do exist between Twelver Shi'ism and the four legal schools followed by mainstream Sunnis, they belong, in a Qutbist perspective, to the category of technicalities. Nevertheless, the insistence of Iranian leaders on a strident Shi'ite motif represents a handicap that is not easily overcome.

More importantly, almost two decades after the triumph of the Revolution, the two main factions of the Iranian establishment are still locked in fierce debates on the legality or religious merits of land distributions and other economic matters. Thus, whereas culture and politics resonate with Islamic overtones, the economy lurches in an open-ended void.

By considering socio-economic and political affairs as mere administrative technicalities, both Sunni and Shi'ite radicalism divest society of its human agencies. Moreover, their moral categories, pronounced to be immutable, reduce complex structures to a set of ordinances that create modern illusions of divine grandeur. Only those with a sense of history suffer the consequences: the ordinary Muslims.

In the early 1990s a number of Islamist movements came to the fore as potent political forces in Algeria, Egypt and the Palestinian occupied territories. The apparent potency of these movements, their popularity and their daily activities led to the belief that they were serious contenders for power, or at least a force capable of disrupting the normal course of political life, such as the Middle East peace process.

The Algerian Islamist Salvation Front (FIS), the Egyptian Islamist Association and Hamas thus claimed the attention of the world media, western governments and the public at large. The Islamist movements of Algeria and Egypt were judged by a number of observers, particularly in the West, to be poised to take over political power in their respective countries, while Hamas, along with its junior partner Islamic Jihad, was feared for its potential ability to undermine peace negotiations and accords between Arabs and Israelis. The Taliban, the Afghan movement of religious students, was also added to the list, particularly after its capture of the capital city Kabul, in September 1996.

In order to achieve their aims, these movements have followed strategies and tactics which are often a combination of peaceful and violent means. Peaceful means include a variety of welfare programmes and facilities designed to win popular support in certain deprived urban areas. These welfare gestures (ranging from health clinics, schools and community centres to outright cash handouts) are, moreover, meant to create infrastructures that function as parallel or alternative agencies of government. By attempting to replace state institutions, or step into the social vacuum left by the failure of official policies, these movements aspire to prepare the ground for an eventual seizure of power. Moreover, social welfare often goes hand in hand with violent and terrorist attacks. By assassinating prominent figures, deemed to be harmful to Islam, blowing up military and civilian targets and trying to deal a severe blow to certain sectors of the national economy, the duty of *jihad* is assumed to have been largely fulfilled. Violence is thus wrapped in a religious cloak and sanctioned by innumerable textual citations. This last function has been performed on a number of occasions by Shaykh 'Umar 'Abd al-Rahman, the spiritual leader of the Egyptian Islamist Association, currently jailed in the United States, who sanctioned the disruption of the tourist industry in Egypt in order to hasten the downfall of President Husni Mubarak.

Whereas in Egypt radical Islamist groups shun the electoral process, considering participation in either municipal or parliamentary elections a dogmatic error, and the largest Palestinian Islamist organization, Hamas, holds an ambivalent attitude towards democratic practices, the Algerian FIS favoured upon its foundation in 1989 the idea of electioneering as a tactical weapon. Thus the FIS has so far taken part in local and parliamentary elections (1990 and 1991) capturing on both occasions a majority of the votes. However, after the first round of the Algerian national elections (26 December 1991), the Algerian government decided to cancel the second round of voting, declared a state of emergency, and imposed direct military rule.

## National Dialogues

In all three cases, a national dialogue was proposed as the best mechanism to resolve differences of opinion between opposition groups and their respective governments. Such proposals, suggested either by western officials or human rights organizations, were accepted in principle by the Presidents of both Egypt and Algeria. The Egyptian President, Husni Mubarak, while welcoming the idea of dialogue, insisted on excluding religious groups and parties, a stance which effectively ruled out the inclusion of the moderate Muslim Brotherhood, under the leadership of its new guide, Mustafa Mashhur (elected in 1996), not to mention the more radical Islamists. In other words, the Egyptian government is committed to a policy of eradicating the threat of political Islam to the extent of conducting regular police raids on Islamist hideouts, torturing suspects and meting out execution sentences after summary military trials.

This attitude of the Egyptian government was the target of criticism by American officials who wished to see more attention being given to underlying social and economic problems (see, for example, *The Sunday Times*, 20 February 1994). The Algerian experience of conducting a national dialogue bears similar overtones, particularly after the re-election of President Liamene Zeroual in November 1995. Following the cancellation of the second round of voting in 1992, the Algerian government banned the FIS as a political party and imprisoned its president, 'Abbasi Madani, and his deputy 'Ali Belhajj (or ibn Hajj). The new Algerian constitution, drafted by Zeroual and his associates, reiterates this stance by excluding all religious parties from direct participation in the political process. The FIS, a coalition of disparate factions and associations, has so far not managed to respond with a coherent policy. Intermittent contradictory statements issued or endorsed by its jailed and exiled leaders indicate a certain disarray in its ranks. The other more radical Algerian organization, Groupes Islamistes Armes (GIA) has adopted a strategy of total confrontation, leading to suicidal attacks as well as the liquidation of moderate or lukewarm Islamist leaders.

Both Britain and the United States supported the idea of a national dialogue in Algeria, whereas France seems to adhere to a more cautious approach, throwing its diplomatic and financial weight behind the Algerian government.

The situation in the Palestinian West Bank and the Gaza Strip is more complicated, given the different political nature of national and regional factors. Both Israel and the new Palestinian Authority, under the leadership of Yasser Arafat, adopted in the initial stages a carrot-and-stick policy. However, with the signature of the 13 September Peace Accord between the PLO leader, Yasser Arafat, and the late Israeli Prime Minister, Yitzhak Rabin, on the White House lawn in 1993, Hamas, along with Islamic Jihad and other secular Palestinian organizations announced its outright opposition to the projected self-rule authority in the West Bank and Gaza. Consequently, it boycotted parliamentary elections held in January 1996. Nevertheless, Arafat was elected president of the self-rule legislative Council with overwhelming support, while the candidates of his organization, Fatah, gained the majority of the council seats.

However, the imprisoned leader of Hamas, Ahmad Yasin, did not rule out the possibility of taking part in future elections. This is at least the impression one gains from a number of letters smuggled out of his prison cell and addressed to the leadership of his organization. (For further details, see the weekly magazine *al-Wasat*, London, no. 92, November 1993: 10–13.)

Be that as it may, the assassination of Yitzhak Rabin in November 1995, by a Jewish fundamentalist zealot opposed to the peace process, preceded less than one month by the liquidation of the Secretary General of Islamic Jihad, Fathi Shiqaqi, at the hands of Israeli intelligence agents, and followed in January 1996 by the killing of Yahya 'Ayyash, a key military figure and bomb-maker for Hamas, unleashed a new cycle of violence. In late March and early February of the same year, both Hamas and Islamic Jihad launched suicide bomb attacks in the heart of Jerusalem and Tel Aviv. The new Israeli Prime Minister, Shimon Peres, responded by sealing off the West Bank and the Gaza Strip. The withdrawal of Israeli occupation forces from their last stronghold in Hebron was halted, giving rise to widespread fears about the collapse of the peace process.

Such fears were confirmed when Shimon Peres and his Labor Party lost the parliamentary elections two months later, and Binyamin Netanyahu, the leader of the right-wing coalition, Likud, was duly elected as the new Prime Minister. His manifesto called for resuming Jewish settlement in Palestinian territories, opposing the creation of a Palestinian state and rejecting even a partial withdrawal from the Syrian Golan Heights. Netanyahu's hard-line policies led to clashes with ordinary Palestinians and the new police force of Arafat's authority, so much so that the US President, Bill Clinton, felt obliged to convene a hastily arranged summit meeting in the White House between the Palestinian and Israeli leaders in order to establish a temporary truce. While Arafat regained some of his lost popularity as a result of his objections to Likud's policies, the future of fundamentalist politics in the West Bank and the Gaza strip still belongs to the activists of Hamas and Islamic Jihad. Their ideological commitments only tend to reinforce radical positions acted out against the background of continuing political crises, a declining economic performance and the persistence of the question of Palestinian national rights. This political and social impasse can be seen in operation throughout the Middle East, especially in countries such as the Sudan, Afghanistan and Lebanon.

The Sudan, after a brief experiment with democracy between 1985 and 1989, succumbed to a military dictatorship answerable only to Hasan al-Turabi's Islamic Front. Its version of one-party rule and the application of the *shari'a* have galvanized the traditional religious parties under the leadership of Sadiq al-Mahdi and Muhammad 'Uthman al-Mirghani into a broad coalition with other secular and nationalist associations in order to restore democracy and bring about a peaceful solution to the civil war between the Christian and pagan south and the Arab-Muslim north. Hasan al-

Turabi's version of an Islamist state, straddling radicalism in the political sphere and reformism in legal procedures, continues to dominate a fragmented civil society tottering on the verge of economic collapse and social upheaval.

Lebanon emerged from its long civil war (1975–90) only to be faced with rebuilding a devastated landscape, restoring a semblance of social and political normality and coping at the same time with the presence of an Israeli security zone in the south. Hence, despite the fact that the fundamentalist Shi'ite organization, *Hizb Allah*, has participated in two parliamentary elections, winning as a result a number of seats, it continues to insist on carrying out the duty of *jihad* against Israeli threats and occupation by proxy. *Hizb Allah*'s insistence on a religious and national obligation causes enormous embarrassment to the Lebanese government, forcing it to forego its policy of disarming all militias by treating the Party of God as an exceptional case. Enjoying Iranian financial support, and backed by Syria in its military tactics, Hizbullah plays the internal Lebanese political game with an astuteness reminiscent of the most notorious tradition of the old republic, while simultaneously adhering to the strictest programme of a militant Islamist movement.

## Seekers of Religion

Nevertheless, the Lebanese civil war did come to an end and its Islamist groups, both Sunnite and Shi'ite, have joined the political and electoral process. Afghanistan, on the other hand, is still in the grips of a bloody factional and tribal war which has been taking place ever since the downfall of its communist president, Muhammad Najibullah, in 1992. The Afghan Mujahidin, professing an Islamist ideology that failed to escape its articulation in tribal configurations, waged a successful guerrilla warfare against the occupying Soviet army, thanks to generous material and military assistance from the United States, Saudi Arabia, Pakistan and a host of other countries. Their victory, however, did not mean the end of either tribal or regional conflict. On the contrary, the fiercest battles were fought between various guerrilla groups under the banner of Islamism. The first clashes occurred between the forces of Gulbudin Hekmatyar's Hizb-i Islami and those of Burhanuddin Rabbani, the spiritual leader of Jama'at Islami and the President of the new regime. Having been defeated despite his assumption of the post of

Prime Minister, Hekmatyar was driven out of Kabul, hoping to reinstate himself by subjecting the capital to constant bombardment. His sojourn south of Kabul was cut short by the advancing Taliban, a guerrilla group which emerged in 1994 from the religious schools run by Afghan refugees in Pakistan. Thus in July 1996, Hekmatyar returned to the capital, reached accommodation with the President and resumed his duties as the legitimate Prime Minister. His return to a city devastated by constant pounding only served to highlight the helplessness of a population on the verge of famine, with increasing numbers of war widows and children without shelter or adequate food. The crisis was further compounded by the rapid devaluation of the national currency whose banknotes were still being printed in Russia.

The Taliban, drawn from remote tribal areas, were indoctrinated by their leaders to uphold and practise an extreme version of Islamic fundamentalism, ultimately derived from medieval texts composed during the decline of high Muslim culture. Such a system of indoctrination and inculcation, refined in the medieval environment of central Asia, was revived by the Taliban and transplanted into an environment that was becoming increasingly at odds with its ethos. An inevitable conflict between two versions of Islam was thus the outcome of the Taliban's challenge. Having as their guiding principle the rigorous application of *shari'a* rules as spelt out in obscure legal manuals, they ended up by creating a mongrel creed that combined the worst features of modern warfare and medieval conservative discipline. Theirs was a daily experimentation with dystopian models (on the decline of high Islamic culture see the illuminating remarks in Hodgson, *The Venture of Islam*, Vol. 2, 1974: 437–45).

The Taliban, backed by US funds and Pakistani logistical facilities, offered themselves as a new neutral force capable of pacifying the country and restoring stability to its social fabric. From their base in Qandahar, in south-east Afghanistan, they began their slow progress towards the capital, defeating in the process an array of local forces. With the fall of Kabul, their leader, Muhammad 'Umar, issued from his headquarters in Qandahar one decree after another. Within a few days, girls' schools were closed and women were denied the right to work or appear in public without full veils, covering the head and the whole body, including their ankles.

In a capital where almost half the female population were attired in western clothes, and a considerable number worked in government offices, and many of the medical staff, including doctors, were women, a curtain of darkness descended on Kabul. Neighbouring countries were also alarmed and voiced their opposition to the rule of the new masters. Iran objected to the harshness of a regime that seems to be distorting the image of religion in the name of Islam. However, Iranian fears were rooted in more mundane considerations: a growing Pakistani influence in Afghanistan coupled with the luring presence of American diplomatic and economic interests, thereby bypassing Iran as the natural trade route between central Asia – particularly Turkmenistan with its vast natural gas resources – and the Indian subcontinent. Russia was another regional power that voiced its concern at the ascendancy of a Pashtun-dominated government enmeshed in long clashes with the two leading minorities of Afghanistan: the Uzbeks and the Tajiks. Both enjoyed longstanding relations with central Asia and the former republics of the Soviet Union – Uzbekistan and Tajikstan. Russia's fear of the spread of Islamic fundamentalism over its southern sphere of influence reactivated its alliance with the former communist general, Abdul Rashid Doestam, who controlled northern Afghanistan, a predominantly Uzbek autonomous region.

As the forces of Rabbani's government withdrew towards the north-east under the command of the Tajik general, Ahmed Shah Mas'ud, the Defence Minister of the ousted government, Afghanistan's military map became demarcated along clear-cut ethnic lines. However, this de facto partition entered a phase of reshuffling and rearrangement in view of the popular discontent voiced by leading members of the Pashtun majority. Thus, disparate forces forged a political alliance under the umbrella of the Supreme Council of Afghanistan. Fighters loyal to Doestam, Rabbani-Mas'ud and a Shi'ite warlord, 'Abdul Karim Khalili, embarked on a new guerrilla campaign designed to defeat the Taliban militia and its commander of the faithful: Mawlana Muhammad 'Umar. However, this was a fragile alliance that failed to withstand the Taliban's strategic superiority.

## The Lure of Ideology

In Egypt, Islamist organizations, apart from the moderate Muslim Brotherhood, continue to voice their opposition to state institutions and government policies in dogmatic statements. Dogmatism, wedded to the notion of waging *jihad* until final victory, forms an underlying principle that seems never to vary or reduce in intensity. This tendency of depicting the world as two irreconcilable camps, destined to confront each other as long as God's sovereignty is not fully established, permeates the world of Islamic fundamentalists even under the guise of political programmes and democratic ideals. A case in point is the *Charter* published by Hamas in August 1988 and the electoral *Manifesto* adopted by FIS in March 1989.

The *Charter* of Hamas ('Abd al-Rahman, 1989: 91–117) highlights the fact that the Islamic Resistance Movement in the Palestinian occupied territories is a branch of the original Muslim Brotherhood established by Hasan al-Banna in 1928. It goes on to describe the society of the Muslim Brotherhood as a worldwide organization and the largest movement in the modern history of Islam. It holds Islam to be an inclusive system of thought, government and social life. It is thus the final arbiter of its strategy as well as a metaphysical doctrine whereby a comprehensive conception of the cosmos and humankind is articulated and delineated. Its doctrinal, political and judicial concepts are as a result emanations from an all-embracing ideology. It is an ideology that subsumes under its rubric artistic creativity as well as the ideal of martyrdom.

In this sense Islam, according to Hamas, shelters under its wing both the duty of *jihad* and the modern obligation of patriotism. It does so because the liberation of Palestine is first and foremost a religious duty decreed for all Muslims by the *shari'a*. The restoration of Palestine to its rightful owners is therefore an urgent task for which Muslim men and women must co-ordinate their efforts and unify their ranks. Being a religious endowment (*waqf islami*), Palestine is entrusted in perpetuity to all the generations of Muslims until the day of resurrection. *Jihad* becomes in this context an obligation incumbent on every Muslim (*fard 'ayn*). Conquered by force in the early days of Islam, its validity as a religious endowment abrogates whatever decision is made by an Arab state, king or president, to cede any part of the Palestinian land.

Hamas reiterates in article seven of the *Charter* its rejection of secularism or the idea of a secular state, embracing Muslims, Jews and Christians, as envisaged by the PLO in its *1968 Charter*. Whereas secularism is rejected, patriotism is, however, adopted as long as it complements the religious doctrine. In addition to the material ties characteristic of all patriotisms, the patriotism of

Hamas is, more importantly, suffused with a divine dimension, binding together earth and heaven under the banner of God.

The *Charter*, moreover, underlines the necessity of offering material and moral assistance to the needy. Thus, welfare politics, armed struggle and patriotic exultation fuse into a programme of immediate and ideological clarity.

Such visions of doctrinal purity and tactical policies inform the political literature of the FIS. Upon its foundation in 1989, the FIS came out with a preliminary political manifesto. Apart from its electioneering purpose, it served to establish the identity of the FIS by claiming to be the only association capable of representing all the interests and aspirations of the Algerian people and their neglected Islamic heritage. It proclaims radical solutions designed to dismantle corrupt state institutions and replace them with ones built on *shura* or consultation. The idea of *shura* is supposed to put an end to political oppression and pave the way for social equality. FIS's adoption of Islamic consultation underlines its aim to abjure another superficially similar system: western democracy. It does so by defining democracy thus:

> It is one of the means used to urge and coerce the individual to reconcile himself to the rule of oppressors. Thus, it is not the opinion of the majority that determines the boundaries of right and justice. Rather, it is God, may He be praised, who determines and delimits [...]
>
> (al-Shaykh, 1993, p. 89)

The *Manifesto* declares the abject failure of all modern ideologies, be they Eastern (communism) or western (liberal democracy). Islam is then offered as the only viable solution. Appealing to the untapped potential of the Algerian people, it calls for total revolutionary change in the fields of politics, industry, commerce, agriculture and education. The example of the founders of Islam (*al-salaf*) is repeatedly invoked wherever a new policy is proposed, particularly in the domain of censorship or strict control of the media.

Moreover, the *Manifesto* reclaims the legacy of the Algerian war for liberation from French rule (1956-62), singling out its Islamic credentials in its final victory over the forces of colonialism. Lamenting the decline of the Algerian armed forces as an ideological power, it proposes a programme of indoctrination aimed at restoring their fighting morale and military efficiency (al-Shaykh, 1993: 204-5).

While the *Manifesto* was largely a device to project the general political image of the FIS, elaborating some of its policies and their Islamic significance, its other periodical publications, particularly after 1991, allowed the Algerians to become better acquainted with its method of struggle. Such a method was made all the more urgent with the various attempts of the Algerian government to amend the national electoral laws, thereby obstructing the emergence of the FIS as the leading party in parliament. Thus was born the idea of civil disobedience, the brainchild of 'Ali Belhajj, Madani's second-in-command, and renowned throughout Algeria for his fiery speeches and uncompromising principles. Born in 1956 in Tunisia, he returned to Algeria after independence only to be disillusioned with the persistence of French culture and influence despite the Islamic slogans of the revolution. In the early 1980s he joined the Islamic Movement for Combating Social Evils, under the leadership of Mustafa Abu Ya'li (d. 1987). The Movement called for armed struggle in order to enforce its policy of forbidding alcohol, prostitution and gambling. In 1983 Belhajj was sentenced to a four-year term of imprisonment for his involvement in violent activities and disruption of public order. In 1989 he founded, together with 'Abbasi Madani, the Islamic Salvation Front.

'Abbasi Madani (b. 1931) was a veteran of the liberation war against France and a founding member of the National Liberation Front, the sole ruling political party in Algeria until 1988. Madani graduated with a degree in philosophy from the University of Algiers, and obtained a doctorate in comparative pedagogy from the Institute of Education in London. In contrast to Belhajj, he is considered a moderate Islamist who favours gradual change and the idea of national reconciliation. Both were sentenced in 1991 to 12 years for incitement and encouragement of civil disobedience.

Shortly before their arrest, the FIS published an anthology of articles dealing with the principles and practical aspects of civil disobedience. By launching such a campaign, the FIS aimed at de-legitimating the authority of the Algerian system of government. Denouncing the state as being un-Islamic and corrupt, it proceeded to articulate its strategy and tactics in order to seize political power.

Civil disobedience was thus considered an intermediate stage situated between political action, on the one hand, and armed struggle on the other. Political action was left behind since it represented a lame tactic, lacking the necessary ingredients to achieve a successful result. Full armed struggle remained a deferred strategy that could be activated once civil disobedience had run its course.

This strategy was carried out in June 1991. It was meant to culminate in a general strike, having as its principal aim the complete paralysis of public life throughout Algeria. In the event, the state used the armed forces to launch a pre-emptive attack which brought Algeria under direct military rule. Consequently, Algeria entered a vicious circle of violence which has so far claimed the lives of more than 50,000 victims. Nevertheless, the FIS has, to a large extent, been discredited as a viable political force, while its Islamist rivals have been driven into an extreme course of action which may turn out to be no less suicidal than its intermediate stage of civil disobedience.

Between 1990 and 1996, the Soviet Union collapsed and disintegrated into independent states with severe economic problems and recurring political crises. Iraq invaded Kuwait in 1990, threatening the oil supplies to the West. The United States, heading a coalition of European and Arab military forces, defeated within a few months the Iraqi army, forcing President Saddam Hussein to retreat into his country.

A number of resolutions, passed by the Security Council of the United Nations, were immediately applied, resulting in widespread sanctions which seemed designed to punish the Iraqi civil society, while leaving the authority of Saddam Hussein largely intact. Be that as it may, Islamic fundamentalism did enjoy an exuberant moment of resurgence between the invasion of Kuwait and its eventual liberation. This was largely due to the enmity engendered by the presence of foreign troops in Muslim lands, such as Saudi Arabia, and the mistaken perception that a latter-day Saladin had finally emerged to vindicate the enduring message of Islam.

Another brief moment of exuberance was experienced when Necmettin Erbakan, the leader of the Turkish Islamist Party, Refah, managed to convince the leader of the secular True Path Party, Tansu Ciller, to enter into a parliamentary coalition. The coalition brought modern Turkey its first Islamist Prime Minister in June 1996. However, Erbakan's party gained a Prime Minister only to lose an ideology. The application of Islamism was ruled out while secularism had to be upheld, a stipulation agreed to by Refah.

Nevertheless, Erbakan's sheer ability to hold such a lofty office in one of the most vigorous secular countries of the Islamic world encouraged others to look for a similar outcome. Although

Erbakan's success came about by peaceful means, the party of Jama'at-i-Islami in Pakistan, originally founded by al-Mawdudi, stepped up its defiance of Benazir Bhutto, the Prime Minister. Its leader, Husayn Ahmad, went as far as to call for Bhutto's resignation, accusing her government of being corrupt and un-Islamic. However, it seems possible that the unfolding events in Afghanistan, particularly as the final fate of the Taliban was still hanging in the balance, had a direct effect on the ambivalent attitude of a Prime Minister who originally supported 'The seekers of religious knowledge' in Afghanistan, then found herself confronted by misogynists defying all known human and divine laws and injunctions.

By 2002 a new Turkish 'Islamist' party, Justice and Development, put forward a mild version of Erbakan's programme and made certain to reiterate its adherence to the secular legacy of the republic. It won in the same year the Turkish parliamentary elections by a wide margin over its rivals, gaining 363 seats out of 550. Pakistan, in the meantime, fell under military rule in 1999 and did not return to a semblance of civilian authority until 2008, following the assassination of Benazir Bhutto after her return from exile to Pakistan a year earlier to reclaim her former position. As for the Taliban, their fate was sealed for giving refuge to the perpetrators of 9/11 attacks in 2001. Although they seemed to have recovered some lost ground, it is far from certain whether they will be able to stage a comeback, given the presence of more than 50,000 NATO forces in the country.

From the Sudan to Afghanistan, the Islamic world is still being torn by its desire for democracy and the drive for a sense of national dignity. Certain Islamic fundamentalists brand the former as being a form of western hegemony, while hijacking the latter under the mantle of doctrinal purity and authenticity.

# Chapter 8

## Elections or Armed Struggle: Ballots or Bullets?

By the late 1990s it was becoming increasingly clear that radical Islamism or Islamist radicalism had reached an impasse. Although Iran under its Islamist system of government had managed to weather the storm of its war with Iraq, as well as a campaign of political assassinations launched by the Marxist–Islamist organization Mujahedin-i-khalq, one of its former allies, in addition to western sanctions and poor economic performance, and while Afghanistan fell under the authority of a new Islamist regime led by the Taliban, Islamist radicalism as defined in this study, particularly in its Sunni version, seemed to have failed in its endeavour to gain power in a key Muslim country. Consequently, the story of radical Islamism by the turn of the twenty-first century appeared to diverge into two separate parts, and with a growing chasm of strategy and tactics between their respective entities. In other words, radical Islamism has now split into two factions: one faction confining its struggle to a particular national territory or nation-state, and the other considering the entire globe to be its legitimate field of operation. The first faction has, moreover, come to accept, albeit in varying degrees of open commitment, the idea of gaining power by peaceful means, including elections, whenever they become available. On the other hand, the second faction is no longer interested in local or national political programmes and has set its sights on confronting the world, particularly its western parts, under the leadership of the United States, by forming an international organization armed with an equally global strategy based on violent confrontations and terrorist attacks.

Hence, what we have are two movements which have common intellectual and ideological origins, with both Sayyid Qutb and Abu al-Ala al-Mawdudi acting as their revered founding fathers. However, seen with hindsight, one could consider Sayyid Qutb, with his puritanical and abstract notions of the universal role of Islam as the inspiring and spiritual leader of the international movement, while al-Mawdudi with his long-protracted immersion in the politics of India and Pakistan could still act as a model for the second national trend.

It is for this reason that various students of Islamist movements have recently adopted a more nuanced designation to differentiate between the above-mentioned trends. Hence, the first trend is still being dubbed Islamism or political Islam, denoting thereby a movement that has decided to join the political process of its country of origin and give up strategies of violence or armed struggle as the means to attain power. On the other hand, the second trend is now almost universally labelled 'jihadist', with its ideology being described as jihadism. In this scheme of things, jihadism becomes equated with a single, clear-cut method of struggle, having violence as its hallmark and dominant identity. Although *jihad* has been assumed to denote a number of connotations, extending from spiritual struggle or personal endeavours of moral rejuvenation to the practice of some kind of self-defence, be it individually or collectively, and culminating in a coordinated effort to spread the word of God by all means, it is clearly restricted in its new contemporary context to a particular type of practice, with the intention of committing acts of violence as its most obvious sense.

To be more precise, one could single out three different schools of, or approaches to, jihadism.

1. *Jihad* is an ideology that stands on its own and should not therefore be confused with Islam as a religion or its theological system. This definition is supposed to refer to Islamist organizations and groups, such as al-Qa'ida. In other words, Islam is left out as an inspiration or legitimate frame of reference by those who wish to distance it from violence or undermine the message of its adherents.

2. *Jihad* becomes part of Islam only under certain conditions, such as devising a defensive policy against foreign occupation. More importantly, it has to be declared by a legitimate Muslim authority or government. In other words, jihadism is here integrated into mainstream or realist policies and strategies

initiated by official governments or movements embracing national liberation and self-determination for their own people. This stance is normally associated with modernist or moderate Islam.

3. *Jihad* is the sixth pillar of Islam (the other five being oneness of God, fasting, pilgrimage, prayer, and *zakat* or alms-giving). Consequently, it is valid under all circumstances without having to justify such validity under the false rubrics of being offensive or defensive. This is a more sophisticated definition than (1), but with the proviso that such an opinion should be pronounced as such by official or qualified Muslim scholars and authorities. More importantly, it is not seen as an ideology, but rather as a tool of preserving the community or assuring its survival.

It is ironic that neo-conservatives in the United States and Jihadists concur on this last point. Here is the American neo-conservative scholar, Daniel Pipes, advancing his own definition:

What does the Arabic word *jihad* mean? [. . .] It means the legal, compulsory, communal effort to expand the territories ruled by Muslims at the expense of territories ruled by non-Muslims. The purpose of *jihad*, in other words, is not directly to spread the Islamic faith but to extend sovereign Muslim power (faith, of course, often follows the flag). *Jihad* is thus unabashedly offensive in nature, with the eventual goal of achieving Muslim dominion over the entire globe.

(*New York Post*, 31 December 2002)

And this is Ayman al-Zawahiri, al-Qa'ida's second-in-command, confirming Pipes' diagnosis in a message addressed to President Obama in the wake of his election in 2008:

You also must appreciate, as you take over the presidency of America during its Crusade against Islam and Muslims, that you are neither facing individuals nor organizations, but are facing a Jihadi awakening and renaissance which is shaking the pillars of the entire Islamic world; and this is the fact which you and your government and country refuse to recognize and pretend not to see. And I tell all Mujahideen everywhere: Allah has granted you success and honored you by making you the most important cause of that, so be resolute on the path of Jihad until you meet your Lord while He is pleased with you.

(English Translation of Zawahiri Message,
Fox News, 19 November 2008)

The spiritual founder of al-Qa'ida, Abdullah Azzam declared: 'Jihad is the most excellent form of worship, and by means of it the Muslim can reach the highest of ranks'. He goes on to say:

Anybody who looks into the state of the Muslims today will find that their greatest misfortune is their abandonment of Jihad (due to love of this world and abhorrence of death). Because of that, the tyrants have gained dominance over the Muslims in every aspect and in every land. The reason for this is that the Disbelievers only stand in awe of fighting.

Interestingly, Azzam gives a direct answer to those who try to differentiate between two types of *jihad*:

The saying, 'We have returned from the lesser jihad (battle) to the greater jihad (jihad of the soul)', which people quote on the basis that it is a hadith, is in fact a false, fabricated hadith which has no basis. It is only a saying of Ibrahim Ibn Abi 'Abalah, one of the Successors, and it contradicts textual evidence and reality.

(Azzam, 2001, Part I: Section 5)

However, one of the most favourite sayings for jihadists, but which could equally be fabricated, is: '*Jihad* shall continue until the day of judgement'.

What we now have is what some writers call 'the global Jihadist Movement' (see e.g. Torres *et al.*, 2006: 399). On the other hand, older Islamist organizations, based in a particular country, such as al-Nahda in Tunisia, al-Jama'a al-Islamiyya in Egypt, al-'Adl wa al-Ihsan ( Justice and Good Deeds) in Morocco, The Islamic Salvation Front in Algeria and the Muslim Brotherhood in Syria, confine their theatre of operations to their own national territories, and more often than not envisage change as a peaceful process, resulting either from elections,or the mobilization of mass movements and protests to effect such change. By becoming purely national parties, these movements have virtually joined the political process, albeit at different levels of engagement and credibility. Such a transformation of Islamist movements, whereby they could be said to have joined the mainstream currents, has given more prominence to hitherto fringe groups and accentuated their significance as representatives of a new brand of Islamism dubbed Jihadism. Jihadism, particularly after the attacks of 9/11 2001, has largely been associated with al-Qa'ida, led by the Saudi Usama Bin Laden and his deputy, the Egyptian Ayman al-Zawahiri.

How did this transformation take place? What particular factors were at play in bringing about such bifurcation within Islamist radicalism?

It would be useful to point out that, in line with our general argument, Islamist movements are still in a defensive position, with globalization, or the latest manifestation of western dominance, acting as a new stimulus. Hence, the adoption of democratic practices and ideas or the insistence on launching violent acts of defiance under the banner of Jihadism, take on an international character, with Islamists and jihadists espousing one or the other in its global dimensions.

As we have seen, in the last two chapters, these radical Islamist movements espoused a vague programme, at both the theoretical and practical levels, with the implicit belief that their societies were innately receptive to and supportive of their message to restore Islam as the focal point of governance and social life. More importantly, they modelled themselves on secular parties, be they nationalist, secular or communist, and adopted similar platforms with a pronounced Islamist overtone. In their initial activities, these Islamist groups believed in some sort of violent or military struggle as the most effective means of setting up an Islamist state. Referring to this type of activity as *jihad*, they believed themselves to be on the threshold of seizing power, particularly after the gradual decline of secular parties or the increasing corruption and repressiveness of state agencies and political leaders. Although these groups belonged to a general trend of Islamism, their mode of operation and political programmes were not the same and tended to be the product of their particular national history and type of local systems of government. Hence, what set apart Hamas in Palestine, Hizbullah in Lebanon, the Muslim Brotherhood in Syria and the Taliban in Afghanistan was more significant than the general appeal to Islamic notions that appeared to give them a common identity. As a matter of fact, these and other similar groups very rarely cooperated with each other or tried to coordinate their efforts to achieve their aims. Unlike communist parties, they lacked a common strategy and a shared vision of their long-term goals. Nor did they have a single patron as the communist parties did with the former Soviet Union.

It was in this context that these Islamist groups were unable to carry out a concerted programme of action or offer adequate responses to the increasingly repressive state institutions of various Muslim countries. By the end of the twentieth century, their main slogan of waging *jihad* in the name of a higher cause was being gradually replaced by a more subtle approach, more concerned with winning popular approval by stressing their political and social agenda. This shift was the result of effective counter-measures by various Muslim states, often violating standard human rights but largely ignored by the international community. One could go further by pointing to a failed strategy that had reached a dead end by the mid-1990s, with not a single Islamist movement managing to seize power apart from the Taliban in Afghanistan, which in itself was not a representative of these movements.

Although one could cite Hamas and Hizbullah as two eminently military movements, still engaged in some kind of *jihad*, their political history is a clear indication of this dramatic shift. Both originated in the 1980s as a reaction to Israeli military occupation of both the Palestinian territories and parts of Lebanon respectively. Hamas, a Sunnite group, advocated *jihad* as its own Islamist brand of armed struggle to bring about the liberation of occupied Palestine, whereas Hizbullah, a Shi'ite party, fought against the Israeli military occupation of Lebanese territory, particularly in the south. Martyrdom was extolled by both groups as the highest form of religious devotion and both considered their struggle to be a profound commitment to the tenets of Islam. However, such martyrdom was simply a continuation of a long line of practices stretching back to the early days of various Arab nationalist movements. Even dying in the name of Islam to liberate one's own country was an integral part of nationalist slogans throughout the twentieth century in the Muslim world. What gave these Islamist movements a distinct colouring was their coupling of military means and political aims and referring both to an original source anchored in Islam as an ideology rather than as a memory or example, as was the case with secular organizations. In this sense, these two organizations can be classed as national liberation movements not dissimilar to other patriotic groups in either Latin America or Africa. They both have a civilian and a military wing and are fully integrated into the political process of their systems of governance, with Hamas running for and winning legislative elections in 2006 and Hizbullah participating in Lebanese elections since the early 1990s (Hamzeh, 1993; Hroub, 2006: 139–50). Perhaps Sinn Fein and the Irish Republican Army before its dissolution constitute the closest example of such arrangements.

Apart from Hamas and Hizbullah, for the various Islamist groups operating in Iraq, (excluding al-Qa'ida), Somalia, Chechnya, Indonesia, India, Yemen and Nigeria, and in spite of their advocacy of armed struggle in confronting their local adversaries, be they state institutions or rival tribal groups, a national agenda can be clearly discerned in their grievances and political fields, with the national territory acting as an ultimate frame of reference, even in the absence of state institutions. However, the bulk of Islamist movements which came into existence in the 1970s and 1980s, particularly after the Iranian Revolution of 1979, have shifted the debate to a different terrain whereby all key radicalist concepts and practices derived from Islamic texts or experiences have been reinterpreted and updated. This was particularly the case in Egypt, with Sayyid Imam al-Sharif, the first Amir or commander of the Egyptian Islamic Jihad organisation, acting as the representative of a new current of revisionism. In 2007 he issued a number of pamphlets and publications from his prison cell in Torah prison, Southern Cairo, denouncing the killing of civilians and minorities as being totally un-Islamic and contrary to the teachings of the Prophet. He singled out the 9/11 attacks as being both 'immoral and counterproductive'. This is all the more significant since al-Sharif, or Dr Fadl (medical),was formerly the main ideologue of al-Qa'ida. Leaders of another radicalist group, the Egyptian al-Jama'a al-Islamiyya, have composed a series of studies under the title *Tashih al-Mafahim* (*Corrections of Concepts*). These revisions were said to be the positive outcome of counter-radicalization programmes run by the governments of Egypt, Jordan, Saudi Arabia and Yemen. In July 2009, the Libyan Islamist Fighting Group declared its defection from al-Qa'ida, citing its strategy of indiscriminate killing of civilians as well as its failure to alleviate political oppression and social malaise as major deficiencies. Entitled *Corrective Studies in Understanding Jihad*, vetted by the veteran Muslim scholar, Yusuf al-Qardawi, and running to 420 pages, this recantation is further evidence of a widespread revulsion against indiscriminate bombings and the random killing of innocent civilians, including the 2004 Madrid and 2005 London bombings. Perhaps the only exception is the Algerian Salafist Group for Preaching and Combat which announced in 2006 that it had become a local branch of al-Qaʻida under the name 'al-Qaʻida of the Islamic Maghrib'. It launched in 2007 and 2009 a number of suicide attacks throughout Algeria, targeting military personnel, foreigners and civilians.

Thus, failure of strategy, coupled with ruthless responses by state authorities and security services paved the way for a revisionist assessment of *jihad* and its weight in the general elements of implementing a particular political programme. Such measures coincided with the rise of a new wave of democracy immediately after the invasion of Afghanistan by NATO forces in 2001 and the occupation of Iraq by a coalition of forces led by the United States in 2003. In both cases the regimes of the Taliban and Saddam Hussein were overthrown and were supposed to be replaced by a new political system presided over by properly elected governments and the rule of law. Before the two experiments began to unravel a few years later, with democracy being sidelined or downgraded as a permanent choice and war objective, local responses ranged from outright resistance to fresh revaluations of national and religious cultures. Although such a process had already started in the early 1990s, it received its impetus and was confirmed as a result of the occupation of both Afghanistan and Iraq and the rapid disappearance of their authoritarian regimes. As early as 1992, Rashid Ghannoushi, the Tunisian Islamist leader, published an extended study on the nature of governance in Islam. In it he explicitly singled out democracy as 'the best mechanism or system of government which enables citizens, through its use, to practise basic freedoms, including political freedom'. He goes on to state: 'the Highest ideal of democracy is for the ruled to become rulers so as to be able to achieve by themselves for themselves what they aspire to' (Ghannushi, 1992: 75–7). Such an acclaim of democracy was premised on the assumption that a similar concept and process did exist in early Islam under the name of *shura* or consultation. This argument has been put forward by leading contemporary Islamic intellectuals, clerics and activists such as Yusuf al-Qardawi, 'Abd al-Salam Yasin Tariq al-Bishri, Fahmi Huwayda and many others.

The Moroccan 'Abdul Salam Yassine, for example, considers *shura* to be an abstract concept left to Muslims to decide its form and content. Offering his own interpretation, he goes out of his way to show how democracy could be integrated into an Islamic mode of governance by showing that it is diametrically opposed to oppression, be it political or social. In this sense, it has nothing to do with matters dealing with the existence of God or the nature of revelations. At the same time Yassine stresses that democracy is 'a form of dialogue having as its purpose the resolution of political disputes by civilized political means' (Yassine,1994: 57–62). However, Ghannushi, Yassine, al-Qardawi and their school of thought assume that secularism is an alien western concept and should not be made part of a democratic package. Such an assumption stems from their differentiation between a religious and an Islamic government, by arguing that Islam is more than a religion in the Christian sense of the word. Hence, secularism is relegated to its peculiarly western history and environment, whereas democracy is given a universalistic character by finding its equivalent in Muslim modes of governance, which in turn are supposed to apply to all societies. This line of argument is deployed in order to reclaim Muslim culture by insisting on considering Islam to be the ultimate frame of reference and authority, even under a freely elected government. By doing so, democracy is robbed of its main characteristic, i.e, the free expression of the will of the people and their entitlement to legislate their own laws and accept, if they so wish, those that are already in place irrespective of their origin. In other words, democracy in this context is made to mean the inescapable choice of Islam as the ultimate authority in the state. Or as the Sudanese Islamist leader, Hasan al-Turabi, avers after extolling the virtues of democratic rule: 'Democracy in Islam does not mean the absolute authority of the people, rather it is people's authority provided the *shari'a* is obeyed' (al-Turabi, 1988: 86). Hence, *shura* could be equated with democracy, but it goes beyond its formalities and western strictures or limitations, particularly in the spiritual field. In other words, it could be said that democracy is universal, but its applications are determined by local cultures. Nevertheless, adoption of elections and acceptance of pluralist politics by these movements represents an advanced stance which is undoubtedly at odds with the puritanical message of jihadism. However, the question remains as to the nature of the Islamic system and the existence of a clear commitment to the political process and the inevitable rotation of power.

# Al-Qa'ida

Much has been written about al-Qa'ida, its origins, ideology, organization, mode of recruitment and operations. As to origins, various accounts trace its initial emergence to the Soviet invasion of Afghanistan in December 1979, the subsequent resistance organized by local mujahideen groups and the military, financial and logistical support extended to these groups by the United States, Saudi Arabia and Pakistan. Between 1979 and 1989 Arab volunteers, motivated by religious and political allegiances, began to arrive in Afghanistan to fulfil what was perceived to be their Muslim obligation, or *jihad*, against an atheist regime and foreign power. During those years two names stand out for their role in paving the way for the emergence what became known after 1995 as al-Qa'ida. The first was 'Abdullah Azzam (1941–89), a militant Islamist of Palestinian origins. As a former member of the Jordanian Muslim Brotherhood, a committed Palestinian militant and a graduate of al-Azhar University, 'Azzam combined in his political loyalties the stance of the scholar and the passionate commitments of an activist. While studying at al-Azhar in Egypt in the early 1970s Azzam seems to have drifted towards the extremist fringes of the Muslim Brotherhood and disciples of Sayyid Qutb. These included the future deputy of al-Qa'ida, Ayman al-Zawahiri. After teaching Islamic topics at King Abdul Aziz University in Jeddah until 1979, and where Usama Bin Laden happened to be a student, he was drawn to Pakistan, first as a university lecturer in Islamabad, and shortly thereafter as an activist in Peshawar in the North-West Frontier and close to Afghan borders. His departure from Saudi Arabia came in the wake of the occupation of the Grand Mosque in Mecca in November 1979 by a group of millenarian Islamists. It seems that the Saudi authorities decided to expel him after ending the Meccan episode, although he was not directly implicated. Before his arrival in Pakistan, he had issued a statement calling on all Muslims to join the battle for the liberation of both Palestine and Afghanistan. In this statement he considered *jihad* to be an individual duty incumbent on all Muslims, rather than a collective obligation: if undertaken by some, others would not be required to join in. In Peshawar, 'Azzam opened Maktab al-Khadamat ('Services Office') to receive foreign, mainly Arab, fighters and organize their recruitment and eventual departure to the battlefield in Afghanistan. It is thought that this Services Office, which was charged with compiling a database (al-Qa'ida means 'base' in Arabic) of all the volunteers, formed the nucleus of what later become the organization of the same name. It was during this period that Bin Laden, a Saudi millionaire, became a close associate of 'Azzam and both worked for the same cause, with the latter articulating the ideological dimensions of *jihad* and acting as the intellectual mentor, while the former offered financial assistance, administrative expertise and a growing network of donors across the Muslim world and beyond. By March 1989, after the Soviet withdrawal from Afghanistan, various Islamist groups within the country began jostling for power, often with deadly encounters. It was at this juncture that both 'Azzam and Bin Laden seem to have fallen out over the future of their presence in Afghanistan or their return to their countries of origin, with the former favouring integrating his volunteers into local factions, while the latter wanted to preserve their separate status. It was during this period, in November 1989, that 'Azzam was assassinated in Peshawar in mysterious circumstances. The culprits have never been identified. Thus the roots of al-Qa'ida go back to this transitional episode, with Bin Laden searching once again for a new territorial base and an alternative intellectual mentor.

After the Soviet withdrawal, Bin Laden toyed with the idea of working in Saudi Arabia, while using Yemen as a new safe haven or launching pad. His plans were cut short by the Iraqi invasion of Kuwait and the rejection by the Saudi authorities of his offer to organize his own military brigades to liberate the Emirate as a close ally of the Saudi royal family. Kuwait was instead liberated by western forces, using Saudi Arabia as their base. It was then that Bin Laden moved to the Sudan, with his Saudi citizenship revoked in 1994. In 1996, as a result of Saudi and American pressure, he was expelled and went back to Afghanistan. His arrival coincided with the ascendancy of the Taliban as the new masters of Kabul. In the meantime, he had met Ayman al-Zawahiri, the leader of the increasingly beleaguered Islamic Jihad, the organization which had plotted the assassination of the Egyptian president, Anwar Sadat, in 1981. In other words, al-Zawahiri, a medical doctor, was soon to replace 'Azzam as the new ideologue and strategist of those dubbed 'Afghan Arabs' (Atwan, 2007: 68–70). After his organization's failure to assassinate the new Egyptian President, Husni Mubarak, in 1995, and the public outrage at the massacre of 58 western tourists and four Egyptians in the Ancient city of Luxor in 1997, al-Zawahiri began his journey from being a fighter against his 'near enemy', or national government, to an internationalist holy warrior launching *jihad* from his new haven in Afghanistan against the 'far enemy', or the United States of America. In 1998 The Saudi millionaire and the Egyptian medical doctor issued a statement announcing the formation of the World Islamic Front for *jihad* with the aim of fighting 'Jews and Crusaders'. Elaborating 'Azzam's articulation of *jihad* as an individual duty, but widening its scope in new directions, the statement urged every Muslim to consider the killing of 'Americans and their allies', be they civilian or military, as an individual obligation (Burke, 2007: 175–6). Suicide attacks were soon to follow with those on the American embassies in Nairobi and Dar-es-Salaam in August 1998 being the most spectacular before 9/11.

It was at this stage that American and European responses became more co-ordinated and information on the new organization taken more seriously. Unfortunately, the new approach coincided with the rapid deterioration of Iraq as a viable society, owing to harsh sanctions imposed on that country by various western nations. It was also a time of growing Palestinian frustration with the 'peace process' and the extreme right-wing policies of Israeli governments. Moreover, despite the rise of a new fundamentalist power in Afghanistan, the United States, having seen the dismantling of the Soviet Union, looked at its former theatre of *jihad* and Mujahideen as a backwater not worthy of the attention of a superpower, secure in its newly-won position and no longer required to be on the alert for a similar formidable enemy. Hence, the American response to the bombing of its embassies was to launch Tomahawk missile attacks on a pharmaceutical plant, touted as a military target, in the Sudan, and a number of training camps in Afghanistan. These attacks made Bin Laden and his deputy into Muslim heroes overnight, contributing in the process to their ability to attract new recruits, with European Muslim youths becoming for the first time amenable to the litany of grievances which Bin Laden became apt at reciting, using media outlets for airing his views, such as the Arabic al-Jazeera satellite station and various internet websites.

After 9/11 Afghanistan was occupied and most of al-Qa'ida's core leadership, except for Bin Laden and his deputy, were either killed or captured. Other attacks followed in Bali, Madrid, London, Istanbul and other European and Asian cities.

By the end of 2003 and after the occupation of Iraq, coupled with the capture of Saddam Hussain, in the same year, a new phase began with increasing monitoring and surveillance, often characterized by intrusions into the private activities of ordinary citizens in the West. This was particularly the case in the United States with unauthorized telephone tapping and the interception of email messages and private correspondence. Registered Muslim charities operating in western countries were being increasingly monitored or proscribed as indirect channels of funding for various Islamist groups – even those with no history of launching attacks outside their national territories, such as the Palestinian organisation, Hamas.

In the course of waging a 'war on terror', as it was called by the Bush administration, a number of human rights abuses resurfaced and became topics of heated debate across the world. These included extraordinary rendition, the detention of suspected terrorists at Guantanamo Bay and the torture of Iraqis in Abu Ghurayb prison.

Extraordinary or irregular rendition is the legal term given to the extrajudicial transfer of a person from one state to another where suspected terrorists are tortured or subjected to harsh techniques of interrogation (Garcia, 2009: 13). Thus, whereas rendition could be a legally acceptable method of handing over persons from one state to another openly and publicly, its irregularity stems from its secrecy whereby a person is kidnapped and handed over to the authorities of another country known to torture suspects, and not abiding by the United Nations Convention Against Torture and Other Cruel, Inhuman, or Degrading Treatment or Punishment (CAT), particularly Article 3. It is believed that hundreds of such persons were kidnapped by various US agencies and handed over to various countries, such as Jordan, Morocco, Egypt and Khuzestan.

Guantanamo Bay detention camp was opened in 2002 to imprison non-American persons who were deemed to be international terrorists. Being located in Cuba, but under US control, the rules governing the administration of the camp was deemed beyond the application of the Third Geneva Conventions relating to the treatment of prisoners of war – hence the classification of the detainees as 'enemy combatants'. It is also worth mentioning that some of the detainees were mere children at the time of their capture. It is estimated that more than 400 terrorists were held at the camp, with some alleging torture and other degrading treatment, before their release. Although the status of the camp was put under review by the new American administration under President Obama in 2009, no final decision has been made as to its ultimate future, except ordering its closure as soon as circumstances permit.

In 2004, a year after the occupation of Iraq, photographs of American military personnel performing bizarre acts of abuse against Iraqi prisoners detained in Abu Ghurayb were displayed by various media outlets across the continents. These showed American male and female prison guards taking pleasure in inflicting acts of humiliation and torture on helpless Iraqi prisoners. Subsequent investigations by official and unofficial parties confirmed that these guards were following instructions and guidelines given to them by the Defense Department. After several hearings in Congress and thousands of press reports and articles, as well as the prosecution of some junior guards, this shocking operation seems to have come to an inglorious end.

## Prospects

It could be contended at the end of the first decade of the twenty-first century that Islamic fundamentalism in all its various trends, schools and organizations is no longer a single ideology or method of operation. Those who believe in gradual change and some form of democracy are no longer pronounced 'fundamentalists', but 'political Islamists', while those who still profess the practice of violence and armed struggle are dubbed 'jihadists'.

In 2009, press reports and unattributed statements began to highlight the gradual weakening of al-Qa'ida as a fighting force capable of sustaining high-level attacks on western targets. While this may be true as far as its shrinking theatre of operations and the disillusionment of some of its supporters are concerned, other causes or factors may account for its apparent decline in comparison with its former ability to launch large-scale strikes. One reason could be its provisional decision to throw all its resources and recruits into its battle on the side of the Taliban. For it is quite certain that both al-Qa'ida and the Taliban appear to feel that they have finally achieved strategic parity with NATO forces and that now is the time to take the offensive and turn the scales against the enemy. It is for this reason that the outcome of the battles raging at the present time in Afghanistan may decide the fate of both the Taliban and al-Qa'ida.

# Appendix

## *General Characteristics of Revivalism, Reformism and Radicalism*

|  | *Historical period* | *Social structure* | *Stimulus* | *Operative concepts* | *Method of struggle* |
|---|---|---|---|---|---|
| *Islamic revivalism* | 1744–1885 (from Wahhabism to the death of the Sudanese Mahdi) | Tribes, nomads, bedouins Peripheral communities beyond the reach of central authorities | Contraction of internal and external trade; agricultural stagnation; European commercial expansion | Oneness of God; Mahdiship or renewal; *jihad* | Migration followed by *jihad* |
| *Islamic reformism* | 1839–1954 (from the formal inauguration of Ottoman reforms to the outbreak of armed struggle in Algeria) | State officials, bureaucrats, intellectuals, and members of the urban middle classes | Internal decline; military defeats; industrial and financial expansion of Europe | Consultation, salafism; patriotism. Rejection of medieval religious Islam; Islam as a code of modern standard laws | Education; dissemination of knowledge; reforming state institutions |
| *Islamic radicalism* | 1945–present (from the end of the Second World War to the present) | Rural migrants; middle traders; artisans; students; teachers; state employees; unemployed youths | Consolidation of the nation-state; Marxism; influx of rural migrants into towns and cities; the oil boom; Israeli victories | Sovereignty of God; the vanguard; the family; religious ignorance (*jahiliyya*) | Dissociation and *ijtihad* |

# Guide to Further Reading

## General Historical Surveys

Abu-Nasr, M. (1987), *A History of the Maghrib in the Islamic Period*. Cambridge: Cambridge University Press.

Brockelmann, C. (1973), *History of the Islamic Peoples*. New York: Capricorn Books.

Choueiri,Y. (2005), *A Companion to the History of the Middle East*. Oxford: Blackwell.

Hitti, P. K. (1977), *History of the Arabs,* 10th edn. London: Macmillan.

Hodgson, M. G. S. (1974), *The Venture of Islam: Conscience and History in a World Civilization,* 3 vols. Chacago: University of Chicago Press.

Hourani, A. A. (1991), *History of the Arab Peoples*. London: Faber & Faber.

Lapidus, I. M. (1988), *A History of Islamic Societies*. Cambridge: Cambridge University Press.

Udovitch, A. L. (ed.) (1981), *The Islamic Middle East, 700–1900: Studies in Economic and Social History*. Princeton, NJ: Darwin Press.

Waines, D. (1995), *An Introduction to Islam*. Cambridge: Cambridge University Press.

## The Genesis of Islam

Cook, M. A. (1983), *Muhammad*. Oxford: Oxford University Press.

Crone, P. (1987), *Meccan Trade and the Rise of Islam*. Oxford: Basil Blackwell.

Rodinson, M. (1971), *Mohammed,* trans. A. Carter. Harmondsworth: Penguin.

Watt, W. M. (1961), *Muhammad, Prophet and Statesman,* Oxford University Press, Oxford, 1961.

## The Arab Caliphate

Cahen, C. (1977), *Islam des origines au debut de l'empire Ottoman*. Paris: Bordas.

Donner, F. M. (1981), *The Early Islamic Conquests*. Princeton, NJ: Princeton University Press.

Kennedy, H. (1986), *The Prophet and the Age of the Caliphates: The Islamic Near East from the sixth to the eleventh century*. London: Longman.

Lassner, J. (1979), *The Shaping of 'Abbasid Rule*. Princeton, NJ: Princeton University Press.

Manuan, R. (1979), *L'Expansion musulmane (VIIe-XIe siecles)*. Paris: Presses Universitaires de France.

## Militarist Islam and the Crusades

Ayalon, D. (1978), *Gunpowder and Firearms in the Mamluk Kingdom*. London: Frank Cass.

Bosworth, C. E. (1963), *The Ghaznavids: Their empire in Afghanistan and eastern Iran, 944–1040*. Edinburgh: Edinburgh University Press.

Cahen, C. (1968), *Pre-Ottoman Turkey*. London: Sidgwick & Jackson.

Holt, P. M. (1986), *The Age of the Crusades: The Near East from the eleventh century to 1517*. London: Longman.

Irwin, R. (1986), *The Middle East in the Middle Ages: The early Mamluk Sultanate, 1250–1380*. London: Croom Helm.

Klausner, C. L. (1973), *The Seijuk Vezirate: A study of civil administration, 1055–1194*. Cambridge, MA: Harvard University Press.

Lyons, M. C. and Jackson, D. E. P. (1982), *Saladin, The Politics of the Holy War*. Cambridge: Cambridge University Press.

## The Ottoman, Safavid, and Mughal Empires

Habib, L. (1963), *The Agrarian System of Mughal India 1556–1707*. Bombay: Asia Publishing House.

Hodgson, M. G. (1974), *The Venture of Islam*, vol. 3. Chicago: University of Chicago Press.

Inalcik, H. (1973), *The Ottoman Empire: The Classical age, 1300–1600*. London: Weidenfeld & Nicolson.

Itzkowitz, N. (1972), *Ottoman Empire and Islamic Tradition*. Chicago: University of Chicago Press.

Jackson, P. and Lockhart, L. (eds) (1986), *The Cambridge History of Iran*, vol. 6. Cambridge: Cambrige University Press.

Pierce, L. P. (1993), *The Imperial Harem: Women and sovereignty in the Ottoman Empire*. Oxford: Oxford University Press.

Savory, R. (1980), *Iran Under the Safavids*. Cambridge: Cambridge University Press.

# Islamic Revivalism

Ahmad, M. (1975), *Sayyid Ahmad Shahid: his life and mission*. Lucknow: Academy of Islamic Research and Publications.

Algar, H. (1969), *Religion and State in Iran 1758–1906*. Berkeley, CA: University of California Press.

Dobbin, C. (1983), *Islamic Revivalism in a Changing Peasant Economy: Central Sumatra 1784–1847*. London: Curzon Press.

Evans-Pritchard, E. E. (1949), *The Sanusi of Cyrenaica*. Oxford: Oxford University Press.

Habib, J. S. (1978), *Ibn Sa'ud's Warriors of Islam*. Leiden: Brill.

Holt, P. M. (1971), *The Mahdist State in the Sudan*. Oxford: Oxford University Press.

Last, M. (1967), *The Sokoto Caliphate*. London: Longman.

Martin, B. G. (1976), *Muslim Brotherhoods in 19th-Century Africa*. Cambridge: Cambridge University Press.

Ziadeh, N. A. (1958) *Sanusiyah: A Study of a Revivalist Movement in Islam*. Leiden: E. J. Brill.

# Islamic Reformism

Adams, C. C. (1968), *Islam and Modernism in Egypt*. New York: Russell & Russell.

Ahmad, A. (1967), *Islamic Modernism in India and Pakistan*. Oxford: Oxford University Press.

Akhavi, S. (1980), *Religion and Politics in Contemporary Iran: clergy-state relations in the Pahlavi period*. New York: State University of New York Press.

Gibb, H. A. R. (1975), *Modern Trends in Islam*. New York: Octagon Books.

Hourani, A. (1983), *Arabic Thought in the Liberal Age, 1798–1939*. Cambridge: Cambridge University Press.

Keddie, N. R. (1972), *Sayyid Jamal ad-Din al-Afghani: A political biography*. Berkeley, CA: University of California Press.

Kerr, M. H. (1966), *Islamic Reform: The Political and Legal Theories of Muhammad 'Abduh and Rashid Rida*. Berkeley, CA: University of California Press.

Mardin, S. (1962), *The Genesis of Young Ottoman Thought*. Princeton, NJ: Princeton University Press.

Noer, D. (1973), *The Modernist Muslim Movement in Indonesia, 1900–1942*. New York: Oxford University Press.

Smith, W. C. (1957), *Islam in Modern History*. Princeton, NJ: Princeton University Press.

Zebiri, K. (1993), *Mahmud Shaltut and Islamic Modernism*. Oxford: Clarendon Press.

## Islamic Radicalism

Cole, R. I. and Keddie, N. R. (eds) (1986), *Shi'ism and Social Protest*. New Haven, CT: Yale University Press.

Esposito, J. L. (ed.) (1983), *Voices of Resurgent Islam*. Oxford: Oxford University Press.

Ettienne, B. (1987), *L'Islamisme radical*. Paris: Hachette.

Jansen, G. (1986), *The Neglected Duty: the Creed of Sadat's assassins and Islamic resurgence in the Middle East*. London: Macmillan.

Piscatori, J. (ed.) (1991), *Islamic Fundamentalism and the Gulf Crisis*. Chicago: American Academy of Arts and Sciences.

Sidahmed, A. S. and Ehteshami, A. (eds) (1996), *Islamic Fundamentalism*. Boulder, CO: Westview Press.

Watt, W. M. (1989), *Islamic Fundamentalism and Modernity*. London: Routledge.

## Jihadism, Democracy and Global Islam

Atwan, A. B. (2007), *The secret History of Al-Qa'ida*. London: Abacus.

Burke, J. (2007), *Al-Qaeda*. Lodnon: Penguin.

Mandaville, P. (2007), *Global Political Islam*. Lodnon: Routledge.

Roy, O. (2004), *Globalised Islam*. London: Hurst & Company.

Zubir, Y. H. and Haizam, A-F. (2008), *North Africa*. London: Routledge.

# Bibliography

'Abd al-Halim, M. (1979), *al-Ikhwan al-Muslimun,* vol. I. Alexandria: Dar al-Da'wa, Alexandria.

'Abd al-Halim, M. (1982), *al-Ikhwan al-Muslimun,* vol. II. Alexandria: Dar al-Da'wa.

'Abd al-Hamid, Sultan (1978), *Mudhakkirat,* trans. and ed. M. Harb. Cairo: 'Abd al Hamid.

'Abd al-Nasir, J. (n.d.), *al-Mithaq.* Beirut: Dar al-Masira.

'Abd, al-Rahman (1989), *al-Qadiyya al-Filastiniyya bayna Mithaqayn,* (The Palestinian Question Between Two Charters), Maktabat Dar al-Bayan, Kuwait, p. 246.

'Abdallah, 'Umar, F. (1983), *The Islamic Struggle in Syria.* Berkeley, CA: Mizan Press.

'Abduh, M. (1971), *Risalat al-Tawhid,* Cairo: Dar al-Ma'am.

'Abduh, M. (1979), *al-A 'mal al-Kamila,* ed. M. 'Amara, vol. I, 2nd edn. Beirut: al Mu'assasa al-'arabiyya li al-dirasat.

'Abduh, M. (1980a), *al-A'mal al-Kamila,* ed. M. 'Amara, vols. II and III. Beirut: al-Mu'assasa al-'arabiyya li al-dirasat.

'Abduh, M. (1980b), *The Theology of Unity,* trans. I. Musa'ad and K. Cragg. New York: Books for Libraries.

'Abduh, M. (1981), *Risalat al-Tawhid.* Beirut: al-Mu'assasat al-arabiyya.

Abir, M. (1971), 'The "Arab Rebellion" of Amir Ghalib of Mecca, 1788–1813'. *Middle Eastern Studies, VII* (2): 185–200.

Abu al-Khayr, 'Abd al-Rahman (1980), *Dhikrayati ma' Jama'at al-Muslimin: al takfir wa al-hijra.* Kuwait: Dar al-Buhuth al-1lmiyya.

Afghani, J. al-Din and 'Abduh, M. (1958), *al-'Urwa al-Wuthqa,* 2nd edn. Cairo: Dar al-' Arab.

'Aflaq, M. (1989) 'Taqyyim shamilli ai-wad' al-'arabi'. *Ad-Dastour,* 17 April: 15–19.

Alavi, H. (1986), 'Ethnicity, Muslim society, and the Pakistan ideology', in A. M.

Weiss (ed.) *Islamic Reassertion in Pakistan*. New York: Syracuse University Press, pp. 21–47.

Anderson, B. (1993), *Imagined Communities*, rev. edn. London: Verso.

Anderson, L. (1986), *The State and Social Transformation in Tunisia and Libya, 1830–1980*. Princeton, NJ: Princeton University Press.

Anis, M. (1966a), *al-Judhur al- T arikhiyya li- Thawrat 23 yulyu*. Cairo: Dar al Nahda.

Anis, M. (1966b), 'Tarikhuna al-qawmi fi al-mithaq'. *al-Katib*, 63, June: 69–74.

Arjomand, S. A. (1984), *The Shadow of God and the Hidden lmam: Religion, political order and societal change in Shi'ite Iran from the beginning to 1890*. Chicago: University of Chicago Press.

Asad, M. (1964), *The Message of the Qur'an*, vol. I. Mecca: Muslim World League.

Atwan, A. B. (2007), *The secret History of Al-Qa'ida*. London: Abacus.

Azzam (2001) *Ilhaq bi al-qafila (Follow the Caravan or Join Our Ranks)*, Part I, Section 5, 2nd edn. London: Azzam Publications.

Baer, G. (1970), 'The administrative, economic and social functions of Turkish Guilds'. *International Journal of Middle East Studies*, I: 28–50.

Baghdadi, 'Abd al-Qahir (1980), *Kitab usul ai-Din*. Beirut: ????

Banna, H. (1938), 'Khutwatuna al-thaniya'. *al-Nadhir*, 1 (I) (1357): 3–5.

Banna, H. (1943), 'Wihdatuna al-kamila'. *Majallat al-Ikhwan al-Muslimun*, 23, 22 dhi al-qu'da (1362): 3–4.

Banna, H. (1945), *Hay'at al-Ikhwan ai-Muslim in*. Cairo: ????

Banna, H. (1957), *al-Salam fi ai-Islam*. Cairo: Oar al-Fikr al-Islami.

Bayyumi, Z. S. (1979), *al-Ikhwan al-Muslimun wa al-Jama'at al Islamiyya, 1928–1948*. Cairo: Maktabat Wahbah.

Berkes, N. (1964), *The Development of Secularism in Turkey*. Montreal: McGill University Press.

Braudel, F. (1973), *The Mediterranean and the Mediterranean World in the Age of Philip II*, trans. S. Reynolds, Vol. II. London: Fontana.

Brown, L. C. (1967), *The Surest Path: The Political treaty of a nineteenth century Muslim statesman*, Harvard Middle Eastern monograph series. Cambridge, MA: Harvard University Press.

Burke, J. (2007), *Al-Qaeda*. London: Penguin.

Carrel, A. (1935), *L'Homme, cet inconnu*. Paris: Libraire Pion.

Choueiri, Y. (1989), *Arab History and the Nation State 1820–1980*. London: Routledge.

Choueiri, Y. (2001) *Arab Nationalism*. Oxford: Blackwell.

'Constitution of the Islamic Republic of Iran' (1980), *The Middle East Journal*, 34, *winter: 181–204*.

Cordell, O. O. (1977), 'Eastern Libya, Wadai and the Sanusiya: A Tariqa and a trade route'. *Journal of African History*, XVIII: 21–36.

Coulson, N. J. (1978), *A History of Islamic Law*. Edinburgh: Edinburgh University Press.

Crabbs, J., Jr (1975), 'Politics, history and culture in Nasser's Egypt'. *International Journal of Middle East Studies*, 6: 386–420.

Dajjani, A. S. (1967), *al-Haraka al-Sanusiyya, Nash'atuha wa Numuwuha fi al-Qarn al- T asi 'ashar*. Beirut: Matba' at Oar Lubnan.

Davis, I. C. (1981), *Utopia and the Ideal Society: A study of English utopian writing, 1516–1700*. Cambridge: Cambridge University Press.

Davison, R. H. (1988), *Turkey: A short history*, 2nd edn. Huntingdon: The Eothen Press.

Dobbin, C. (1974), 'Islamic revivalism in Minangkabau at the turn of the nineteenth century'. *Modern Asian Studies*, VIII: 319–45.

Dobbin, C. (1983), *Islamic Revivalism in a Changing Peasant Economy: Central Sumatra, 178–1847*. London: Curzon Press.

Fadl-Allah, M. (1978), *Ma' Sayyid Qutb fi fikrihi al-siyasi wa al-dini*. Beirut: Mu'assasat al-Risala.

Faraj, M. 'Abd al-Salam (1982), *al-Farida al-Gha'iba*. Amman.

Farrukh, 'U. (1980), *Tajdid al-Tarikh*. Beirut: Oar al-Bahith.

Foucault, M. (1977), *The Order of Things*. London: Tavistock Publications.

Garcia, M. J. (2009) *Renditions: Constraints imposed by Laws on Torture*, Congressional Research Service Report, 22 January. Washington: Congressional Research Service.

Ghannushi, R. (1984), *Maqalat*. Paris: Dar al-Karawan.

Ghannushi, R. (1988), 'Min Awraq al-Ghannushi'. *al-Majalla*, 440, 441, 442, 443, 445.

Ghannushi, R. (1992), *al-Huriyyat al-'Amma fi al-dawla al-islamiyya*. Beirut: Markaz Dirasat al-Wahda al-'Arabiyya.

Ghorbal, S. (1958), Ideas and movements in Islamic history, in K. W. Morgan (ed.) *Islam: The Straight Path: Islam interpreted by Muslims*. New York: The Ronald Press, pp. 42–86.

Goldschmidt, A. (1968) 'The Egyptian Nationalist Party: 1892–1919', in P. M. Holt (ed.) *Political and Social Change in Modern Egypt*. London: Oxford University Press, pp. 308–33.

Graham, Major-General F. G. I. (1909, 1974), *The Life and Work of Sir Syed Ahmed Khan*. Karachi: Oxford University Press.

Hamzeh, N. (1993), 'Lebanon's Hizbullah: from Islamic revolution to parliamentary accommodation'. *Third World Quarterly*, 14 (2): 321–37.

Hanna, S. and Gardner, G. H. (1969), *Arab Socialism: A documentary survey*. Leiden: E. Brill.

Hardjono, loan. (1983), 'Rural development in Indonesia: the "top-down" approach', in D. A. M. Lea and D. P. Chaudhri (eds) *Rural Development and the State: Contradictions and dilemmas in developing countries*. London: Methuen, pp. 38–63.

Harputlu, K. B. (1974), *La Turquie dans l'impasse*. Paris: Editions Anthropos.

Hawwa, S. (1977), *Jundu Allah: Thaqafatan wa Akhlaqan*. Amman.

Herring, R. J. (1979), 'Zulfikar Ali Bhutto and the "Eradication of Feudalism" in Pakistan. *Comparative Studies in Society and History*, 21: 519–57.

Hitler, A. (1969), *Mein Kampf*, trans. R. Manheim. London: Hutchinson.

Hodgson, M. (1974), *The Venture of Islam: Conscience and history in a world civilization*, vol. 01. Ill. Chicago: University of Chicago Press.

Holt, P. M. and Daly, M. W. (1983), *The History of the Sudan: From the coming of Islam to the present day*, 3rd edn. London: Weidenfeld & Nicolson.

Hooglund, E. J. (1982), *Land and Revolution in Iran, 1960–1980*. Austin, TX: University of Texas Press.

Hroub, K. (2006), *Hamas*. London: Pluto Press.

Hussain, A. (1985), 'Pakistan: the crisis of the state', in M. Asghar Khan (ed.) *Islam, Politics and the State: The Pakistan experience*. London: Zed Books.

Ibn 'Abd al-Wahhab, M. B. (1976), *al'Aquida wa al-Adab al-Islamiyya (Doctrine and Islamic Rules)*, Part I. Riyad: UMISI.

Ibn 'Abd al-Wahhab, M. B. (1978), *al-Rasa'il*, Part V. Riyad: UMISI.

Ibn Badis, 'Abd al-Hamid (1968), *Kitab Athar ibn Badis*, Vol. II (I). Algiers: al-Sharika al jaza'iriyya.

Ibn Khaldun (1900), *Muqaddima*, 3rd edn. Beirut: al-Matba'a al-Adabiyya.

Ibn Khaldun (1967), *The Muqaddima: An introduction to history*, trans. F. Rosenthal. London: Routledge & Kegan Paul.

Imam, 'Abdallah (1981), *'Abd al-Nasir wa al-Ikhwan al-Muslimun*. Cairo: Dar al-Mawqib al-'Arabi.

'Isa, S. (1972), *al-Thawra al-'Urabiyya*, Beirut: al-Mu'assasa al-'Arabiyya.

Al-Jabarti, 'Abd, al-Rahman (n.d.), *'Aja'ib al-Athar*, Vols I and II. Beirut: Dar al-Faris.

Keddie, N. (1983), *An Islamic Response to Imperialism: Political and Religious Writings of Sayyid Jamal ad-Din 'al-Afghani*. Berekely: Universoty of California Press.

Keyder, C. (1987), *State and Class in Turkey*. London: Verso.

Khan, A. M. (1965), *History of the Fara'idi Movement in Bengal 1818–1906*. Karachi: Pakistan Historical Society.

Khumayni, Imam (1979), *al-jihad al-Akbar*, trans. HusaYn Kurani. Tehran: Ministry of Islamic Guidance.

Khumayni, Imam (1981), *Islam and Revolution*, trans. and annotated by H. Algar. Berkeley, CA Mizan Press.

Khumayni, Imam (1982), *Mukhtarat min Aqwal al-lmam al-Khumayni*, vols. II and III. Tehran: Ministry of Islamic Guidance.

Khumayni, Sayyid Ruhollah al-Musawi (1964), *Tahrir al-Wasila*, vol. I. Najaf: Matba'at al-Adab.

Kurd 'Ali, Muhammad (1934–6), *al-Islam wa al-Hadara al-'Arabiyya*, 2 vols. Cairo: Lajnat al-Ta'lif wa al-Tarjama wa al-Nashr.

Lambton, A. K. S. (1953), *Landlord and Peasant in Persia: A study of land tenure and land revenue administration*. London: Oxford University Press.

Lambton, A. K. S. (1964), A reconsideration of the position of the *Marja' al-Taqlid* and the religious institution. *Studia Islamica*, XX: 115–35.

Laroui, 'Abdallah (1967), *L'ideologie arabe contemporaine*. Paris: François Maspero.

Laroui, 'Abdallah (1981), *Mafhum al-dawla*. Casablanca: al-Markaz al-Thaqafi al-'Arabi.

Malik, H. (1980), *Sir Sayyid Ahmad Khan and Muslim Modernimtion in India and Pakistan*. New York: Columbia University Press.

Marx, K. and Engels, F. (1974), *The German Ideology*, Part 1. London: Lawrence & Wishart.

Mawdudi, S. Abul A'la (1962), 'al-'Adala al-ijtima'iyya'. *ai-Muslim un*, 7 (9): 867–77.

Mawdudi, S. Abul A'la (1963), 'Bayna al-hadaratayn al-gharbiyya wa al-islamiyya'. *al Muslimun*, 8 (2, 3): 134–8, 254–7.

Mawdudi, S. Abul A'la (1976), *Jihad in Islam*. Lahore: Islamic Publications.

Mawdudi, S. Abul A'la (1977), *Minhaj al-inqilab al-Islami*. Cairo: Dar al-Ansar.

Mawdudi, S. Abul A'la (1978a), *Bayna al-da'wa al-qawmiyya wa al-rabita al-islamiyya*. Cairo: Dar al Ansar.

Mawdudi, S. Abul A'la (1978b), *The Economic Problem of Man and its Islamic Solution*. Lahore: Islamic Publications.

Mawdudi, S. Abul A'la (1979a), *A Short History of the Revivalist Movement in Islam*. Lahore: Islamic Publications.

Mawdudi, S. Abul A'la (1979b), *Islamic Way of Life*, 11th edn. Lahore: Islamic Publications.

Mawdudi, S. Abul A'la (1980), *Towards Understanding Islam*. Beirut: The Holy Qoran Publishing House.

Mawdudi, S. Abul A'la (1981/1401), *Nadhariyat al-Islam al-Siyasiyya*. Beirut: Mu'assasat al-Risala.

Mawdudi, S. Abul A'la (1982a), *Unity of the Muslim world*, 5th edn. Lahore: Islamic Publications.

Mawdudi, S. Abul A'la (1982b), *Rights of Non-Muslims in the Islamic State*. Lahore: Islamic Publications.

Mawdudi, S. Abul A'la (1983), *First Principles of the Islamic State*. Lahore: Islamic Publications.

Mitchell, R. P. (1969), *The Society of the Muslim Brothers*. London: Oxford University Press.

Mughniyya, M. (1979a), *al-Shi'a fi al-Mizan*, 4th edn. Beirut: Dar al Ta'aruf.

Mughniyya, M. (1979b), *al-Khumayni wa al-Dawla al-Islamiyya*. Beirut: Dar al-1lm li al Malayyin.

Munir, M. (1980), *From Jinnah to Zia*. Lahore: Vanguard Books.

Mustafa, 'Abd al'Aziz al-Haj (1984), *Mustafa al-Siba'i Rajul Filer wa Qa'id Da'wa*. Amman: Dar Ammar.

Mustafa, Ahmad 'Abd al-Rahim (1965), 'Hawla tarikh misr al-hadith'. *al-Hilal*, 73 (9), August: 10–13.

Mustafa, Ahmad 'Abd al-Rahim (1967), 'Nadwat i'adat kitabat al-tarikh al-qawmi'. *al-Majalla al Tarikhiyya al-Misriyya*, XIII: 345–69.

Mut'ini, 'Abd al-'Azim (1980), *Jarimat al-Asr? Qissat Ihtilal al-Masjid al-Haram*. Cairo: Dar al-Ansar.

Nadawi, Abu al-Hasan 'Ali (1961), *Islam and the World*, trans. M. Asaf Qidawai. Lahore: The Academy of Islamic Research Publications.

Nadawi, Abu al-Hasan 'Ali (1977), *Madha Khasira al- 'Alam bi-Inhitat al-Muslimin*, 10th edn. Cairo: Dar al-Ansar.

Nietzsche, F. (1979), *The Use and Abuse of History*, trans. A. Collins. Indianapolis, IN: Bobbs Merrill Educational Publishing.

Pakdaman, H. (1969), *Djamal-Ed-Din Assad Abadi dit Afghani*. Paris: V.P. MaisonneUe et Larose.

Parvin, M. and Hic, M. (1984), 'Land reform versus agricultural reform: Turkish miracle or catastrophe delayed?'. *International Journal of Middle East Studies*, 16: 207–32.

Peacock, J. L. (1978), *Muslim Puritans, Reformist Psychology in Southeast Asian Islam*. Berkeley, CA: University of California Press.

Peters, D. (1953), 'Muslim brotherhood –terrorists or just zealots?' *The Reporter*, 17 March: 8–10.

Plumb, J. H. (1969), *The Death of the Past*. London:  Macmillan.

Qutb, M. (1964), *Jahiliyyat al-Qarn al- 'Ishrin*. Cairo: Maktabat Wahbah.

Qutb, S. (1978), *Ma'rakat al-Islam wa al-Ra'smaliyya (The Battle Between Islam and Capitalism)*, 5th edn. Beirut: Dar al-Shuruq.

Qutb, S. (1980), *Khasa'is al-Tasawwur al-Islami*, 7th edn. Beirut: Dar al-Shuruq.

Qutb, S. (1980/1400), *al-Islam wa Mushkilat al-Hadara*, 6th edn. Beirut: Dar al-Shuruq.

Qutb, S. (1981), *Fi Zilal al-Qur'an*, rev. edn, 6 vols. Beirut: Dar al-Shuruq.

Qutb, S. (1981/1401), *Ma'alim fi al-Tariq*. Beirut: Dar al-Shuruq.

Qutb, S. (1983), *Hadha al-Din*, 8th edn. Beirut: Dar al-Shuruq.

Qutb, S. (1986), *Muqawwimat al-Tasawwur al-Islami (Fundamentals of the Islamic Conception)*. Beirut: Dar al-Shuruq.

Rajaee, F. (1983), *Islamic Values and World View: Khomeyni on man, the state, and international politics,* vol. 01. XIII. London: University Press of America.

Razi, Fakhr al-Din (n.d.), *Usul al-din,* ed. and introduction by T. A. Said. Cairo: al-Azhar.

Ricklefs, M.C. (1981), *A History of Modern Indonesia.* Basingstoke: Macmillan.

Rida, R. (1907), 'al-Istibdad'. *al-Manar,* 10 (4), 11 June: 279–84.

Robed, B. (1986), *Troubles on the East Bank.* New York: Praeger.

Rouleau, E. (1967), 'The Syrian enigma: what is the Ba'th7'. *New Left Review* 45: 53–65.

Sa'id, R. (1967), *al-Asas al-Ijtima'i li al-Thawra al-'Urabiyya.* Cairo: Madbuli.

Salim, J. (1982), *al-Tanzimat al-Sirriyya li Thawrat 23 Yuliyu.* Cairo: Maktabat Madbuli.

Satloff, Robert B. (1986), *Troubles on the East Bank,* Praeger, New York and London.

Sayyid, J. (1963a), 'Tarikhuna al-Qawmi fi Daw' al-Ishtirakiyya'. *al-Katib* 29, August: 87–92.

Sayyid, J. (1963b), 'Tarikhuna al-Qawmi bayna al-Haqiqa wa al-Tazyif'. *al-Katib, 26, May: 103–10.*

Sayyid, J. *et al.* (1966), 'al-Thaqafa wa al-Thawra'. *al-Katib* 63, July: 27–32.

Sayyid, J. (1973), *Hizb al-Ba'th al- 'Arabi.* Beirut: Dar al-Nahar.

Shadi, S. (1981), *Safahat min al-Tarikh,* Part I. Kuwait: Sharikat al-Shu'a' li al-Nashr.

Shafi, M. M. (1969), *Distribution of Wealth in Islam.* Karachi: Begum Aisha Bawany Waqf.

Shah, M. R. (1979), 'How the Americans overthew me'. *Now:* 7–13. December, pp. 21–34.

Shahidullah, M. (1985) 'Class formation and class relations in Bangladesh', in D. L. Johnson (ed.) Middle Classes in Dependent Countries. Beverly Hills, CA: Sage.

Shaykh, Y. M. (1993), *Ajnihat al-Inqadh (The Political Wings of the Islamic Salvation Front).* Beirut: Mu'assasat al-'Arif li-al-Matbu'at.

Sourkes, T. L. (1967), *Nobel Prize Winners in Medicine and Physiology 1901 1965.* London: Abelard-Schuman.

Sulaiman, I. (1986), *A Revolution in History: The Jihad of Usman Dan Fodio.* London: Mansell Publishing.

Symonds, R. (1950), *The Making of Pakistan.* London: Faber & Faber.

Syrian Ministry of Culture (1966), *Kayfa Naktub Tarikhana al-Qawmi.* Damascus: Syrian Ministry of Culture.

Toprak, B. (1981), *Islam and Political Development in Turkey.* Leiden: E. J. Brill.

Torres, M. R., Jordan, X. and Horsburgh, N. (2006), 'Analysis and Evolution of the global Jihadist movement'. *Terrorism and Political Violence,* 18: 399421.

Tunisi, Khayr al-Din (1978), *Muqaddimat Kitab Aqwam al-Masalik fi Ma'rifat Ahwal al-Mamalik,* ed. Ma'n Ziyadah. Beirut: Dar al- Tali'a.

Turabi, H. (1988), *Nadharat fi al-Fiqh al-Siyasi.* Khartoum: al-Sharika al-'Alamiyya li Khadamat al-'Ilam.

Upton, J. M. (1970), *The History of Modern Iran: An Interpretation.* Cambridge, MA: Harvard University Press.

Vatin, J-C. (1983), *L'Algerie politique: histoire et societe.* Paris: Presses de la Fondation Nationale des Sciences Politiques.

Wilber, D. N. (1963), *Contemporary Iran.* London: Thames & Hudson.

Winder, R. B. (1954), 'Islam as the state religion'. *The Muslim World,* 3 and 4 (XLIV): 215–26.

Yakan, F. (n.d.), *al-Islam.* Beirut: Mu'assasat al-Risala.

Yassine, A. S. (1994), *Hiwar m'a al-Fudala' al-Dimuqratiyyin.* Casablanca: no publisher.

# Index